40 ACRES – WATER ON 3 SIDES – TIDES & TAXES RISING

# HANSEN'S LANDING

*old house, run-down cottages
rotting dock, some good timber*

## JAN WALKER

Chapter Quotations from Famous Quotes at Brainy Quotes
www.brainyquote.com

This is a work of fiction. Any similarity to persons living or dead (other than the author's deceased Norwegian father and uncles) is not intended.

Cover Design by Mary E. Smith, Harbor Design, 2018

ISBN: 978-1-7322963-1-2 2018953088
LCCN: 2018953088

Publisher's Cataloging-In-Publication Data
(Prepared by The Donohue Group, Inc.)

Names: Walker, Jan (Janet D.)
Title: Hansen's Landing : 40 acres - water on 3
    Sides - tides & taxes rising : old house, run-
    down cottages, rotting dock, some good timber /
    Jan Walker.
Description: Gig Harbor, WA : Plicata Press LLC,
    [2018]
Identifiers: ISBN 9781732296312
Subjects: LCSH: Norwegian Americans--Washington
    (State)--Poulsbo--Fiction. | Real estate
    development--Washington (State)--Poulsbo--
    Fiction. | Families--Washington (State)--
    Poulsbo--Fiction. | Family secrets--Washington
    (State)--Poulsbo--Fiction. | Suquamish Indians-
    -Washington (State)--Poulsbo--Fiction. |
    Poulsbo (Wash.)--Fiction.
Classification: LCC PS3623.A35936 H36 2018 | DDC
    813/.6--dc23

For Descendants of Norwegian Immigrants . . .

A Celebration of Their Families and Their Foibles

Also by Jan Walker

Fiction

*History Lesson: The Walls Know Where the Body Lies*

*The Whiskey Creek Water Company*

*A Farm in the South Pacific Sea*

*Romar Jones Takes a Hike: Runaway or Missing Person*

*An Inmate's Daughter*


Nonfiction

*Unlocking Minds in Lockup: Prison Education Opens Doors*

*Teach Inside: Parenting, Family and Reentry Activities For Prison Classrooms*

*Parenting From a Distance: Your Rights and Responsibilities*

*My Relationships, Myself*

# HANSEN'S LANDING

*A people without history is like wind on the buffalo grass.*

*Sioux proverb*

1880's

## Prologue
## The Old Ones

Helgar Hansen left Hardangerfjord, Norway, south of Bergen, to join his cousin Arvid, in America, where second sons—and third and so on—could own land. On Arvid's South Dakota prairie acres littered with bleached bones, Helgar's ankles puffed and ached, and his feet itched even when winter lay on the land. His felling and limbing axes remained unused in his travel trunk, their blades protected by shirts and pants newly mended for his journey. Atop them rested a folded and worn newspaper story about forests and logging camps, and sawmill towns begging for hands. Arvid had heard of such, but he'd married and fathered children, and found contentment raising wheat and cattle.

Helgar stayed in South Dakota long enough into spring thaw to help his cousin plow, plant and herd, before setting out for Washington Territory. He traveled by train and boat to Poulsbo, a Norwegian community, where he bought forty acres with salt water on three sides and evergreen trees so thick sunlight never touched the earth. There he put his axes to work felling trees, clearing enough land to build a house.

He sent some of his first earnings back to Bergen, to his sweetheart Magna. She joined him on that peninsula of land that jutted into the salt waters of Puget Sound and bore him seven sons strong enough to log the land for the next settlers. Both of them kept journals for that next generation of Hansens who would be born American but remain Norwegian.

Only Magna wrote of their three daughters buried on the land, and her prophecy that one day a daughter strong enough would be born to the land she named Hansen's Landing, America.

*Life is pleasant. Death is peaceful. It's the transition that's troublesome. Isaac Asimov, 1920-1992.*

> *American writer of popular science and science-fiction; biochemistry professor, Boston University.*

April 1992

# 1

# Ragnar Hansen

The day before Ragnar Hansen took to his bed to die, he planted the last of a thousand fir seedlings, a little something to replace all the old growth trees Hansens logged over the years. A little something for Kelda, daughter of the Landing, who would inherit all forty acres with its old house, four run-down cottages, a rotting dock, some good timber, and taxes at one-thousand an acre.

The salt-scented breeze coming off Liberty Bay lifted hair gone too thin over the years to warm his head. Gone white, too, though color didn't matter much when it came to stopping the chill. He figured dying would take a day or two, three at most. Norwegians could do prit-near anything they set their minds to, and he'd set his to joining his six brothers in the beyond. Six brothers and one sister-in-law, Lydia, who'd come to life in his head of late, fussing over the wee tree planting that stirred up aches in his bones in the April air. His hands felt good—rough and soiled with Hansen earth—in spite of the chill.

Calluses that softened with age were toughened up a bit from this planting. They'd started as blisters when he was but five years old and swinging an axe to help bring down a Douglas fir on Hansen land.

Loggers, that's what Hansens were back when, that's all he'd ever been. A simple man who'd run short on cash since buying his two nephews' shares of the Landing. He had his Last Will and Testament prepared and them thousand seedlings planted for forgiveness when Kelda learned the truth of that selling and buying. He had the Indian lawyer, Walkingstick by name, ready to put other growing things in the ground, native plants, while Kelda settled the estate. Way he figured, Kelda would have enough money for a year or two; it would take that long to straighten out the mess. Like as not, after that, she'd have to turn the Landing over to her husband and his construction business.

He pushed himself to his feet and hobbled toward the dock for one last stroll out over salt water. Out there, where steamboats once called in at the Landing, he felt his closest brothers with him. Rolf and Karli not so much older but long since dead, and little Olav who'd rested at the bottom of Pearl Harbor over fifty years.

At the end of the dock he could look back on the Hansen's forty acres still more green than not. Even Kelda's husband, Arne Hedstrom, agreed it wouldn't be right to cut the stand of timber that grew right down to the beach along the inlet side or the cedars at the cove, but that left plenty enough room for Arne to plan on developing a gated community at the Landing.

Ragnar made it halfway across the sloping lawn before he heard a car coming down Hansen's Lane. Hearing was going dim, along with his eyesight. Time was, back when, he could hear a car turn off the county road a good two minutes before it came into view.

"Damn it all to hell," he said without turning, figuring it was Emma Stern butting in when he'd already told her the house was clean enough for a month. A man set on dying doesn't need so much fussing over dust or ironed handkerchiefs for his back pocket. He raised a fist in protest and kept it raised even when the car turned out to be some new sporty thing, its door already opened by a youngster like as not lost. His mind was on a chat with Lydia, only woman he'd ever loved, dead thirty-five years but alive in his head and full of advice. She'd sent Walkingstick, told him so in his head. Maybe she'd sent this red-haired boy, too.

"Mr. Hansen?" the boy called in a voice deep enough to be a man's, ordinary enough to be a Hansen's. "Mr. Ragnar Hansen?"

"*Ja*, that'd be me, but I'm not needing to buy anything, or be saved by some religion neither. You might just as well get back in your automobile and drive on out of here."

4

"I'm not selling anything. I'm from the paper, the *Poulsbo Herald*."

"I already read the paper this week, it comes in the mail, you don't need to be driving all the way down here to deliver."

"No no, I'm not here to deliver, I'm a reporter. I tried to reach you by phone. Your housekeeper said it might be best to drive on out, see you in person."

"Not much news to report," he said, serious Hansen scowl in place. The young man had added his name, something Eklund, and set to going on about Wallace Taylor. Ragnar looked skyward, hoping for wisdom from Lydia. Hard to talk out loud to her with a stranger in ear-shot, so he stayed quiet, deaf-like.

"You see," said the boy/man after a decent wait, "I write the history column—twenty-five years ago, fifty years ago, that kind of thing. Wallace Taylor's body washed up on a beach sixty-years ago next month. May 1932. My boss figures an unsolved murder is worth some space, and I thought you could comment, him having been your brother-in-law."

Ragnar dusted his hands, reached down and dusted his pant legs from knee to hem for good measure. His bones creaked both bending and straightening. "I have a hard time remembering anything that far back, I'm eighty and some-odd years old, memory's not what it used to be."

"Records show you were married to Ruth Taylor, sister to Wallace."

"Seems to me that was along about 1935, my marriage to Ruth. Her brother was already dead by then, so he couldn't be my brother-in-law. Fell off the ferry from Seattle and drowned long before Ruthie and me married."

The reporter grinned. Damned if he didn't look like a Hansen lad getting into some kind of mischief, trying to look innocent behind his freckles.

"Old reports said suspected murder victim, Mr. Hansen. No water in his lungs. Drowning victims always have water in their lungs."

Ragnar shook his head, one shake, still unsettled at how he'd come to marry Ruth. He'd done it to please Lydia, who'd chosen Olav for herself. Ruth needed a husband, what with her poor health, her dead brother, and their parents not so good in the aftermath. A darned shame it was, Wally's body washing up like that. He poked around in his head for an answer that would satisfy this young reporter.

"Is that so? No water in his lungs. I long been wondering just what happened to my younger brother, Olav, killed at Pearl Harbor. Dead from a bomb blast without a taste of salt water, or dead from drowning? Either way, he left two little boys, one looked a lot like you when he reached his teens."

"I see," young Eklund said.

Ragnar figured that had been enough Hansen confusion to throw the lad off, but Eklund kept right on talking.

"We covered Pearl Harbor in last year's column, sir—the locals that died and some that survived. Fifty years ago, last year. The paper will likely do it again in 2001, when it will be sixty years."

"*Ja?* I plan to be long gone by then. If you're wanting to interview me about Pearl Harbor you'd better get it done with now."

Damned if the youngster didn't muster up another grin while shaking his head and making comments about old Norwegians being clever. Acted amused more than mad and took a new approach.

"Mr. Hansen, let's say, for the sake of the paper's story, that Wallace Taylor was murdered. Who do you think might have killed him?"

The reporter waited, leaving Ragnar no choice but to come up with something. He and his brothers made up truths right and left at the time, to get investigators off the scent of local Indians, they'd been that sure someone from the Suquamish tribe had killed Wallace, payback for death of one or two of theirs.

"My brother Karli, he died sometime back, *ja?* Well, Karli seemed to think Wallace Taylor was robbed of his money pouches and tossed off the ferry. Them empty pouches floated up, too. Could be Wallace Taylor died in the robbery from them pouches. Now, how you'd go about finding out who robbed him all these years later I wouldn't venture to guess."

The reporter's face turned serious. "That was stated in the old accounts in the Bremerton paper at the time. Did your brother Karli have any other opinions about the death?"

"*Ja*, he said for certain it had to do with bootleg whiskey, and no Hansens ever took part in any such bootleg. That'd be the sum of what I know." No need to mention Hansen's homebrewed beer to young Eklund; there was never enough to sell. "Seems to me I remember some Eklunds might have done some bootleg. You related to those Eklunds, lived around here back when?"

"I am," the reporter said, grinning again, "though I grew up in Portland. I've heard stories all my life that make me want to learn more about this area. Thanks for your help, Mr. Hansen. One of these days, with your permission, I'd like to come back to interview you about your family, with or without connections to Wallace Taylor."

Ragnar stood rooted after the reporter left, his eyes fixed for a time on the house, the window of the bedroom where he'd lay himself down to die. His heart sounded in his ears, which felt hot. With luck he'd die right this minute, die of a heart attack like the ones toppled Rolf and Karli. A yacht drifted on the bay, but he saw a steamship, women in long dresses and brimmed hats, men in stiff collars and buttoned vests with fedoras held aloft. The steamer blew its whistle, blasted black smoke that trailed on the echo, and slowed as it neared the Landing dock with guests for the cottages. Seattle folks seeking a break from the city.

"Well, now, what do you make of that, Lydia?" he said to the salt-air breeze as he walked toward the sight. By the time he reached the end of the dock he saw only a yacht. He leaned on the railing, rubbing the stubble on his jaw and watching for Lydia to materialize. The chat with young Eklund left him agitated and that would make taking to his bed just then a problem. He didn't want to die thinking about Wallace Taylor, or even about Ruth.

The breeze changed directions, mingling the scents of evergreen tree resin with creosote from the dock pilings, groaning as waves washed toward shore. Off toward the inlet an old fir soughed. He looked around, certain Lydia sent him the sounds just as she'd sent the message a few months ago about inlet land going back to the Indians, she just hadn't made it clear how to do that. One Indian in particular kept coming to mind. Indian Joe, friend to the Old Ones, Helgar and Magna.

Ragnar saw certain times clear as yesterday, but he couldn't quite get a mind picture of Joe. He rubbed his hands that had worked the land with his dad and brothers, pitched in to help his mother cook and clean and sew, there were no girls for doing that. Clear the land, plant the garden, milk the cows, scrape barnacles from the boats, row a sack of potatoes and a box of apples over to Mrs. Carlson, the widow across the cove, other side of the Landing from the inlet.

He looked for the Carlson place set back from the beach, hidden behind weeping willow trees. He'd always liked the rowing job best. On the water, out on the Sound, he could think and wonder. He could worry too, truth be known, and leave the worry like he'd left many a gunny-sack of barn kittens, weighted down with a rock. He stood stock-still and listened for a steamboat's whistle, for oars dripping water. Looked and listened for Lydia, and heard a head-full of worries. Of late they'd started washing to shore, them worries, them Hansen truths untold. Could be Lydia wanted Kelda to know the ins and outs of that Wallace Taylor mess. Once he'd managed the dying, Kelda could drag out the trunk Karli left filled with Hansen memories. It was all in there, the last of the truths, its lock soldered shut.

The breeze shifted direction once more, and there was Lydia's voice telling him there's a right way to do things, taking to his bed wasn't a Hansen way. He turned from viewing the bay and saw 1992, an old house needing some repairs and paint, a lawn needing mowing, forty-thousand in taxes due.

"Damn it all to hell, Lydia, I could use some help with the telling."

*Everything has been figured out except how to live. Jean-Paul Sartre, 1905-1980.*
*French philosopher, playwright, novelist, political activist & existentialist.*

# 2
# Kelda Hansen

Therapists at Mid-Sound Mental Health often joked that all their phone calls were emergencies, but Kelda startled, dropping her pen, when the emergency-call buzzer rang through to her office. The receptionist rarely interrupted a session in progress.

"Kelda Hansen here," she said, turning away from her clients, a bickering mother and daughter in her office for a pre-counseling interview.

"It's your Uncle Ragnar, he's took a turn, he's took to his bed refusing to eat."

"Emma?" Kelda said, aware that the emergency was in her own family, not one of her client's.

"Yes, it's Emma, come to the Landing for my regular cleaning. This is long distance on his telephone, you'd better come see for yourself the turn he's took."

The line went dead. Kelda put on her professional mask for the sad-faced mother and scowling daughter sitting across from her. Theirs was a court-order case, a domestic dispute that escalated from shouting and shoving to serious assault when daughter tried to stab mother with a kitchen knife. Mid-Sound Mental Health acquired half its clients from the courts, and. Kelda got stuck with most of them based on her years of experience.

"How long's this gonna take?" the daughter asked, her voice a whine. She had dyed-black hair, maroon lipstick, green-polished fingernails and a black V-neck sweater pulled down to display ample cleavage.

"Until the court sees the progress they deem necessary for you and your mother to live in harmony. My role is to listen to both of you, and help you listen to each other." Kelda's jaw ached from being clenched. She scanned the papers on her desk for her clients' names. Mandy and Shawndra Jenkins.

Mandy Jenkins had checked divorced and listed three dependents and two jobs on her application. At thirty she looked used up, her hair worn-out from bleaching, her face creased from smoking and despair. Shawndra's age was listed as fourteen.

"She ain't never listened, not since she started crawling," Mandy said, her eyes on Kelda, her head bobbed toward her daughter.

"Ain't never." Shawndra rolled her eyes.

Kelda's fists clenched against an impulse to shake some sense into the girl. Burnout. She'd warned the agency director. "That seems to bother you, Shawndra."

"Yeah. It's like, dumb sounding."

"You watch your mouth. I left school to have you, you're lucky I'm struggling to keep you in school." Mandy Jenkins had tried glaring at her daughter, but her eyes were wet, her shoulders slumped. She coughed a smoker's hack and pounded her chest.

Kelda dredged up her compassionate look, went through the intake form with practiced patience and explained client journaling as part of the therapy they would be doing. "If you don't know what to write, just note the date and time, and one word. Call the agency if you need to talk to someone, or if either of you feel threatened by the other. Call before it becomes an emergency."

She'd given them notebooks for journaling, a set of sample entries, and the agency's 24-hour phone number. Both Shawndra and Mandy knew an emergency would mean police involvement.

As soon as the door closed behind them Kelda crammed files into her briefcase. She needed to get to the Landing, to her Uncle Ragnar who had been father to her all her life, and mother too, since her fifteenth year. She'd hoped to move back to the Landing when her younger daughter entered college, but Arne, her husband of twenty-five years, argued that two incomes were necessary to meet the girls' expenses. He complained about the old Hansen house, the upkeep it required, the ownership problems with four names on the deed and the fact that two of the owners, Kelda's older brothers, didn't do squat.

She'd tried to assure Arne that she could get work in the Poulsbo area; she even urged him to set up an office there, a satellite to the one he had in Edmonds. Their home and their respective offices were only twelve miles from the Landing as the crow flies but at least an hour and a half by car and ferry. They lived in an Arne Hedstrom Construction home, over four-thousand square feet of luxury, the latest lovely Arne-built house of their married life. Of late she'd found the luxury discomforting.

She grabbed her laptop, pager and cell-phone, and buzzed Rachelle. "Cancel my afternoon appointment and evening class. I'm headed for Hansen's Landing. I can just make the ferry."

Kelda paced the passenger deck of the Rhododendron, stopping to glance back at Edmonds, once a sleepy waterfront town north of Seattle, now in danger of becoming part of a metropolis. Homes started at the water's edge and climbed the hills where thick forests of Douglas fir, western red cedar and hemlock once grew. Her grandfather and uncles helped deplete those forests. Her husband built expensive homes on the hillsides, and reminded her that trees he removed for his developments were second-growth; her family took down the good stuff.

Each thrum of the ferry's engine pulled pain from deep in Kelda's brain to rest behind her eyes. She skirted other passengers and concession machines where trapped air tasted of over-warm bodies and stale coffee, and pushed against a door made heavy by the wind to reach the outside deck. The day was April-clean, with drifting cirrus clouds. She filled her lungs with salty air. It smelled like Hansen's Landing and her youth. Uncle Ragnar couldn't die yet. She still needed him.

According to Hansen family legend, she'd been born to the land purchased by Helgar Hansen and protected by his Magna, who birthed seven healthy logger-sons and three frail daughters. All three girls died within days of their births. After burying her third baby girl among the cedars above the cove, Magna wrote, *"One day there will be a Hansen woman strong enough for this land. She will be born to one of my sons, but her spirit will come through me, from Hardangerfjord. From the islands of Norway. My spirit is the ship that will carry her through life. Men may clear and plow the land, and erect buildings, but it takes a strong woman to manage it all."*

So it was and long had been. Kelda's mother, Lydia Berg Hansen, chose the name from a book Magna brought from Norway in 1889.

*Kelda: from the ship's island. Ronalda: strong. Hansen: patronymic family name for three centuries.*

Her uncle Ragnar was over eighty now, and stubborn. Planting trees during January and February cold, and March and April rain. She begged him to forget that stupid promise. When she arrived for weekends with him, he acted nonchalant and tried to keep her from counting the seedlings, from finding new spots with disturbed earth, but she already knew. She saw him in her mind all week, and felt the stiffness in her own fingers and knees.

The crew directing vehicles off the ferry's car deck held her back in the spot they'd wedged her in; last car on, last car off. That put her at the back of a long, slow-moving line snaking uphill past the Kingston business strip and onto the highway. Lately every driver seemed to know all the old short-cuts. Exhaust fumes seeped into Arne's battered Bronco, the car she was stuck with because their older daughter had her Honda. Kelda checked her cell phone for the umpteenth time to see if it was still charged. She pushed the Landing's code. "Emma? It's Kelda. Is there any change?" She ran the words together, forgetting to breathe.

"He's resting. Did you miss the ferry, then?"

"No, no, I'm on this side, I'm calling on a cell phone. I'm going to run into the Country Market for makings in case he wants beef-barley soup."

"I already give him soup, he's not much interested."

Her phone made its disconnect beep as she wrenched the steering wheel to turn into the market. She tossed it onto the passenger seat, dashed into and through the store and back to the car, driving too fast along the main highway onto Bay Loop Road. The Loop ran east toward Liberty Bay, turned south and twisted a couple more times without ever permitting a glimpse of the Landing. Arne always mentioned that when he schemed. It would lend privacy to an upscale development. Forty perfect acres. Ideal country living.

Hansen Lane ran between Liam and Leah Kerry's place, where sheep grazed, and an abandoned apple orchard with gnarled trees hip deep in grass. A Private-Keep Out sign did less than loose gravel and dust or mud, depending on the weather, to deter drivers from turning down the lane. "Rural life, not country living," she'd say to Arne, but it didn't deter him from his dream.

Kelda sped past the Kerry place, spit gravel and fish-tailed a little by the upper pond on Hansen land. Mallards lifted onto their tail feathers, flapped their wings in protest, then scuttled to the far side where they gathered in the shadows of a cedar stand more than a century old. Magna's cedar grove. She'd made Helgar leave it even when shake mills begged. According to Magna's journal, only one cedar had ever been removed by Hansens, that for a Suquamish Indian to make a dugout canoe.

Kelda took her foot off the gas and lowered the window to breathe cedar scented air. In her childhood imagination, those trees were grand ladies in fine attire dancing the minuet, the pond that reflected their finery a polished ballroom floor. Her two daughters, even when they were young enough to play Let's Pretend, saw just trees.

"Just trees." She coasted into the circle drive, parked behind Emma Stern's old Oldsmobile and opened the car door before the Bronco's engine coughed its last. The great-room windows were dark, sheathed with heavy draperies she and her uncle had made. He could sew a fine seam, and never fussed that it was woman's work. She stayed to the right on the step that needed repair, noting a nest of tools Ragnar had ready for the job.

"Dear God, he's given up waiting for Arne," she said, wondering who she meant to hear. Her brief case and computer banged against the heavy oak door as she pushed it open. "Emma, I'm in the great

13

room. Why is it so dark in here?" Looks like someone died, she almost said, but swallowed the words and hiked the paraphernalia she carried onto the round oak table, the centerpiece on one side of the room. "Emma?" she called again, circling to open the drapes.

"Shh, you'll be waking him up, he's needing his rest," Emma said, bossy as always. "And I drew them curtains on purpose. It's still April, curtains keep the heat bill down. You'd be wise to remember this is an old house, high ceilings, 'specially this room."

"It's well insulated." Kelda stopped herself from talking about the work involved in adding new insulation to that old part of the house. Emma knew about that and every other maintenance, remodel or repair done in the last several decades. She'd known this house before Kelda was born. The great room, twenty-two by thirty feet, was the original house Helgar Hansen built for Magna before she came over from Norway. Kelda believed the Old-ones' spirits warmed it from the office corner that honored them, with some help from an occasional alder fire in the fireplace on the front wall. Alder trees, which grew fast, gave off good heat and left nitrogen in the soil, were the only ones they burned at the Landing.

Old sofas and chairs, arranged to watch the fire and look out onto the view of the bay, divided that half of the room from the great room table and the Old Ones area. The oak floor, sanded down and refinished before Kelda and Arne's wedding, had a worn path down the middle from the entry to the main house hallway and stairs to the bedrooms.

"Is he in the sewing room, Emma?" They had moved a bed into that room, tucked in under the stairs, for Lydia, Kelda's mother, when her heart problems developed. It had served as both guest room and sick room since.

"He'd be in his own bed. I told you he wouldn't let me change the sheets what need changing."

Right, she should have remembered. The wide oak steps gleamed when she flipped on the light switch. They too bore worn spots in their middle. She tiptoed to the top and down the hall to her uncle's room. Emma had closed the curtains there, blocking the view of dock and bay. From this floor, Ragnar could look across to Lemola, a community not even named on a map, the place where four Hansen men first met Lydia Berg. He never closed the curtains. Things must be serious if he let Emma get away with that.

She looked at him, at his head nested deep in his favorite goose down pillow, his thinning white hair invisible against the white pillow case. His arms resting atop a down comforter seemed shrunken, less muscled than a few days ago. True, he'd had on his favorite wool plaid shirt then, one she'd made long ago and patched often. His eyelids looked blue, his face gray. When had he gotten so frail? Pressure built behind her cheek bones and eye sockets. She lifted Ragnar's right hand. The callused palm and scratch roughened back comforted her with its rightness, its normalcy. A working man's hands. Lately working at planting fir seedlings. She watched his eyelids flutter open, watched his eyes absorb her and a smile form. Then the Hansen scowl fell into place. He pushed up a bit on one elbow.

"Damn it all to hell, Kelda, I'm wanting some good Hansen beef-barley soup. That Emma brings me dish water, I'm t'inking by its taste. Chicken soup, says she. Made from an old chicken feather, maybe, say I."

The dropped 'h' in 'th' words, a Ragnar pattern that occurred when he was mad, tired, a little drunk, and increasingly with age, delighted Kelda. She almost laughed before her submerged tears erupted, plopped on the comforter, and soaked right into the fine goose down stuffed into the muslin cover and tufted in place by Ragnar himself.

*Kissing don't last; cookery do. - George Meredith, 1828-1909.*
*English novelist & poet—Victorian era, nominated for the Nobel Prize in Literature*
*seven times.*

# 3
## Arne Hedstrom

Arne Hedstrom shoved aside the family size pizza box and belched. He'd bet soup was on at the Landing. It wasn't that he expected Kelda to have dinner ready when he walked in the door, not every night, four out of five seemed reasonable. A working man needs a hearty, home-cooked meal at the end of the day his mother always said, and Kelda could cook. She'd learned as a kid, cooking for her overfed, chowder head Norwegian uncles. Used to bake bread once a week, fruit pies every Sunday from the time she was ten or twelve. Now she complained that she'd been cooking all her life and was tired of it, but she ran home to the Landing to put on a pot of soup every time the old man sneezed. He knew darn well that's what she was doing over there right now.

Arne figured he'd been a good parent to their two daughters and a good husband to Kelda. Hell, he saw to getting his own dirty clothes into the laundry. What more could a woman want? He just didn't have the knack for cooking; most guys his age didn't. That, and Kelda used old family recipes that required some Hansen genetic memory. "How am I supposed to know what to add, nothing's written down?" he'd said, and she'd handed him a Betty Crocker cookbook. Betty frigging Crocker in a Fifties' hairdo on the fraying cover.

So, there'd been no real dinner tonight because ornery old Ragnar Hansen didn't have the decency to die and let the next generation take over the Landing, do something creative with all that acreage. None last night because Kelda had to teach a group of whining women who'd provoked their husbands long enough to get themselves battered and ordered by the courts to get help or lose their welfare. She didn't need to listen to that crap. Could have gone into the construction business as his partner, gotten him contracts going to women and minorities a few years back. That would have helped with the mess when his dad died and his mother transferred her mania for control onto him. They'd all be a lot less stressed now. But no, not Kelda, stubborn as all the other Norwegians he'd ever known. Kelda had to have her own career, saving the less fortunate from themselves. Well, he'd seen to it she kept the Hedstrom name out of the sob-story business.

And he'd found a partner. Maria Sanchez, minority and female, one hundred percent Mexican though she'd never stepped foot outside the state of Washington. With her name and ethnicity on the bid forms he'd gotten enough of the good contracts. He'd put on a bit of a show for Maria earlier in the afternoon when the call came from Kelda. Made a production of banging the construction phone back onto its hook while she picked her way over a pile of lumber scraps in her size five work boots. Cute little feet, cute little butt in her Levi's, nice bazooms as Kelda's dead Uncle Karli used to say when he described women. Too bad Maria kept hers hidden under her denim work shirt. She'd helped him make some bucks, they just did upscale developments now. Gated communities. They could do that at the Landing. Or build a resort. THE INN AT HANSEN'S LANDING – ARNE HEDSTROM CONSTRUCTION. He liked the concept. Maybe he'd look for an investor, someone with some resort building experience. He needed to get it going, get some investors' dollars rolling in.

Maria had looked up at him, smug little grin, black eyes snapping. "That scowl on your face says trouble. Let me guess; no dinner again tonight." She patted his stomach and laughed.

"Yeah, I like good food." Arne sucked in his gut tight as he could. "But that's solid muscle. An extension of my chest." He'd put on a few pounds, but not the thirty or forty Kelda harped about and used as a reason to change how she cooked.

"I just don't want you having a heart attack on me and leaving me to run this business by myself. Want me to call Gran to make an extra tortilla?"

"No, better not. I imposed last night." They both knew it was the grandmother, not the imposing, that worried Arne.

Maria shrugged and walked away. He saw the silver threads in her blue-black hair, the graying that worried the old grandmother. "My little one needs a husban', you still marrie'?" she'd ask. He'd nod. "Then you hire 'nother partner, you train him good, he can marry my Maria."

Maria would say, "I have Carlos, Gran."

Then the old grandmother would rock her head shoulder to shoulder and rub her hands down the front of her long skirt. "That one."

Carlos Rodriguez was Maria's live-in before he went to prison. He'd worked for Arne. Movie-star handsome, even Arne had to admit: indigo hair halfway down his back; widow's peak; chiseled facial features; skin more tan than Mexican. But Carlos was the epitome of Mexican machismo, and would spend a few more years paying for that. He'd mixed it up with some Indians in a Yakima bar. Been elk hunting with some of Arne's crew, stopped for a few beers, let his hot-head rule. Went to his truck for his rifle. That made it first degree murder. He'd done several years in the penitentiary at Walla Walla before his transfer to the medium security prison at McNeil Island in the South Sound.

Maria made the drive to Tacoma every other weekend or so, complaining afterward about riding the visitors' bus and passenger ferry to the island. Arne supposed they groped each other in the visiting room. He would like to be the one groping Maria, but she managed to dodge him.

Arne had the Sonics and Mariners on split screen, Maria's private number on redial, a golf tutorial on the computer, and a micro-brew in his hand. He belched again. Kelda would make one of her faces at the belch and the amount of pizza he'd consumed. Dinner with Kelda meant sitting at the table, no TV, napkin on your lap. The phone rang. Maria, he hoped, calling now that inmates would be locked up for

18

count. She'd be irritated, bitch a little, ask him if he'd gotten anything to eat; he'd play up the cold pizza for sympathy.

He barked hello, heard Kelda's voice and scowled.

"Just checking in, Uncle Ragnar seems better, I got him a doctor's appointment for tomorrow afternoon."

"Yeah? That mean you're spending tomorrow there too?" He turned up the Mariner's sound so she could hear the crowd cheering. Let her know he was busy.

"I'm not sure, Arne. It depends on what the doctor finds. Right now, I'm getting some soup ready."

"Let me guess, beef-barley, right? Shit, I'm stuck with a cold takeout pizza."

"You don't even like beef-barley soup."

"No, but I love your clam chowder, how long's it been since you made that?" He listened to a long silence before she said, "Goodbye, Arne," and hung up.

He looked at the humming phone. So, Ragnar seemed better, not the news Arne wanted. Not at all. He wanted the old man off the Landing property so he could start developing it, get his mother off his back. Gerda had pushed him to marry Kelda, and had expected to see the Hedstrom name at the Landing as soon as that happened. Twenty-five years later, Gerda was still waiting. He was getting the lecture weekly now, since he'd made the mistake of telling her old Ragnar bought back Kelda's brothers' shares of the place. He'd learned that from Kelda's brother Erik, out on the golf course. Gerda knew, but Kelda didn't, which left Arne walking on the razor's edge of Gerda's German logic. Why in god's name had his Swedish father married a German woman? Her speech ran through his head almost daily.

*'It's not right for your wife to keep that property from you. Forty good acres, Arne, not all logged off like what Hansens sold your father and me. The Landing has salt water on three sides, that's a lot of waterfront, Arne. You married into the Hansen family, you have a right. Washington's a community property state."*

Gerda refused to understand the law no matter how he explained that property owned before marriage could be held separately, and

Kelda had seen to that. Gerda knew land values and had longed to own waterfront on Puget Sound all her life. He'd let her pull the strings, gone along with her plan like his dad had, it kept the peace, but Gerda was aging and tired of waiting. She'd planned it all long ago; she just hadn't expected Kelda, granddaughter of one of the area's biggest logging outfits, to become such a tree hugger.

If he could get started on a development he'd get Gerda off his back, give him some breathing room, give him and Maria a chance to talk some things through, things just hanging in the air between them. Nothing major; hell, he was a married man, father of two beautiful daughters, but Maria would help keep things on an even keel while Kelda went ballistic over losing the Landing. Might even let him move their relationship up a notch.

Kelda would come around in time, she always did. Win-win, way he figured. Him and Maria with a major construction project, Hedstrom name at the Landing, Kelda there to do the cooking. She could feed a construction crew, keep them onsite, get the job done in a few months, year tops.

Hell, she could even set up an antique store with all the old crap the Hansen family had been holding onto all these years, make some money that way and oversee the cooking at the same time. She always managed what needed managing—he'd give her that.

*It takes two to speak the truth - one to speak, and another to hear. - Henry David Thoreau, 1817-1862.*

*American essayist, poet, philosopher, naturalist & abolitionist.*

# 4

# The Landing

"You'd not be tossing them perfectly good carrots and celery stalks in the garbage, Kelda." Emma Stern's fingers plucked limp, boil bleached celery and carrots off the heap of beef bones dripping their last through a strainer.

Kelda raised one arm and twisted to block Emma's reach. "Uncle Ragnar and I like only broth, meat and barley in our soup. The veggies have served their purpose." She loved Emma, but she wanted the house and Uncle Ragnar to herself so she could determine what was going on.

"You haven't even picked them bones clean." Emma dropped a small morsel into the broth. The scrap dented the broth's congealing skin and rested in the wrinkles.

"Hey, that's fat." Kelda removed the offering with a slotted spoon and gave Emma the look that generally sent her off to a task of her own, doing for the Hansens and the Landing. "I'll collect it, fatty bones and all, to send along with you for your dogs."

Emma lived alone with two aging dogs in the old Stern place up across the county road from the Kerry farm, and did cleaning, laundry and assorted tasks for her neighbors. She'd spent most of her life seeing to others. First-born in a large family, Emma helped her mother tend the younger ones who moved on. She cared for her parents through assorted medical crises, handled their estates on their deaths and earned a little money doing for neighbors. She'd started helping the Hansens after Lydia's first heart attack. Ragnar and two other Hansen uncles ate regularly at the Hansen table then. Those three men, reared on generous servings of homecooked food, complained that Emma was stingy with helpings, so Kelda cooked, with help from Ragnar. Emma cleaned, ironed the men's work shirts and pants, and put things left here and there into proper closets and drawers. The uncles, accustomed to managing for themselves, took to leaving things about to keep her busy and out of the kitchen. She fussed at them to keep an ironed hankie in their pockets, they grumbled that she hid their glasses and house slippers. Fuss and grumble—it suited their needs.

Emma snapped a lid on the container of bones and vegetable scraps. "I might consider a bowl of that soup myself, after Ragnar's had his fill."

"There's more than plenty, Emma. I'm just waiting for the fat to set so I can remove it."

"Little fat wouldn't hurt your uncle none. He's been off his eating. Course that could change, with you here serving him."

Kelda saw through Emma's scowl to the love she harbored, and gave her a hug. Soup would be Ragnar's third little meal since Kelda arrived. He'd eaten some of her homemade applesauce with cinnamon stirred in and warmed in the microwave. Later, when he asked if the soup was ready, she whipped up a batch of scones and served them warm, dripping with butter and raspberry jelly. Butter and jelly drips left enough stains on the sheets for Ragnar to agree they needed changing.

"Only a couple months to raspberry season," Kelda said as she tugged a fresh white sheet over the mattress. Kelda saw raspberries as a health barometer. She and Ragnar argued every year over how much of the crop could go for jam or jelly and how much got crushed for his raspberry wine.

"Ah, I think I'll be having a glass of the wine with my soup when it gets ready."

Kelda's heart soared. "You're feeling better." She finger-combed his white hair.

"Some better." But his shoulders sagged as he spoke.

In a moment he added, "There's some papers need going through, some things need deciding, can't be put off no longer. I'm prit-near used up." His eyes clouded and he winced as though the weight of pending decisions landed on his shoulders and dug in their talons.

A piece of her soaring heart broke off and floated around in her chest, bringing pain from stomach to head. "Okay, Uncle, we'll start deciding, you and me. I've saved up leave time for whenever you say." Taking leave would be difficult but she'd manage; she always managed. "Now, let's get you back into bed."

His eyes closed as soon as his head touched the pillow, and he drifted away like a boat cut loose from its mooring. She knew little about failing physical health. The other Hansen uncles to whom she'd been close had died of heart attacks mid-stride. Her mother died so young. Most older people tired easily, slept fitfully, and dozed off and on during the day, but that didn't account for the wincing.

Ragnar had rallied again by the time she brought the soup and wine, and he ate and sipped with his old vigor. At his last medical visit, a couple months back, his doctor had told Kelda to get him to talk, and then laughed with her. Ragnar didn't spend much energy on words. She'd learned as a child to read his eyes, and right then they looked troubled.

Ragnar set down his soup spoon. "April's most gone, dahlias need planting."

"Dahlias need planting." She felt a smile start and grow. "You're worrying about getting the dahlias planted. Is there any ground left after planting all those trees, Uncle?" She watched him grin. Getting a grin from a stoic Hansen, and all but Uncle Karli had been stoic, was like winning the lottery, or beating Ragnar at a game of cribbage.

"Planted them trees here and there. Edge of the forest, out by the cottages, some along the creek. Here and there."

His eyes came back from the depths they'd plumbed earlier and resumed the color of pure delight, a blue so clear it made her think of mountain lakes. "Okay, we'll plant dahlias this weekend. Do you think we can cut back this year? To, say, a hundred or so?"

"*Ja*, I think we can. Give the rest to Walkingstick."

"Who?" Kelda frowned, worried that his mind was failing. He gave cut dahlias away to all the nearest neighbors from mid-July through October, but she'd never heard of Walkingstick.

"Walkingstick. The Indian lawyer, maybe interested in renting the big cottage. I said about him before."

Weariness returned to his posture and voice. The three small cottages had been closed for two or three years now, the big one for several months awaiting roof work and a new bathroom floor before they let it again.

Kelda put her hand on Ragnar's shoulder. "Yes, you did tell me about the Indian lawyer. His name is Walkingstick?" She'd thought he meant a lawyer that worked for the tribe, not an Indian who was also an attorney.

Ragnar nodded, sipped some more wine, shook his head, smacked a little.

"Maybe Arne can work on the cottage this weekend," she said. "While you and I get the dahlias in the ground."

"Walkingstick can work on it himself. Anxious to get a place over here, out of town, can't blame him. He's been living in Seattle." Ragnar sipped again.

"No, I don't blame him, either. Sometimes I think I'd like to live in one of those little cottages myself."

"You come home, you live in the big house, not one of them cottages."

He lifted his glass of wine and his eyes in salute. And something else. A plea? "That was some good soup, Kelda. I'll be getting stronger now."

His actions belied his words. He melted back into his pillows. His eyes closed. Kelda moved the table with their soup bowls and wine glasses away from the bed. He let out a sigh. She pulled up the comforter, fussed a little, dropped a kiss on his forehead and tiptoed away with the tray. At the door she heard him say, "Yes, Lydia."

Damn it all to hell, dying took work, what with a mind still treading water, Lydia offering up bits and pieces of wisdom, and Kelda fussing over him with good Hansen soup. They looked so alike, Kelda and

Lydia, he almost got mixed up which one was there. Serious blue eyes and sandy blonde hair, and Kelda still freckled though she'd tried hard enough to bleach them out with lemon juice all those summers back when. "Yes, Lydia," Ragnar said a second time. Seemed most Lydia messages were about the Suquamish tribe, interested now in their culture and recovering from the government wrapping them up in a package and tying it with reservations laws. She wanted truths told and the inlet returned to the Indians. He guessed she meant the whole Suquamish tribe, though Indian Joe was the name she kept sending, and Lydia should know Indian Joe was long since dead.

He rolled from his back to his left side, to his back again, gave up and got out of bed. Across the bay, he saw lights on the beach at Lemola. Used to be a dance place over there, the very place where Hansens first met Lydia Berg. He fixed his mind on that time, four Hansens still living at the Landing, still owning it together, working together as Hansen Brothers' Logging. Lydia's message floated across the water, rolled along the dock and across the lawn, and climbed right up to his window. *Tell Kelda about her brothers selling out to you. Tell her she will be sole owner of the Landing.*

While Kelda worked at the great room table where she'd stacked files and notes to write up her Mid-Sound Mental Health cases, her brain replayed Ragnar's words. He'd called her Lydia. She opened her laptop computer and searched for the correct client forms. Ghosts occupied most of the chairs around the table where Helgar and Magna and their seven sons once sat. Kelda always felt their presence in this room, but tonight she could almost touch them. They appeared, or she conjured them, when she was worried about her uncle.

She, a therapist, needed help. Grief counseling for her uncle's declining health, marriage counseling for her conflicts with Arne, anger management for her disgust with clients who beat and stabbed those they were supposed to love, then blamed their victims. She'd asked Keith, Mid-Sound's manager, for a leave of absence right after Christmas, and he'd agreed. "Whenever you're really ready, Kel." Why, then, had he assigned her two conflict resolution groups, now in the middle of their ten-week sessions? Because they met at night, and Keith's most recently hired counselor couldn't do nights; she was a single mom. The agency was short-staffed, and in truth no one wanted the groups. The women, ten victims of domestic violence, hadn't yet gotten to the angry stage. They still cried and blew their noses. The men, twelve testosterone junkies court-ordered to learn anger management, still held pissing contests and bemoaned the loss of masculine rewards.

Kelda turned on her computer to write up the mother-daughter case she'd seen that morning. She listened to the quiet, the drone of her computer's hard drive. The lingering smell of soup mingled with cedar kindling ready for building a fire. Ragnar kept kindling and alder in an old copperware canner that Kelda had used when she worked alongside her mother preserving peaches and pears. An antique dealer had tried to buy the canner, and several other old relics her uncle still used, but Hansens had never been anxious to let go of anything for which they could find a purpose, and three generations had used that canner for one thing or another.

The night begged for a fire. Kelda left her work to crumple newspaper and break kindling pieces. Cedar perfume filled the room. She heard a rustling, saw an apparition in the archway that separated the great room from the main house. Ragnar in waffle-weave long-johns. "Uncle!" She left her fire to meet him in the passage. They did their little dance, each helping the other to the great room table, both offering to get a bite to eat.

"Hot chocolate, I'm thinking, and Magna's sugar cookies."

"You haven't finished them yet?" Kelda had baked the cookies two weeks earlier. Ragnar, conservative with things he valued, had frozen most of them.

"I put them back for now, for a time to talk." His blue eyes begged her to make it easy.

She dashed up the stairs for his bathrobe, then fussed at arranging the cookies just so, stirring the chocolate longer than it needed. Ragnar dipped a cookie. Kelda watched and waited. Something about his look alarmed her. A burden that had nothing to do with physical problems. He set the cup down and brushed some cookie crumbs into one hand.

"April's 'most over."

Kelda released her breath. "Yes, we talked about that, remember? We can prepare the ground for the dahlias when we get back from seeing the doctor."

"I remember the talk about the dahlias. It's them property taxes I'm meaning, due the end of April." Ragnar fiddled with his cup.

"Right. The accountant will take care of them." She leaned toward Ragnar. "Won't he? Isn't Ivar Jonasson's son-in-law still doing the books? The guy with the Italian name?"

"*Ja.*" He fiddled with the cup a little longer. Then he looked up, his worried scowl in place. "There's something you'd not be knowing."

Sweat erupted. A chill swept over her. She waited. It never helped to rush Ragnar.

"It's about them taxes. I'll be paying Erik's and Greg's share. I bought back their half of the Landing. Took most all my money. Not much left for earning the interest to keep up the paying. Might be we will have to let Arne do his developing." Ragnar fished in his bathrobe pocket, brought out an ironed handkerchief, blew his nose, shook his head.

For a long moment Kelda felt like she'd been caught in a mudslide she'd watched working its way toward her. She'd known Erik and his wife Patty wanted investments that offered more immediate returns, and that Gregg wanted to buy more land in Alaska. A down-draft forced wood smoke into the room. Kelda pushed away from the table, crossed the room, poked at the wood and listened for wind outside. Her heart beat a tattoo in her ears. "Old Helgar's furious, Uncle. He's trying to choke us with this smoke."

"He's just giving us an excuse for water in the eyes, my *kär a.*"

*Kär a*, the old Norwegian endearment saved just for her. "No tears. We're Hansens. We're not giving up the Landing. Not without a fight. We'll fix up all the cabins for rental. We'll find a way, Uncle Ragnar. You and me."

"You think?" Ragnar nodded three times, a good sign. "You and me, *kär a*, we'll find a way. With Lydia's help."

*How could the drops of water know themselves to be a river? Yet the river flows on. - Antoine de St. Exupéry, 1900-1944.*

> *French writer/poet—amateur pilot—joined US allies in WWII, lost over Mediterranean Sea in 1944.*

# 5

## Raymond Walkingstick

The January day after Raymond Walkingstick retired from his Seattle law firm, he visited Hansen's Landing for the first time in thirty-five years. Hansens and the Landing once gave him reason to live. He needed them again, to renew his spirit. There were times when he felt his spirit had been born at the Landing, though he couldn't explain why, certain that his physical body had been born on the Suquamish Indian Reservation.

He found Ragnar Hansen aged but agile, planting fir seedlings at the edge of the creek that crossed Hansen property. Raymond introduced himself, and nodded when Ragnar said, "Lydia send you?" He changed into work clothes he carried in his truck and used his cane to lower his stiff body to Hansen earth, certain Lydia wanted him to help with the planting.

In his earliest memory, his mother called him Raymond. They lived in a long house built of cedar, with many people and few walls. The house had a high roof that let in slices of light. He played with other children on the beach where they collected clams exposed by their digging sticks. He listened to the elders' stories. Sometimes he floated on the water in a boat and wiggled his bare feet in fish the men pulled in. Afterward, his feet sparkled with silver dots.

Then a man named Raymond Morse came in a smaller boat and took him and his mother away.

In that memory, his mother called him Edward. The man never spoke in words to him, but Edward understood eyes, and he went into the woods when the man gave him the look. They lived many places, always by the sea. His mother and Raymond Morse made houses of driftwood and mats, and paddled off in the small boat. Edward remained on the beach. He played with shells and rocks and sticks, and waited for his mother to come back. When he tired of those playthings, he went into the woods and pulled pieces of bark from cedar trees. In his memory, before Raymond Morse, women wove bark strips. Edward practiced, and soon had a collection of cedar mats. One day, he folded one in half and closed the ends with narrow bark strips he poked through with a twig. He put his favorite rocks inside the pouch.

In the season when the maple leaves change color, Raymond Morse and his mother made their home on an inlet. A stream flowed into the inlet. Edward carried water from the stream to the driftwood house. Raymond Morse caught many silvery fish there. Edward's mother stopped fishing. She stayed on the beach and told Edward stories, and said, "Soon you will have a playmate." A man with light skin and hair came, and then another, but his mother shook her head. "No, Edward, they are not your playmates. They are the men who own the land and trees, and the rocks and shells, and all but fish in the sea."

The men brought food and took away fish. Edward followed the men, though he didn't let them know he followed. Sometimes they stopped by a house with three walls. Most times they went through the woods to a road made of slippery logs. Beyond the road were bushes and a big house, almost as big as the one where he'd lived before he became Edward.

Rains came, and cold. Edward and his mother stayed inside the driftwood and mat shelter. His mother wrapped them in blankets and mats, and held him so he couldn't leave. Edward missed the woods and the things he found pushing up through dry needles and mosses. He missed seeing the big houses.

The men from the houses came again, two at once. A woman came with them and, even then, Edward knew she brought something just for him. The men talked; then the woman said, "I am Lydia Hansen. The men are my husband's brothers." She said other things, important things about a war and bombs, and hiding the fire at night so the Japanese planes wouldn't see them. She talked about a baby. Edward watched her and listened to every word, and saw something in her face when her mouth stretched and her eyes went soft.

Lydia Hansen said, "Come with me." She took one of his hands, his mother took the other, and they followed the men into the woods, to the house with three walls. It had a black box with a fire inside. A kettle atop the box sent steam into the air. The woman gave them tea with sugar stirred in. His mother sat on a bed near the fire box, tears running down her cheeks. The men disappeared, but soon Edward saw them coming through the trees with the mats and blankets and cooking things from the driftwood house.

The men put posts along the opening on the house with the firebox and bed. They nailed up boards and put in a door and a window. Lydia Hansen brought books and read words to him. Soon, he read words to her, and her mouth stretched often, and her eyes went soft.

One day she said, "It is time for the baby to come, Edward. I need your help. I need you to read books to me while I help your mother. It hurts sometimes, when the baby is being born, and then it stops hurting. I will stay with your mother to help her through her hurting time. Will you read me words while I help your mother?"

Lydia Hansen and a woman his mother called grandmother stayed with them through the dark hours, through his mother's screams, comforting him and his mother. Edward helped with words, and with wood for the fire. Afterward, when his mother slept, Lydia Hansen showed him the baby. "This is your sister. Your mother named her Lucy. It will be a very long time before she can read books."

In Edward's opinion, Lucy was worthless as a playmate, but he didn't mind. Lydia Hansen came every day to hold Lucy and listen to Edward read. She talked to Edward's mother about learning. His mother talked too, and cried, and nodded her head. After that, Lydia Hansen took him to a place with many rooms, all filled with playmates and books. There he was called Edward Morse, and had a book of his own. Lydia Hansen said, "The children are your classmates." Her mouth stretched often, her eyes went soft, and she taught him the word. Smile. She smiled out loud when he read past his classmates. "They like you, Edward." He felt his mouth stretch. He knew they liked him because he could run past them in their games and catch the balls they threw.

He learned about the war, a place called Pearl Harbor, where Lydia Hansen's husband died. After the war ended, the man named Raymond Morse left to look for work in a logging camp or shake mill. They never saw him again. Edward's mother said he'd gone to Neah Bay, to his own tribe, and disappeared when a fishing boat sank in the big sea where no land can be seen.

His mother took Lucy and him back to Suquamish where they'd lived before the man named Raymond Morse came to take them away. Their chief, called Seattle by teachers at Edward's school, was buried there. Edward's mother sat on a mat by the grave, clutching Lucy, rocking and crying. Edward was glad for school and books, for cedar trees, rocks, shells.

In time, Lucy didn't want to be held and rocked. Then Edward's mother clutched a bottle. She still rocked, but she cried less. They moved into a house with walls too close and little light. Edward stayed outside, or in the woods, until the sky went black. Men taught him to fish and hunt. Women taught him to gather roots and berries, and to smoke fish. Some of his school mates called him 'squaw-man' or 'dirty Indian,' because he smelled like smoke.

Lydia Hansen taught his class that year. She gave him soap to scrub his clothes and told him to hang them on huckleberry branches in the woods, away from smoke. She helped him find information at libraries even when she wasn't his classroom teacher. She talked to him about things he understood: trees and seasons, math and science, football and baseball. She talked about things he didn't understand: human strengths and weaknesses, sadness and sorrows, sameness and difference.

He grew tall and strong, and won letters in sports. Girls who'd once teased him about being a smelly Indian now teased him another way. Lydia Hansen talked to him about that, too, and about personal responsibility and integrity. He liked having integrity, craved it, and knew it helped him win state honors in debate. His classmates joked that debating was the only time Edward ever spoke. They didn't know he talked to Lydia Hansen.

Edward graduated from high school in the top ten in his class. His only graduation gift came from Lydia Hansen; a collegiate dictionary and thesaurus, and a savings account in his name at a local bank. He wrote her a thank-you note, but it seemed inadequate, so he went to Hansen's Landing to thank her. He drove down the lane in his rusted and dented 1941 Chevrolet, where he entered the Landing house for the first time. It welcomed him, filling him with messages he would spend the next four years sorting.

"Are you still determined to go into the army rather than directly to college?" Lydia asked. Her eyes asked more, said more, told him she worried deeply about men at war.

Edward nodded and almost smiled. "Yes. I will remember what you told me. I will fight for my beliefs, not against other people. It will help me prepare for life away from the Suquamish village."

"You will need that." She put a hand on his arm. "Would you like to see the house on the inlet where Lucy was born? Where you lived for a time during that awful war? My brother-in-law Karli made it into a workshop."

He nodded again, his tongue paralyzed by her simple touch. He'd experienced little touching. He followed her through the woods without knowing where he stepped.

Karli Hansen had added plumbing and moved in many electric wood-working tools, but he kept the stove where Lydia Hansen had boiled water and made tea. Edward ran his hand over the smooth black surface, remembering, knowing she remembered too. "It was my first cup of tea."

He wanted to thank her for rescuing him, his mind, but he didn't know how. He wanted to express his concern for her health. Her eyes, ringed with dark circles, reminded him of his mother's eyes, robbed of depth by alcohol.

Lydia Hansen motioned him to a chair and sat on the bed's edge. "Wars give us reasons to hate. They also give us new technology. Both teach valuable lessons. I know what you learn will stay with you through your life."

"I owe you more than a thank-you, Mrs. Hansen." His feelings at her look and touch confused him. He knew only that it went beyond respect and gratitude, and that it was okay to feel it.

"The way you've been living your life pleases me. That is the best thanks. Come visit me when you have leave, so we can discuss colleges."

Edward nodded, finding it hard to speak, or even breathe, past the sadness of leaving. "Will you hold the books you gave me until I come back?"

"They will be in the great-room at the Landing, with your name on them."

He joined the army, went to Korea, spent his leave time seeing other parts of the world so he wouldn't have to see what was happening to his mother.

When he returned four years later, he drove down Hansen's Landing lane in a better car, though not a new one. He'd been home long enough to know his mother lived a life of despair worse than any he'd seen in Korea. Lucy had dropped out of school, seemingly to drink alongside their mother. Four years in and near war gave him confidence to speak in conversation, not just debate. He longed to talk with Lydia Hansen about his mother and sister.

The young woman who greeted him at the Hansen's great-room door looked like Lydia. She had the same smile.

"You're Edward Morse. I have the picture you sent my mother. I'm Kelda Hansen." She took his right hand in her two; her eyes moistened. "My mother is dead. Lydia is dead. Her heart gave out."

He stumbled back, like he'd been hit and lost his balance, though Kelda still held his hand. She smiled through the tears she didn't let fall, and pulled him to her for a hug. Her touch felt good, like her mother's touch had felt. It alarmed him.

"Come in and sit, Edward. Have a piece of pie and a cup of coffee."

He followed her, stunned and numb, through the great-room and hall to the kitchen, where he sat tongue-tied.

"Blackberry pie," Kelda said. "It's the best. They're the little mountain blackberries. I always find the first ones about this time, just before the Fourth of July. They're so much better than the big ones that come on in the fall. My mother knew all the best patches. She'd even slash brush and stir up places a little, to get them to grow."

She started coffee, patted his arm as she set the pie in front of him. He sat frozen by his body's response to this girl who looked like Lydia Hansen.

"I'll get the books Lydia put away for you."

She returned with them and a sealed envelope with his name written in a hand that must have been shaky.

"Mother said you would come one day. She said that I must be patient if you seemed reluctant to converse with me, that you were always quiet but war would likely leave you solemn. Are you solemn, Edward?"

He looked into eyes so blue he thought he was looking at pieces of the sky. She had golden hair, rosy skin, freckles on her nose and cheeks.

"Yes," he said. "I'm afraid I am."

"Do you need a place to stay? We still have one of the cottages vacant. There aren't so many summer people as years past. Mother said to offer you a room, or a cottage if one was available."

"That's very generous, but I need to stay with my mother and sister. I'm working at the fish market until fall." He was dumbstruck by the girl, but more by the desire to forget his own mother and move into a Landing cottage just to be near her. He knew she carried her mother's spirit. His own spirit had been touched by Lydia's. It had changed his life. In a sense, Lydia Hansen had given him life.

"Oh, it's not all that generous. My brothers are both gone now. You remember them? Erik and Greg? Erik's taking summer classes in college and Greg's up in the mountains at a fire lookout. I could use some help with the yard and garden. It's a job just dragging the hoses to keep everything watered."

"Do you live here alone?"

Kelda laughed, a pleasant laugh that made him want to smile.

"Hardly," she said. "Uncle Ragnar and Uncle Karli both live here, Uncle Rolf comes up from Brownsville almost every night for dinner, Emma Stern is in and out, bossing me around. Do you know Emma? She keeps up the cleaning, so I don't object too much."

"How old are you?" It wasn't what he wanted to ask or say, but it was all he could manage.

"Fifteen." She tilted her head and studied him. "You have such pain in your eyes. Were you injured in the war, or just saddened like I am at my mother's death?"

Her words shocked him. He jerked to his feet, tipping the chair in the process. A screen door slammed, a woman's voice called, "Kelda, are you lost in a book again? The water's running down the road. You'll drain the pond dry and burn up the pump."

"Well, damn, why didn't you just turn it off, Emma?" She shook her head, said, "Come with me, Edward. I'll show you the watering pond and pump system, just in case."

The remainder of that summer he stopped by the Landing after work and on his days off to give a hand where he could. He asked Kelda once if she ever did anything for fun. She answered that she swam every day. One Sunday he wandered out to the dock and found a crowd of young people on the beach. There were assorted boats and water skis, beach towels and ice chests. Kelda was directing the moving of a picnic table with attached benches. She saw him and called, "Edward, come join us."

He went to her, acknowledged introductions, then said he had to go. Kelda's swim suit revealed freckles on her shoulders and chest, right down to the top of her breasts. He found himself wondering where the freckles ended. She was his sister's age, a few months younger. He ought not be looking at her that way.

The last time he saw her, the end of that summer before he started college, she gave him boxes filled with home-canned fruits, jams, green beans, salmon and venison, and told him to come by for more when he'd finished those. "Since you won't take any money for all your help with the garden, you'll have to take some produce and meat."

"You do all this preserving?"

"My uncles help. Uncle Ragnar helps the most. He's a good cook, too. And he mends the clothes and repairs our shoes. You know, like putting on new heels and half-soles."

Again, he was stunned. He'd left for Korea believing the Hansens represented wealth and privilege, a world he'd never enter. He returned to find the Landing embodied hard work and responsibility. The two-plus months he helped out at the Landing changed his view of American life outside an Indian reservation.

He started college that fall, went straight through, summers included, until he earned his law degree. Mid-way he married a woman with connections to two northwest tribes and an interest in tribal politics. He could relate better to politics than to human emotion. It served for them, for a time.

More than one Seattle law firm courted him, even before he completed his studies. They all said the same thing; they needed a bright Indian on staff. Not just any bright man, but a Native American Indian. He became a partner in a small firm where he practiced for thirty years, working for tribal causes. Over the years, he became more Indian than just any man, as though his work altered his soul.

No one had been home that long-ago day when he returned the empty canning jars to the Landing. He left a note of thanks signed Edward, though he no longer used that name. He'd taken back Raymond when he joined the army. The name returned something he'd lost when Raymond Morse entered his life.

He changed Morse to Walkingstick after the accident that killed his wife and son, and left his left leg and hip with injuries requiring several surgeries. Names no longer mattered much, but Walkingstick fit him better than Morse. He'd never known if his mother used a surname before Raymond Morse came into her life. She'd never told him anything about his birth father. He let his hair grow long, braided it, took up the study of ethnobotany, and started a native plants nursery near Poulsbo. In time he adopted a cat he named Seatlh, spelled as the old chief had meant, not as white men spelled it.

While helping Ragnar Hansen plant fir seedlings, Raymond talked about the nursery, the need for land to grow plants for sale. He left it to Lydia, who'd sent him there, to tell Ragnar that the Landing would be a perfect place to do the growing.

*Disease often tells its secrets in a casual parenthesis. - Wilfred Trotter, 1872-1939.*
*English surgeon, pioneer in neurosurgery, studies on social and crowd psychology.*

# 6
# Kelda

Kelda almost let her uncle talk her out of the doctor visit, he felt that much better; later she almost wished she had. Dr. Clauson, known for his straight-forward, no-nonsense, face-the-facts manner, came right to the point.

"Your uncle is old. His joints are arthritic. His knees, hips, and shoulders are all deteriorating, but that's due to age, not to an invasive disease, and none are bad enough to risk surgery. No evidence of cancer. Lungs look good. Heart's sound."

The doctor paused, and Kelda knew she wouldn't like whatever came next. "But?"

"But, he's not eating right, thus losing weight, and he's suffering some level of depression. Surely you of all people must recognize the depression." He peered at Kelda over the top of his glasses.

She almost laughed to mask the shock. "Not eating right? How can he not eat right? I prepare meals and leave them for him. Things he likes. Healthy things, not just cookies, though I always make him homemade cookies." Her arms waved about as she talked. Why couldn't her hands rest in her lap? Why couldn't she just calmly say, *I see, doctor*, rather than blurt out, "And depressed?" Guilt, her old nemesis, tugged at her. She, a counselor, a family therapist, had missed signs of depression.

"Old people get depressed when they're alone. They don't eat right, even when the food's prepared for them. Ragnar told me you cook for him, leave everything ready for heating up. He says that with pride. Says Emma Stern eats the leftovers. Like all older people, he needs more—human contact and care and love almost as much as babies, if they're going to survive. Lots of old folks live on for years in nursing homes, long after their families expect them to die. And want them to die, for that matter. Attention keeps them alive."

"Emma's in and out. I visit every week." Not eating right and depressed. Emma eating the leftovers. The words circled her brain in a holding pattern, looking for a place to settle. Emma certainly wasn't losing weight or suffering any disorders.

"I'm not criticizing you, Kelda. I know you're devoted to your uncle. You do far more than many of your generation. But he needs daily attention now. Maybe a retirement home is the answer. An independent-living place. People his age for company. Meals prepared. Staff to see that he takes his medications on time. Not that he needs much beyond arthritis relief."

"How long do you think he'd last?" Kelda leaned forward, her voice another notch higher. Her face felt hot. She knew it was red, but better a loud voice and red face than tears. "Away from the Landing that's been his life?"

"I don't know, Kelda. He'd have to decide to make the transition. He'd have to choose to live. Right now, I just don't know."

A well of saliva collected in her mouth. She worried about drooling if she said anything more. Dr. Clauson saved her from herself.

"I know it all rests on your shoulders. Ragnar told me about your brothers' decision to sell out their interest in the Landing, the financial strain that's created. You're left with a lot of responsibility. Your uncle, the land, your own family, your career. Your own health. You have to find a balance."

"He's not eating right and he's depressed." She couldn't get past that.

Dr. Clauson smiled. "Some of the independent-living retirement homes are quite nice. Of course, they're expensive."

"I know. My mother-in-law lives in one. We pay her expenses, Arne and me. She thinks Arne's father left money invested for that, but that's not the case." She swallowed. "Uncle Ragnar is not going anywhere. I already told him I'd take a leave from my job and move home." To the Landing, still home in her mind.

"What about your own family?"

"The girls are both in college. Arne can live at the Landing, too. If he chooses." What was she to do about Arne if he still refused? She'd just reverse things, cook meals ahead for Arne to warm up, and live with Uncle Ragnar. Of course, Arne would cheat, eat fast foods, complain to Lauren and Reva that their mother had abandoned him. Arne needed attention, too. She'd spent twenty-five years trying to make up for the poor mothering job Gerda had done.

On the drive back to the Landing Ragnar said, "That was some good Hansen soup you made, fixed me right up. Figure I can get those dahlias in the ground myself."

They'd spent the morning before his appointment sorting tubers, agreeing they'd plant only one-hundred this year. "We need to get the ground tilled first. Or spaded," Kelda said. Her mind was busy making lists: call Keith about a leave of absence; call the accountant about first-half taxes; call Abe Tosenrud, the family attorney, about her trust. Her trust, made up of her share of Lydia's widow's benefits and her father's share of all Hansen Brothers' Logging generated before they sold off everything but the Landing. A trust in her name because her parents died young. Used for her education; borrowed against by Hedstrom Construction in which she had a partnership by marriage and incorporation, a fact Arne used for leverage.

Call Lauren and Reva, put them on warning to watch their spending. Lauren especially, who spent like Gerda. Dear God, how could Gerda believe Knut earned more money all these years after his death than he'd ever earned in life.

Call her brother Erik and tell him she was angry at him for selling out. What good would that do? He'd give her his wise-investment lecture, tell her the Landing was a luxury none of them could afford, she'd get angrier. And hurt. She crossed Erik off her mental list.

She coasted down the lane, enjoying each sprouting bud and new leaf on trees and shrubs, each old-fashioned daffodil that pushed its way through clumps of grass, the sight of water, salt and fresh. The big old Hansen house, white with forest green trim, gleamed in the early afternoon sun like a new coat of paint had applied itself in their absence. The lilac hedge hinted at beauty to come. She could almost smell fragrant blossoms, see them in Magna's old water pitcher.

Fresh tire tracks crossed from lane to dahlia bed, tilled in their absence. How could that be?

"Someone's been here, Uncle."

"*Ja,*" Ragnar said, over his shoulder. He'd opened the passenger door and helped himself out while the tired vehicle coughed and chugged.

"Who?" she called, but he was up the great-room steps and porch, and she still had her handbag and wits to gather. She headed for the kitchen phone, dialed the agency number, and was arguing with Keith about leave time when she saw Ragnar, dressed in work clothes, lugging a box of dahlia tubers across the yard.

"I'll see you tomorrow, Keith," she said, dropped the phone in its cradle, and dashed upstairs to find a pair of jeans and an old shirt.

"Only one-hundred this year," Ragnar said, his hands busy in the box, which he'd set on a cracked resin table that served as work bench for the flower and vegetable gardens. "S'pose you're wanting only pinks and purples, with some white for contrast."

"Now, Uncle, you know I like the reds and yellows too." Those were his favorites, and they fussed every year about how many of each. Kelda urged him into an extra jacket and set gardening gloves by his elbow. "You sort, I'll plant. I don't want you down on the ground getting your bones all chilled. Doctor said it's not good for your arthritis."

Tulips and hybrid daffodils, edged with two hundred or more double lavender primroses, bloomed on the dahlia side of the lilac hedge. The Old-one's journals noted the arrival of the first primrose plant, brought as a welcome by Mrs. Carlson, the widow across the cove, the year Magna arrived from Norway. Every March, the one just past included, Ragnar potted up plants in full bloom for community plant sales. Dear God, he'd done that and planted all those fir seedlings. No wonder he'd ached enough to crawl into bed.

Kelda counted gardening as one of her hobbies, the Landing yard her garden. She poked a trowel into tilled soil, lifted dirt, set a tuber and name-stake. The homes she'd shared with Arne were professionally landscaped with low-maintenance in mind. Their street-front yards all looked alike, though the shrubs got more expensive along with the houses. In their first two or three homes, Kelda had free-reign in the back yards, but that ended as they moved into increasingly expensive developments, and backyards became courtyards off master bedrooms or breakfast rooms. Waterfalls, pools, streams, gazebos and pergolas filled the space she'd once considered hers. She learned to plant flowers in pots, and move them out of view when their beauty faded.

She'd gotten only six tubers and stakes in the ground before Ragnar was down on his knees at the beginning of another row, the sleeves of his favorite navy and red plaid shirt rolled up, soil clumped under his fingernails and clinging to the white hair on his hands. The jacket she'd insisted he wear lay atop the table. He dug in the compost-enriched earth, set a tuber, covered it. They worked in tandem silence as they'd done in gardens for all the years Kelda could remember. Her dearest uncle, the one who'd set aside his own grief to see her through her mother's death. A bad time shored-up with love.

He checked name stakes, arranging by color, planting several of a tuber he called Lemon Meringue, a bright yellow with white tips. "Makes my mouth water for a pie just seeing the name on the tuber."

By the time they finished, Liberty Bay reflected pink from the setting sun, and Ragnar's depression lay buried somewhere under one-hundred and ninety-eight dahlia tubers. Kelda helped him stand and held one arm while he pressed his hands into the small of his back. He groaned, but a hint of grin softened his face. Her own back and limbs ached. They limped to the work table like two people staggering to the end of a three-legged race.

"What happened to our agreement? Only one-hundred this year?"

Ragnar stood a little straighter. "Way I figure, we kept it, and one to spare. Planted ninety-nine each." He grinned, then winced.

They limped and groaned their way to the back of the house, to the laundry room he called his mud-room. Ragnar collapsed onto a chair old Helgar had built. Kelda kneeled to untie his shoes. Her knees creaked.

"Oh, *kär a.*" Ragnar patted her hand.

"It's just knees popping. They need a little oil. I'll get us a drink."

"You're just keeping me sitting to catch my breath," Ragnar said, between sips of raspberry wine.

"I'm busy worrying backward. I'm thinking about you out in the rain and cold planting those dumb trees."

"Ah, now you don't want to be calling trees 'dumb.' Or the planting, either. It's right and good for the old and infirm to plant trees." Ragnar winced a little, moved his bottom so the weight shifted off his right hip. "And I had help with the tree planting. Walkingstick worked right alongside me. Was him got most all those thousand trees here to the Landing. Was him came down and plowed up the dahlia ground. He'll take the extra tubers."

"Walkingstick." She said the name for its sound and feel. "Oh, the extra tubers. I left them out on the table. Now, you stay put while I gather them." Her words trailed behind as she dashed back out to the dahlia bed.

Her low back ached, a pain shot down her left leg, she longed for a bath and bed, but Ragnar needed dinner, Arne needed to know she was spending another night, and her unfinished agency paperwork had to get done. She regretted telling Emma not to come until tomorrow. Not that she'd let Emma cook Ragnar's dinner, but the two of them could play cribbage while she wrote up notes and a formal plan to use the vacation and comp-time she had coming.

She loaded trowels and gloves into the box holding dahlia tubers, at least another one-hundred, and carted the box off to the garage corner that served as potting shed. The air in the space built for Model T autos, and filled with Ragnar's old pickup and garden tools that ranged from old to antique, smelled like leaked oil. Arne thought the pickup could be restored and sold to a collector, given its condition and low mileage.

Arne had similar thoughts about Karli Hansen's tools stored in the basement, where Ragnar kept them cleaned and oiled, and protected with tarps. Her Uncle Rolf's tool and dye collection was there, too. Arne had recently said there was a fortune in equipment in that basement, reminding her that it would need to be sold before they tore the old house down and started building an upscale gated community. Kelda had stared at him until he turned his back and stomped away.

A fortune in equipment? Maybe she and Ragnar could sell a few things, bank the money and buy some time. She hummed her way inside, considering what she'd prepare for dinner. Something that nourished body and spirit.

*It is hard to fight an enemy who has outposts in your head. - Sally Kempton, 1943 ...*
*Yoga, meditation and spiritual philosophy teacher.*

# 7
# Arne

The phone hadn't stopped ringing all morning, every call bringing bad news. And now this. Arne Hedstrom punched Off and threw the cordless phone in the general direction of the base unit. It skittered along the glass topped desk and spun to rest against a roll of building plans. "Shit!"

"Careful, there," Maria Sanchez said. "Remember your blood pressure. Your face is so red your yellow crewcut's turning pink."

"We Anglos call it blonde, not yellow." He ran one hand over the neatly trimmed cut he'd gone back to after years of fighting a cowlick in his thick, straight hair. "I swear, you're as bad as Kelda, all the time reminding me about my blood pressure."

"I'm just watching out for my interests. We Hispanics call it covering our ass. Anything happens to you, I know where I stand with this corporation."

"You're the vice-president, for crissakes."

"Vice-president, good at business details, marginal with tools, minor shareholder. Or is it minority shareholder? That's the part that worries me. You and Kelda own the company. You sell the company, I'm gone."

"Why would I sell the company, Maria? It's a growing company." He knew she'd been listening to his side of the phone conversations, all of them about money, most about projects in progress, the last a courtesy call from a friend who also happened to be the Hansen Landing accountant.

Maria shrugged. Arne watched her body move under her shirt. He'd always been attracted to dark-haired, olive-skinned women, but his mother swore to disown him, never let her eyes touch his again, if he ever brought around another female with hair darker than light brown. She'd told him that years ago, when one of his relationships ended. Kelda met his mother's guidelines just fine at that time: a natural blonde with a vested interest in waterfront property.

"So, what sent your temper into overdrive this time? Somebody hang a door backward?"

"Shit." Arne thought about the phone call. "Kelda fired the accountant."

"She fired Mac?"

"No, not McCluskey. Petrulli. Tony Petrulli, old Ragnar's accountant, been handling all the Hansen Landing books for the past two or three years. Took over when his father-in-law died. Old Norwegian, name of Jonasson." Arne snickered. "Norwegians are losing some of their chokehold on old Poulsbo. From Jonasson to Petrulli." Not that it was doing him any good. Just the opposite; it got harder every day to pry Kelda's fingers loose from her hold on that land.

"So?"

"Never mind, Maria, it's a family matter."

"Well, excuse me."

Arne saw the hurt look as she turned her attention to the papers on her own desk. What could he tell her? That Petrulli kept him informed about Ragnar's finances? Hell, he played golf with Petrulli, they discussed things out on the course. Things got said, filed, forgotten. After he heard about her brothers selling, Arne got Tony Petrulli to help him prepare a plan to offer Kelda for caring for her uncle and managing the Landing. After he comforted her, of course. He knew she'd be upset when she got that piece of news about her brothers. Been waiting for her to hear, see what she did. He sure as hell didn't expect her to fire Petrulli, take over the books herself.

"Kelda's taking a leave-of-absence of sorts from the agency. Going to stay at the Landing most of the time, which leaves me high and dry, but there you have it. Kelda's made up her mind." That should ease some tension. Maybe get Maria to feel sorry for him, his wife almost abandoning him.

Maria turned his way again, and frowned. "What do you mean, 'leave of absence of sorts?'"

"She has to finish up with those night groups, a few more weeks, she's just started a new mother-daughter case. And there's another family case no other therapist will take on. One of those court order things. Father, daughter, and son. Looks like the old man's been diddling the daughter, got her pregnant, son helped her get an abortion. Whoever did the abortion left her bleeding, she ended up in the hospital. Doctor reported it to the authorities, prosecutor stepped in, but they can't make a case."

Maria's frown turned into a squint-eyed scowl. "Kelda told you all this? I mean, aren't there some privacy laws? Or professional ethics? Or something to protect a family?"

"Hell no, Kelda didn't tell me. You know Kelda. I read it in the paper, community news section. It's a common name. Smith. I saw a file on her desk. Intake file, nothing much interesting in it, but the names are the same as the article. Father name's Hap, daughter's name's Cameo."

"You snooped in Kelda's papers? Why am I not surprised?"

"Oh, come off it, Maria. You collect tidbits about Carlos's prison buddies all the time. His letters, the parts you read to me, are full of inmate crap, getting fucked over by the man. He mentions names and cases, you pass it along. Shit. We talk more about that than work."

Maria ignored that. Turned her back again. Arne unrolled plans for a doctor's clinic. He had a crew out demolishing four old houses on the site. World War II houses, hadn't been lived in for a couple years. Kelda didn't get all upset when he developed sites that had been built on before. Easier, actually, taking out old buildings rather than trees. Property owners knew the value of trees these days. Wanted to negotiate timber sales themselves, get top dollar for their evergreens.

He couldn't get his mind off Petrulli's call. He'd hoped the accountant would spring some information from the Hansen's attorney, maybe find out just how much money Kelda had tucked away in that trust that he'd hoped to have converted to a joint investment long ago. Petrulli said old Abe wouldn't say and might not know. The bank handled the trust, but old Abe had helped set it up. He knew what went into it. Knew that Hedstrom Construction had once borrowed against it.

Arne checked his watch. He needed to stop by the retirement home where his mother lived before she went to lunch. The Kensington, expensive as its name implied. Gerda Hedstrom expected to hear that Hedstrom Construction was taking over the Landing. He'd let the news about Ragnar buying out Kelda's brothers slip, then gotten Gerda's promise to be patient just a bit longer.

"I only want what's legally mine. Yours, too, as Knut's son. Those old Hansens cheated us."

She believed a business partnership that involved boats and land existed between Knut Hedstrom and Karli Hansen, and kept at Arne about making things right.

"I'm working on that, Gerda," he'd say, careful to use her given name, always avoiding the truth. Knut Hedstrom and Karli Hansen were drinking partners, that was all. Knut's alcoholism wasn't as long-running as Karli Hansen's, but Knut didn't have Ragnar and Kelda around to take care of him, manage his affairs.

Arne should have been seeing to things for Knut and Gerda, but he'd been caught up in growing his company. He'd figured he was close to taking over the Landing this time, and then Kelda pulls this fast one. Now he'd have to tell Gerda they had another glitch.

Knut Hedstrom, a Swedish man, married Gerda Wagner, a German woman, against both families' wishes. They moved to the Kitsap Peninsula in 1942, when the navy yard in Bremerton and government installations at Keyport and Bangor ran shifts around the clock for the war.

That made them late-comers. Fifty some years later than Hansens. Fifty some years too late to get choice land. Knut worked in the navy yard first, then later at Bangor, as a carpenter. After the war, when there seemed to be plenty of money, he built a three-bedroom house on five acres west of Hansen's Landing. Land purchased, already cleared, from the Hansen brothers. Arne could still hear Gerda going on about that.

*"You paid those Norwegians too much for the land, Knut. Cleared land. The value was in the timber. The Hansens kept the good land. The waterfront."*

*"This is good land, Gerda. Look at the vegetables we're growing."*

Knut loved the place, loved being around other Scandinavians, albeit most were Norwegians who liked to poke fun at Swedes like him.

*"I've no axe to grind with the Hansens. They've been fair. They're my friends, their sons are our boys' friends. Just once be happy with what we've got, and keep in mind the Hansens have their own struggles."*

Arne hadn't noticed any struggles. Maybe his older brother did, but they rarely talked. Arne went through school with Erik and Greg Hansen, the grade between them, played football with both his junior year. Hansen's Landing was known for beach parties in those days, and Arne attended his share. Kelda was in junior high, a typical bratty younger sister. Except she could already cook. Best potato salad he ever had, up to that time, Kelda made when she was twelve or thirteen. Lydia Hansen's heart was already acting up, Kelda took over the household tasks. Guess that could have been a struggle.

And old Ragnar's wife, Ruth, who spent most of her life in mental hospitals. None of the high school crowd had paid much attention to any of the women. In fact, they never went to the house. Hung out in the boathouse shelter, out in front by the Landing dock, or in Karli's workshop over on the inlet. The property Gerda most coveted.

Karli Hansen was the fun uncle, always a little drunk, kept homebrew under his power saws, shared it with the football players. He wasn't all that concerned with laws about drinking age, but he made the guys stay at the Landing until they were sober enough to drive. And they had to clean up their own messes.

Karli's shop had a kitchen of sorts. An old wood-burning stove, sink with cold water, 1930s refrigerator. And a little room with a toilet and sink. Girls called it a powder room. Guys mostly peed in the woods. Erik said the Hansen uncles fixed up the shop for some Indian family during the war. Supposed to have been some baby born in it.

A whole stand of evergreens hid Karli's workshop from the main house, made it a great place for necking parties. That's about all you could get from girls in the mid-fifties, a little necking. Maybe some serious petting if you were going steady. Arne got his fair share, always with the best looking and most popular girls. Cheerleaders. Kelda liked to remind him how few of those girls went on to college. High school represented their acme. Leave it to Kelda to point that out. Acme. Shit.

With Gerda on him all the time, Arne grew jealous of Erik and Greg having all that land. "Hey, man," Greg said, "you've got your own father. We barely knew ours. And there's still three Hansen uncles. By the time they divide this up, there won't be much left."

"You Hansens own land other places." Arne knew that from Gerda, too.

"Some timber rights. Not much land. The uncles keep selling to pay for Aunt Ruth's special care. You know, Uncle Ragnar's wife. She went over the edge when her baby died." Greg shrugged off Erik, who tried to hush him.

Far as Arne knew, the Landing parties ended the year he graduated and started college on a football scholarship. Erik was already in California on academic scholarship, taking special classes through the summer, and Greg was off hugging trees somewhere. Arne lost touch with the family, except through Gerda's updates, clear in his memory as if she was speaking that moment:

"Kelda's home from Washington State University for Christmas, Arne. She brought some Hindu friend with her, do they celebrate Christmas? You should call her. You were so close to the Hansen boys."

"Kelda brought a new boyfriend home from Brazil, or maybe Argentina. At least this one's not as dark as the last one. Of course, she says they're just friends. I'm sure the uncles would love to have you stop by, they must be worried she'll marry one of those dark-skinned foreigners."

"Kelda's in Hawai`i, visiting her current boyfriend. A Hawaiian, I guess, but still dark skin and hair. WSU seems to have a lot of foreign students. Of course, Hawai`i's not quite foreign now that it's a state. Emma Stern, you know she helps out at the Hansen place? She says Kelda has this fascination with Pearl Harbor. Well, it's to be expected. Her father died there."

"Rolf Hansen died. Not even sixty years old. Kelda's back home, taking care of Ragnar and Karli. They're the only old Hansen brothers left, they own all the land now. Kelda's teaching some classes at the community college while working on her master's degree, you really ought to stop by, Arne."

At times, Arne wished he'd never heard of the Hansens of Hansen's Landing. Or that Kelda had just stayed in Hawai`i, married that Hawaiian, dark skin and all. Then Gerda wouldn't have started on this property thing. Arne had done quite well on his own, but Gerda never noticed. She stayed stuck in an old belief that the Hansens cheated Knut Hedstrom out of land, and Arne was the one needed to make it right.

"Shit." Arne rolled up the plans, tossed the pencil he'd been using into the desk drawer, looked over at Maria. "I'm going to run by Gerda's, then check on the crew. You'll see me when you see me."

For a moment, Arne thought his mother was having a heart attack. Her hand pressed her chest. Diamonds caught the light. Shit, a year's wages on one finger. But she recovered enough to drag out her old trump card.

"Well, dear, it's time to remind Kelda, and the rest of the world, about that old murder the Hansens covered up. You know those nasty uncles killed that man. Wallace whatever, Ragnar's brother-in-law. Crazy Ruth's brother. Killed him, and robbed him of all his money. Maybe land too, it's hard to say, but what does it matter? It's the murder that counts. How would Kelda like that news to get out? Or even the news that she had a crazy aunt?"

"Forget it, Gerda, that's sixty years ago. Nineteen thirty-two, for crissakes. It's just a matter of time 'til Kelda gives in. I told you, I've got a plan. There's no money to keep up those taxes. None. Nada. Hell, I doubt they can pay the first half out of Kelda's trust, there can't be that much left." Except the Hedstrom Construction debt. Arne felt the pressure in his chest, the heat on his face. Best way to pay a debt like that, borrow more from the same source, make a bigger splash, then pay it all off on the winnings.

"Arne, dear, I'm not getting any younger. I want your father's fair share, that's all. Is that too much to ask?"

Arne groaned. There were things about Knut that Gerda would never need to know if Arne just got Kelda to come to her senses on the Landing. He looked at his watch, though sweat or heat waves made his eyes too blurry to see. Must need glasses. Shit. "Look, Gerda, gotta go check on the crew, just trust me on this a little longer. Okay?" He kissed the air near her cheek, and turned to leave.

"We'll see, dear."

Now, what the hell did that mean? Arne used every curse word he could remember as he pulled his truck into traffic. He'd been hot for another girl when he married Kelda. Not that Kelda hadn't been a good wife. No complaints except that blue eyes, blonde hair, and freckles hadn't been his fantasy. He liked his women a little more exotic, a little less wholesome, and a lot less independent. Shit.

*The afternoon knows what the morning never suspected.* –

*Swedish Proverb*

## 8

## The Landing

Ragnar figured Lydia must be satisfied for the moment, he'd slept that well. Here he was in the old breakfast nook on a sunny Saturday morning, drinking coffee and eating scrambled eggs, hash browns and toast with homemade jam, listening to Kelda explain her delayed leave of absence.

"Work two days," she said. "Mondays and Wednesdays noon to nine, more or less, for the next five weeks, and then a real leave."

"That makes for twelve-hour days, *kär a*, what with the ferry rides." Ragnar watched her eyes. They looked strained, like the migraine made them, but not near so bad as Lydia's looked after she got that rheumatic fever that developed from some infection going around the school where she taught. "You say Arne's going to come and go?"

Kelda's eyes got busy with a drip of jam running off her toast. He gave one nod. He'd known that would be the biggest worry—what to do about Arne, who'd been promising to help with the Landing for all the years he could remember, but who'd found excuses when Kelda asked. She wanted new roofs on all four cottages so they could rent them for income to help with taxes. Ragnar could do most all the fixing on his own, but roofing needed a couple men, at least one some younger than him.

Kelda had been through the accounts and said she could handle bill paying just fine, they could cut that accountant expense. Said she knew just where things stood. That did his heart good. Ivar Jonasson had been his friend, but when Ivar upped and died and his son-in-law took over the firm, costs went up. Seemed the son-in-law charged for unwanted advice. Bad investment, he'd said, when Ragnar bought out Erik and Greg.

Kelda gave a Hansen nod. "Arne will complain about living here for a time, but he'll show up for dinner. Now, let's get this breakfast mess cleaned up so we can walk the property and think out loud about making the Landing pay its way."

Ragnar pushed away from the table. "We'll leave these dishes, give Emma something to do, keep her from making a mess of the living room. You get into your hiking boots, we'll go on over to The Indians, take a look at Karli's shop." He grabbed plates and headed for the kitchen.

"You mean the inlet?" Kelda said. "I remember Mother called the inlet *The Indians*, for the families that camped there to fish the fall salmon run. Right?"

Ragnar waited without answering, given that Kelda's look said she was far away in thought. Now what made him say *The Indians* when he meant the inlet? Lydia, that's what. There she was, reminding him that was Indian land. He didn't know what Lydia had in mind, but it looked like she might be sending the message to Kelda.

"Which brings up another issue," Kelda said. "The creek needs to be cleaned out and restored. I know there are salmon stream reclamation projects going on, but I don't think there's any money allotted. Not that there'd be any expense—just physical labor, which I can do."

"Now, *kär a*, you can't be doing it all."

"And why not? I'm a Hansen."

With that declaration, Kelda followed her uncle on the narrow path through native rhododendrons, evergreen huckleberry and sword fern to Karli's old workshop. Windows caked with grime and siding that needed a coat of paint gave it a forlorn look. Inside, tarps covered what remained after Ragnar moved the most valuable tools to the basement of the big house. She peeked under the tarp covering a cast iron wood stove.

"Stove's in good shape," Ragnar said. "Work benches too, far as that goes. Could hook up water for the sink and toilet. Doubt there's anyone wants a workshop away off out here. Should have torn it down when Karli died. Maybe should tear down the house, too."

And on that note, he left her to go outside, hands shoved into pants pockets and eyes wet with unshed tears. She gave him time to remember when Karli's workshop hummed with saws and sanders. The building could be salvaged, though for what purpose? More likely they would need to tear it down, break up the concrete floor and have it hauled to a recycle center. More work, more expense, no income.

One of Arne's schemes suggested they short-plat the Landing property to keep the house and yard a separate parcel, build upscale homes around it.

"Fence it in," Arne said. "Fence all the way to the water to keep one patch of beach private."

She'd seen one place in Edmonds where that happened. An old couple held on to their home, sat inside and watched heavy equipment clear everything to bare earth, new houses with new landscaping go in around them, until their old home became a prison of sorts.

Better to sell out, make a clean break. But not yet, not while Ragnar lived, and it seemed he'd decided to go on living after that business about taking to his bed to die. She went out, locked the door, and hooked her arm in Ragnar's. "Walk me out to the dock, Uncle, and tell me about those old steamboats that called in at the Landing."

Later, while Ragnar rested in his recliner and Emma fussed with laundry and floor scrubbing, Kelda set out to assess what it would take to make the three small cottages livable. As she stepped onto the porch of the first cottage at the top of Hansen Lane, she heard a vehicle and felt a vibration. Old post and block footings needed to be replaced. A loaded lumber truck rumbled by, stopped long enough for the driver to roll down the window and shout something she didn't understand. He drove on to the large cottage, the one Ragnar had said the Indian man wanted to rent.

The truck door opened, a young man jumped out and pushed a pencil behind his ear. "This the two-bedroom cottage at Number One Hansen's Landing?"

"Yes. But we haven't ordered any lumber. We haven't even decided whether we're going to fix them up or tear them down."

The man shrugged, reached back into the truck for a clip board. "If this is Number One Hansen's Landing, the load gets dropped here, cottage nearest the bay proper. Just want to check, make sure it's the right stuff."

"We have not ordered any materials." Spoken with exaggerated spaces between the words.

You Ragnar Hansen?"

"That's my uncle."

"Or Kelda Hansen? Say's Ragnar slash Kelda Hansen on the invoice."

"I'm Kelda, but . . ."

"Must have ordered then." He closed the truck door, and pulled on a cinch holding a nylon strap in place. The load groaned.

"No. Wait. I'm managing this property, and we have not ordered any lumber." She again enunciated each word as if the man's problem might be with the English language.

"Here's the invoice." He shoved the clipboard into her hand, loosened a second cinch. "It's marked paid. My job's dropping the load."

She scanned the top page, then the one under it, where 'paid' was written in large, loopy letters. "This says Raymond Walter something or other. This is not for Hansen's Landing." She tried to shove the clipboard back into his hands, but he was lifting and whipping one of the nylon straps. He frowned, grabbed the clip-board and shook his head.

"Raymond Walkingstick. Walkingstick Nursery."

"I thought Walkingstick was a lawyer."

"Yeah, he is."

"Oh. Well. That makes all the difference in the world." Her sarcasm was wasted. The man's biceps bulged as he pulled sheet-rock from atop the load. She marched toward the house to ask her uncle just what was going on. Halfway there she heard another vehicle. A black pick up. Walkingstick, no doubt. She changed directions, marched toward him, hands on hips, ready to set things straight.

For thirty-five years Raymond Walkingstick carried a picture of a fifteen-year-old girl in his heart. When the subject of that picture turned and walked toward his truck, he saw the girl in the woman and wished something of the young man he'd been, just stepping out into life, remained in him. At that moment, he hated the cane and the lame leg that required it.

She stopped just out of the pickup's path and glared. Nothing Ragnar had said about Kelda prepared him for the anger he saw; nothing prepared him for the leap in his heart. The lumber yard's driver let a piece of sheetrock slide down his body to rest on his foot, balanced it, waved, lifted it over his head. Walkingstick turned off the pickup's engine, opened the door, and eased out, cane first. Kelda kicked a round rock out of the crushed gravel while he steadied himself. He took it for what it was, a gesture to avoid staring at another's frailty.

"Hello," she called, taking long strides to reach him, as though to save him from stumbling toward her with his cane.

He switched his cane to his left hand, offered his right. "I'm Raymond Walkingstick, you'd be Kelda Hansen."

"I know who I am and figured out who you are. I'm not interested in shaking hands until you tell me what's going on."

Her eyes looked sad, sadder than they had that summer when her mother died. He felt the pain in his chest, right where he'd felt excitement flutter a moment ago. "Your uncle didn't tell you? I'm renting this cottage." He pointed his cane to let her see he could stand up straight without leaning on it.

"He told me you wanted the cottage. He said we needed to do some roof repairs. He didn't tell me we were going to rebuild the whole damn thing." Her hands left her hips, punched air.

"If it's the expense, I've paid for the materials." He returned the cane to his right hand, shifted his feet on the uneven gravel, and kept his face serene, his lawyer's face that no one could read.

"It's not the expense, it's a matter of ownership. You can't just come in here and tear into the place, making changes to suit your whim. It's Hansen property." She looked down for a moment, then back at him. "And we can't have you buying materials. That's not how we do things."

"Your uncle agreed to the repairs. As for buying the materials, that was decided by a cribbage game. Loser pays." He took off his dark glasses, let her see his eyes, though he doubted they showed much after years of hiding everything.

She tucked her lips between her teeth for a moment, maybe trying to hide the smile he saw lighting her eyes. "You played cribbage with Uncle Ragnar? For who had to pay? Nobody beats Uncle Ragnar in cribbage."

"I know. He gave me several dozen chances. Maybe several hundred."

"Well, it won't do." A grin took possession of her face, still freckled, and softened her eyes. "He's been playing cribbage since he was five. Almost eighty years. He cheats, steals pegs while you're concentrating on your cards, just to take your measure."

"I know he's very practiced. He's still teaching me. In the end, it doesn't really matter who pays for the materials. The cottage and I have come together at a time when both our souls need restoration."

"Oh, dear god, are you a left-over Hippie?"

"No, a left-over attorney, I'm afraid. Now owner of a small native-plants nursery."

"Well, you should have waited on the materials. We could have gotten them wholesale. Through our construction business. Because we will pay for them, Mr. Walkingstick, simply by refusing rent money."

"My retail license gives me a decent discount, and your uncle and I have a gentlemen's agreement that will be honored. But, cost is not the important factor."

"It's always important."

A ringing bell pierced the air. He saw fear consume her; saw it in her eyes before she turned, watched it in her body as she ran for the house. He leaned on the cane for a moment, enjoying the sight of her, using the time to center himself. He knew Ragnar's spirit could decide to leave his body at any time, so he sent his own spirits' energy with her.

The bell. Kelda was in full run before she heard Emma stretch her name. They'd always used the bell at the Landing. It could mean dinner's ready; it could mean an important phone call; it could mean an emergency. How much time had elapsed since she left Uncle Ragnar tucked into his chair? Was he in the throes of a heart attack? Her heart pounded so hard she might be in the throes herself. She pressed one hand to the stitch in her side and muttered, "Walkingstick. Gentlemen's agreement. Cost isn't an important factor."

She'd watched him coming down out of that big black pickup, his silver hair combed back from his face. He'd turned enough for her to see the thick braid that reached down his back almost to his belt. It gave him back power the cane took away. In profile, he reminded her of pictures she'd seen of Crazy Horse. His sunglasses irritated her. When he took them off, she saw eyes she'd seen before, honest and sad. She worked her memory, but couldn't place him, and knew no amount of stress would make her forget a name like Walkingstick.

"Call 911," she yelled, but Emma had disappeared from the great room porch. "Emma?"

She staggered through the door and bumped into Emma's soft body. "Uncle Ragnar?"

"It's these contraptions, all ringing and beeping. Your uncle's snoozing in his chair. He said to tell you he'd be liking some scalloped potatoes with the German sausage for dinner tonight, if you're of a mind."

Kelda collapsed onto a chair, gasping for a decent breath to fill her lungs. Emma had jammed her cell phone into one hand, her pager into the other. Arne's office number showed on the pager. She'd forgotten to call him the night before as promised. In truth, she'd forgotten Arne existed, except at some transitory level. She'd forgotten her daughters and her subliminal worries about them. Her home, her job, her life prior to three days ago, had all vanished from conscious thought. She'd returned to the Landing and slipped into a new role, or back into an old one.

She pulled herself up out of the chair and navigated, weak kneed, around the big oak table to the corner that served as the Landing office. It was watched over by a portrait of the Old-ones. There, in the center of the desk, rested her To Do list with an attached Post-It note to call Arne. God, she needed a note to herself to remember to call her husband. As she punched in his office number, she heard Emma at the door explaining to Walkingstick. "Them phone things of hers going, one after the other, her husband having one of his fits."

Arne barked, "Hedstrom Construction," so loud she moved the phone from her ear and spoke from a distance. "Hello, Arne, I've been running, I'm out of breath, Uncle's okay, and I'm fixing scalloped potatoes for dinner if you want to come." She closed her eyes and leaned her forehead into one hand to hide from her shame at forgetting him. Then she felt a slight smile, and moved her hand to cover her mouth. Arne was telling her stuff she didn't really care about, but she'd heard the change in his voice. "So, do you want to come for dinner?" she asked.

"Yeah, okay, I'll come over."

"Oh, Arne? Bring your tools. There's a renter moving into the big cottage. You could take care of a few things in minutes that would take me hours." She felt Walkingstick's eyes on her, and knew he'd heard. Well, she needed to stay in control of the Landing. Better if Arne did the work than a tenant. Right's right, as Emma would say. She looked away from Walkingstick's dark eyes to busy herself with papers. For some odd reason, she felt like going to the man and wrapping her arms around him. She looked at the Old-ones' portrait and would swear her grandmother winked.

Kelda tried to hide her smile when her uncle helped himself to a third serving of scalloped potatoes before passing the casserole to Raymond Walkingstick. "Damn it all to hell, Kelda, you sure got the right scald on these here spuds. Even kept Arne from the TV long enough to eat one whole dishful himself. One good thing them

Germans came up with. Sausage. Damn, that man can eat more than three Hansens put together.

"Need a casserole size of a washtub," Emma Stern said, accepting a second helping herself.

Kelda watched and listened. Her uncle had given his head three little shakes with his compliment. Not shake back and forth, but a shake to the right and pause three times. That had long been accepted as praise in the Hansen family, and by many Norwegians who conserved words, especially words of approval. She grinned at the 'three Hansens put together' description. That's how they spoke of themselves in the years three of them gathered at this table. Rolf, Karli, and Ragnar. They'd been here in her infancy and through her childhood. When Arne complained about her strong attachment to them, she explained attachment theory, which irritated him as much as the Hansen's closeness.

"The food is excellent, Kelda," Raymond Walkingstick said. "It's entirely understandable that a man Arne's size would consume a fair portion. Thank you for including me."

Kelda gave him her warm professional smile to make up for her earlier behavior. "That sounds like a legal argument." Those eyes. She squinted, tilted her head, dropped her counselor voice. "Edward? You're Edward Morse. From the summer my mother died. You helped me take care of things around here that summer."

"Why, yes. Didn't Ragnar explain?"

"Explain how?" Ragnar said, as he fished another potato slice out of the hot dish. "He's the Indian lawyer, like I already said."

Kelda saw the twinkle in Ragnar's eyes, and knew there was more to the story. She turned to Raymond, giving Ragnar time to come up with an explanation. "So, what happened to Edward Morse?"

Raymond paused, fork poised in the air, face looking carved from granite.

Kelda knew that it would be a long story, and that it was somehow woven with her own.

*Memory is the diary that we all carry about with us. - Oscar Wilde, 1854-1900.*

*Irish playwright and novelist.*

# 9
# Kelda

While Raymond Walkingstick explained that Edward was his middle name, and Morse not his biological father, Kelda thought about the confusion and loss children endure when life changes as it had for Raymond. She spoke to that, in professional mode again, and listened with pride as Raymond said complimentary things about Lydia. More than complimentary, he spoke with love and wonder. Her uncle's fork reached out to spear a piece of sausage from her plate; she half-heartedly swatted at him. Her thoughts were on that summer, and what Raymond, as Edward Morse, had meant in her life.

At fifteen she was mature in many respects, responsible certainly, but had never dated. Her brothers always had their carefree friends around. That's how she saw them and most high school males in the late fifties. The young man she'd known as Edward differed in every respect. He understood sadness and sorrows. He watched her, but startled at her touch, lowered his head when their eyes met, turned away when he saw her in a bathing suit. Emma had harped at her.

*He might be older, but you're more mature. He's just back from a war, he's not so used to young women bouncing about, touching arms, giving hugs. He's from the tribe, you have to be careful. Kelda, you need to cover up that chest of yours.*

Had she done any of it on purpose? Touched, or hugged, or put on a swimsuit on a warm afternoon? She thought not; she was trying to find normalcy after her mother's death. Boys who came to the Landing to swim or tie up boats at the dock were always a little older and a little uneasy around her in her lingering sorrow. They draped themselves around other girls or huddled with her brothers and their friends. When they spoke to her, it was generally to ask what there was to eat.

Remembering, she began wondering if her intrigue with Raymond as Edward led to her interest in cultural differences in college. Not just interest, but infatuation in some cases. She wanted to learn from them, to better understand all human nature, not just white people, and certainly not just Norwegian men who'd earned their income cutting down entire forests.

She'd brought any number of foreign exchange students home to Hansen's Landing during breaks that were too short to let them return to their own countries, or in one case to Hawai`i. It dawned on her now that she'd chosen them in some futile search for a man like the one she'd known as Edward for those two summer months. Dear god, she was a therapist, and she just figured that out.

"Oh, Christ," Arne shouted, from the living room where he'd turned on Ragnar's TV. "Geez, these umpires, get worse all the time." He rejoined them at the dining room table. "What's for dessert, Kelda? You make some pies?"

"No, she didn't make no pies," Emma said. "Pies take a lot of work. Besides, I just done the kitchen floor."

"There's a wine cake and whipped topping," Kelda said. "You can add a dollop of raspberry jam, if you like."

"That'll do." Arne headed for the kitchen.

"Go easy on the jam and use the lo-cal whipped topping," Kelda called after him.

"Shit."

"Arne, we're still eating."

"Yeah, don't blame you, it's good."

"No sense wasting your breath, *kär a*. He's Swede and German, half 'n' half, one's stubborn, other's obstinate." Ragnar shook his head, paused, shook again for good measure.

"He is a test," Emma said.

Ragnar pushed himself back from the table. "Let's you and me play a little cribbage, Walkingstick."

"You're on, if you'll handicap me. Let me help clear the table."

"Be off," Emma said. "I don't want no man messing in the kitchen."

Kelda laughed and looked at Raymond. "Welcome to Hansen's Landing, Raymond Walkingstick. Thank you for your kind words about my mother."

Raymond nodded and lowered his eyes. Ragnar winced as he stood, and Raymond took his elbow so that each helped steady the other. Kelda listened to them talk, not to the words but to the tone. Could Raymond's appearance in her uncle's life contribute to keeping him alive? Had it been doing so during these last months? The two men settled with the cribbage board between them. Behind her, in the kitchen, Arne and Emma argued about his having another piece of wine cake.

Arne stomped out of the kitchen. "Why do you keep that cranky old woman around?"

"Because she's Emma. She's part of Hansen history. Her energy nourishes us, even when it's perverse, Arne." She watched her husband of twenty-five years shake his head. A good-looking man, even with the extra pounds. Together they'd produced attractive daughters. Pretty, popular, sophisticated Lauren, who majored in finance in college, intending to make scads of money, invest it, and play. And earthy Reva, an accomplished photographer at twenty, who wanted to travel to the four corners for *National Geographic*. Arne saw to it she had the finest cameras and equipment money could buy.

"Nourishes us," Arne mimicked. "Shit, Kelda, why can't you just talk like other people. Lighten up."

She handed him a stack of dirty dishes. "There, lightened up already."

He grinned at that, carried the dishes to Emma, and cut another piece of wine cake when she turned to set the dishes on the counter.

Emma grabbed a dish towel and swatted him. "You best be getting out of this kitchen and tend to the cottage business, Arne Hedstrom, or I'll be taking a broom to you."

"I'll wash what won't fit in the dishwasher," Kelda said. "You can dry, Emma. Do you remember Raymond from that summer? How sad he looked?"

"Shoot, yes, I remember. He come home from that mess in Korea to a worse mess on the reservation. That and he took a shine to you, but he was gentleman enough to keep it to himself, with you but fifteen and him in his twenties. Shine's still there, from the looks of things, and so's the gentleman."

"Oh, Emma."

"Oh, Emma nothing. I'll make us another pot of coffee and we can talk a minute about them times. What worries me, you've got a sad look yourself, and it's not just your uncle. I think it's time you give up that job of yours. No part-time, just quit and tend to your uncle, and most of all tend to yourself a little."

Coffee and reminiscing with Emma, and later Arne's presence in her Landing bedroom, made for a restless night for Kelda. Arne overfilled the room. He groused about the narrow bed, the distance to the bathroom, then turned on his pre-sex charm. She was lost in the past, the months before and after her mother's death, and not interested in love-making. Arne rubbed her back, something he rarely did these days. It worked as he'd hoped, and soon he slept.

Unlike Arne, making love left Kelda more awake, more on-edge. She took an Afghan and slipped down the stairs to the great-room to commune with the Old-ones. "Is Emma right? Do I need to give up my job?" She'd swear they nodded. She pulled a journal from the shelf and curled up to read the mixed Norwegian and English, and the translations first by Lydia and then by Kelda herself.

It had taken her grandfather almost a year to clear the land for the first house, the room where she snuggled in the overstuffed chair. He'd fallen hemlock and used whole trunks to shore up a root cellar he dug where he stored apples, potatoes, carrots, a few beets and winter squash. He wrote that mills wouldn't buy hemlock, considered a weed by timbermen.

He built a skid road of hemlock too, and rented a man and oxen team to drag fallen Hansen trees down to the beach. He rafted his own logs, traded building work for a boat, and delivered the logs to mills at Port Gamble and on Bainbridge Island. He practiced English words, and learned about the mechanical animal called a steam-donkey that whipped logs around and dragged them out of the forest, using only fuel for feed. Wood a-plenty for burning for the steam.

Kelda came to the part that always shamed her, a prideful shame, if such a thing were possible. Old Helgar wrote that by listening more than talking he'd learned there was timber for the taking all up and down Washington Territory. He paid men who wanted land cleared for farming cash for their timber, hired help when he needed it to log the land, and earned good money toward bringing Magna over from the old country.

When Magna arrived in April 1890, Washington had become the forty-second state of the United States. The pastor of the Poulsbo Lutheran Church married them on a Sunday, right after the regular service. On Monday, Helgar plowed a new plot of land for Magna to plant flowers, which she wrote nourished the soul.

"There, Arne," Kelda whispered, "that's why I talk the way I do. It's genetic."

Arne, Ragnar, and Raymond Walkingstick started work in earnest on the big cottage the next day, and Kelda saw the reason for all the materials delivered to the site. The bathroom floor and walls had serious dry rot problems, and Raymond wanted to tear into exterior walls to add more insulation. Kelda vacillated between worry and elation over Ragnar's participation in the project. She went through the three small cottages, and found no serious interior problems, just tired decor. Each had a small bedroom, small bath, and an open area that combined kitchen, dining and living areas. She couldn't imagine anyone wanting to rent them by the month, or even for a weekend. She returned to the house where she started a pot of spaghetti sauce and refigured the Landing's finances. She was interrupted while deep in thought by calls from her daughters.

Lauren called first. "Mother? I had a message on my machine from Daddy. He says you're quitting your job to take care of your old uncle, and that I should postpone grad school, is that true?"

"I've always thought you should postpone grad school, Lauren. Spend some time in the work-world."

"Mother." Lauren dragged out the word. "My goals are very clear. I've explained."

Kelda held the phone away from her ear while Lauren ran down a list of mild expletives. "Lauren, unless there's something your father hasn't told me about the company's finances, I think we're only asking that you watch your discretionary spending. Clothes, meals out, parties. And, you might find a part-time job rather liberating."

When Reva phoned, Kelda knew Arne was up to his old game of getting at her through their daughters.

"Should I register for fall classes or not?"

"Yes, of course you should register. Your education fund is secure. But you should also dust off the budget you and I worked out before you started school."

"What's that supposed to mean?"

"Reva, what would you do if you had to survive on your own? If suddenly you had no help from your dad and me."

"First, get a part time job. Then, if necessary, sell some of my photographic equipment, I guess. Is that what you want me to say?"

"Could you sell some of your gear and still use your talents to support yourself?"

"Mother, I hate it when you do that. You know I don't spend and accumulate nearly as much as Lauren."

Kelda pictured her younger daughter stamping her foot. "That's true. And I appreciate you for that."

After a silence, Reva said, "Is Daddy moving to the Landing too, or are you two going to separate?"

Kelda held the phone out and looked at it. "I don't think we're at either/or here. I think your dad will come and go. He's not exactly happy about that. You may know better than I just how unhappy, since he called you and Lauren."

Reva laughed. "Unhappy is an understatement."

"It won't hurt him to live at the Landing for a time."

"No, but it will drive you crazy, Mother, with Gerda calling every five minutes to see if he's torn down the house and built her a resort."

Kelda frowned, wrote resort with three question marks. "A resort? So, it's a resort now, not just a gated community?" She heard Reva groan. "Never mind," she said. "There's time to get into all that. Right now, I'm just trying to figure out finances for the short term. For as long as Uncle Ragnar's alive . . ." Her voice broke, her eyes smarted. "For as long as my uncle remains alive and well enough to live in this house, on Hansen land, there will be no resort, no gated community. Gerda will have to wait."

On Monday morning, the first of her two long days each week, Kelda carried hot cereal and buttered raisin toast to the dining room. Arne, smug after two nights of love-making, had gulped coffee and left without breakfast. Morning mist that developed into rain skittered against the windows. She'd pushed the furnace thermostat to a higher setting than Ragnar allowed himself, and draped a wool sweater across his shoulders. "That cottage is going to be cold today, Uncle. I don't think you should work out there. There's assorted left-overs for Emma to heat, but she'll have to come up with something when they run out."

Ragnar poured milk on his cereal, took a bite of toast. "Damn it all to hell, you'd be fussing too much over an old man. The working's good for me, and we don't need Emma's cooking. Me and Walkingstick can batch on days you're gone. Eat beans."

"Uncle, you don't like beans."

"No, but I like Walkingstick okay. Help me be remembering to explain the toilet donut thing. He'll have to drive out and get a new one. He's not done remodeling before, he'll end up with the toilet leaking, floor will rot all over again. Might just as soon leave the toilet sit in the bathtub as put it back with an old donut."

He ate fast, anxious to get to work. His face looked gray, but that may have been a reflection of the morning.

"April is the cruelest month." Kelda brought his work boots and got onto her knees to push them onto his feet and tie them, talking while he protested, and urged him into a sweater over his wool shirt, a jacket over that. They walked arm-in-arm to the cottage. Ragnar held an umbrella over her head.

Cold, dank air wafted up through the mess that had been the bathroom floor. Two-by-fours served as walks from doorway to tub. Kelda waited while her uncle and Raymond commiserated about what first, before catching Raymond's eye and signaling for him to follow her outside.

"The air in there is not good for my uncle to breathe. Don't let him stay too long. There's some food for warming. Enough for the three of you, for one meal at least. He doesn't want Emma to cook, but she'll come heat it up. Don't let her skimp on his portions. Here's the agency phone number, and my cell phone, and Arne's cell and office numbers." She narrowed her eyes. "Why are you smirking?"

Walkingstick took the paper with the phone numbers and shoved it into his shirt pocket. The smirk softened into a smile. "I'll properly tend to your uncle, Kelda."

"Okay, it's just that I'm concerned." Concerned. She was worried sick.

Walkingstick nodded to her, but answered something Ragnar said. They didn't need her there, handing out instructions like Ragnar was a toddler. "Uncle? Remember about the toilet donut," she called past Raymond.

"*Ja,* and you remember not to worry 'bout me and Walkingstick, we'll fix them beans, like I said."

"He doesn't like beans. I've left a note for Emma to find something in the freezer when leftovers run out. Something that will be easy for him to fix. Something nutritious."

"I will lend a hand. It's my turn to provide a meal."

She wanted to say more, but Raymond's look told her to go and let them manage on their own. She left them, worry still knitting her brow. She needed to unknit it, to relax or a headache would move in, making her day worse.

*All our reasoning ends in surrender to feeling. - Blaise Pascal, 1623-1662.*
*French mathematician, physicist, inventor, writer and Catholic theologian.*

# 10
# The Agency

Kelda drove a bit too fast on the narrow road that led to the Kingston ferry dock, feeling a little miffed. Her uncle and Raymond had each other and a task they both seemed to relish. Not the first task they'd undertaken together. For all she was grateful to Raymond for his part in keeping Ragnar alive through planting a thousand fir seedlings, she had a right to worry. That big cottage had a history Raymond knew nothing about, and she didn't like feeling dismissed by him.

Was she trapped by Hansen history, as Arne often said? Did she wallow in Hansen lore? A thirty-minute ferry ride gave her too little time to ponder that; she had the Shawndra/Mandy Jenkins case history to read before she met with them, and, more troubling, Hap Smith and family to prepare for later in the afternoon.

She was at her desk, still stewing a bit, when Rachelle buzzed her to say her clients were in the therapy room.

They sat on the far ends of an attractive sofa, the space between them representing their problems. A coffee table held fresh flowers and a box of tissues. Shawndra glared; Mandy watched her hands, which she'd rested on her lap. Kelda greeted them and waited for them to respond through their anger and sadness. Nothing.

"Have you been writing in your journals?" she asked

Shawndra flung her journal across the table. Mandy's head fell forward in shame. Kelda wanted to gather the defeated woman into her arms, and send the under-dressed, over-painted child out into the streets. "I can see you're angry, Shawndra. Mandy? Have you been writing too?"

"Some." Mandy dug in a cracked vinyl handbag, found a used tissue, worried it with her fingers.

"Perhaps you handle your feelings differently than Shawndra handles hers." Kelda focused on Mandy, ignoring her daughter. "Tell me what you were feeling while you wrote"

"She can hardly spell," Shawndra said. Today her lipstick was blood-red and drawn into points aimed at her nostrils.

Kelda felt patience dissolve like sugar in boiling water. She breathed in and found her voice of professional reason. "I will not permit you to abuse your mother, even verbally, in my presence. You're here because you tried to stab her. She does not have to tolerate your behavior because she's your mother." She watched Shawndra until the girl lowered her head.

"Mandy? Your feelings when you wrote in the journal?"

It took another thirty seconds, but Mandy finally looked up from her hands. "Tired, mostly. Sad."

Shawndra started a sigh, but aborted it when Kelda's eyes caught hers.

"Do your jobs tire you, Mandy?"

"Some." Mandy shifted in her chair. "Not so much. Sometimes it's nice to go to work."

"What makes going to work nice?"

"I can forget the . . . the other stuff for a bit."

"The other stuff?"

"Yeah." Mandy's eyes met Kelda's. "Her, mostly. I can forget for a few minutes at a time how hard it is."

"What makes it so hard?"

"She's so, I don't know, she's just mad all the time."

Kelda turned to Shawndra. "Let's talk about that, Shawndra. Why are you so angry?"

"Geez. Why am I so angry?" Shawndra rolled her eyes and sucked in her cheeks. "I don't have a father, at least I've never met him. We live in a dump. She expects me to watch the boys so she can go to her minimum wage job and forget about the shit she piled up around us."

Shawndra's head moved from side to side as if she had glider springs
in her neck. Her mouth contorted. She scrunched her eyes.

Silent tears ran down Mandy's cheeks and dripped onto her chest.

"That's very clear, Shawndra. You know you're angry, and you've
identified some reasons. Now, let's look at the feelings behind the
anger." She waited until both agreed they would work with her to talk
about anger, its triggers and expression. Shawndra acted out; Mandy
turned it inward, and felt sad and tired. Though both said they
understood, Kelda knew it was temporary awareness; it made sense in
a therapist's presence, but would be difficult to remember the next
time a conflict arose.

After they left, Kelda made notes on the case management form
and posted an alert for possible medical evaluation. She was sad and
tired herself. Tired of counseling people who tried to solve disputes
with knives and guns. On that note Rachelle opened her door, said,
"The Hap Smith family is here, Kelda," and tried to send a warning
message with her eyes

The Smith family. Common name, uncommon case for the
agency. Keith refused to pass it on to another therapist on the grounds
that four sessions with Kelda made it too late to change. Truth was
they'd all met Hap Smith, whom they suspected had raped his
daughter. Cameo. 'Li'l Camie,' Hap called her. The prosecutor was
sure Hap was the perpetrator but couldn't make a case. Cameo
wouldn't talk.

The Smith case started with a hospital report of a botched
abortion, and a police report of a father-son domestic dispute. Tory
got his sister to the hospital in the nick of time; she was hemorrhaging.
Hap ranted about losing his grandchild. Father and son almost killed
each other in the ensuing argument that included a tug-of-war with a
rifle. Cameo was placed in foster care; she ran away, was returned, ran
again. A judge ordered the family into counseling.

Hap entered the therapy room first, pulling Cameo with him. Tory
shuffled along behind.

"Hey, Miz Hansen, you're looking good enough to eat. I'nt she,
Tory?"

Kelda felt her face heat with anger. "Mr. Smith, I will remind you only once that such comments are inappropriate and detrimental to resolution of this case." She locked eyes with the man until he looked away. This case would be her undoing. She'd lose it and strangle the man herself. "Please sit down. All of you."

Cameo sat on the edge of the sofa, head down, eyes veiled behind one open hand. Tory's eyes moved from Kelda to his sister, and then to his father, as he sprawled on the rest of the sofa, leaving a chair at the end of the table for Hap. His loathing for his father was palpable.

"No offense meant, doctor," Hap said. "I'm just trying to keep things upbeat here so's we can get this matter settled. Way I see it, sooner we learn who done the butchering job on Li'l Camie, sooner we get justice. That'd be your job." He grinned, showing ragged and missing teeth.

"She's told you she's not a doctor, and she's not the police," Tory said. He resembled a playground slide, slouched as he was, head back, body curved, legs out.

Kelda took them through their paces. Tory answered for himself and Cameo. They went to school, and to the restaurant where Tory bussed dishes. Cameo hung out until Tory got off. Then they went home, where Hap, who worked at a scrap-metal recycling plant, 'rustled up some grub' for them, and watched a little TV.

"Tell me about your weekend." Kelda knew weekends worried Tory. Cameo had to clean the house and do laundry before taking her homework to the restaurant.

Tory shrugged. Hap said, "Just another weekend." Cameo kept her eyes down, but nodded when Kelda asked her for a response.

"Mr. Smith, Tory, I want to talk with Cameo alone first today. Help yourselves to coffee and juice. Tell Rachelle if you need anything else. Tory, I'll see you when Cameo and I are through."

"Hows about me?" Hap asked.

"You'll be last today, if we have time."

Hap left muttering. Cameo remained a statue.

"Cameo, you're still letting Tory and your father speak for you when I ask you about your week. I want to hear from you." Kelda waited what seemed an eternity before saying, "Are you ready to talk about the man who got you pregnant?" Cameo's head moved to one side. "Cameo, the case worker and police suspect your father got you pregnant. If that's what happened, your father broke a law. It's not your fault. Please look at me so I know you understand that it's not your fault." After another eternity, Cameo lifted her head and fanned her fingers so Kelda could see her eyes. Then she dropped her head and hid behind her hand-veil again.

"Are you sad about your baby? About aborting your baby?"

Cameo's head moved a little. "No," she whispered. "And I don't care about my uterus neither. I don't want no kids, kids just suffer." She raised her hand enough to see the tissue box, pulled out two, blew her nose. "Can I go now?"

"Where do you want to go?"

"Home, I guess."

"I can help find a home with a woman who will take care of you." Kelda watched Cameo shake her head. "I'll leave that for now, but before you go, there are some things I want you to hear." Kelda explained laws and options, and asked Cameo to nod if she understood. She watched Hap's reaction when Cameo returned to the waiting room. He leered, knowing nothing of import had transpired.

By the time she'd finished with Tory and Hap, Kelda had a full-blown headache and a growling stomach. She headed for the staff room. "I need aspirin, food, and time to discuss this mess with Keith. But first I need to call the Landing."

Rachelle followed her. "Emma called here. Your uncle agreed to a snooze after lunch. The Indian fellow's going to eat you out of house and home. Emma put a match to the great room stove, otherwise you'll be in the poor house, the furnace was turned that high."

Kelda laughed, then groaned and grasped her head. Rachelle pulled aspirin out of the cupboard and retrieved water from the refrigerator. "Coffee's fresh. I knew you'd need it. Let me see if Keith's available."

Kelda ate some crackers to quiet her stomach, washed them and the aspirin down with coffee and carried a second cup into Keith's office.

"So, you're reporting no progress." Keith Burgess had his chair tilted back and his feet on an open desk drawer.

"None at all."

Keith rubbed his shaggy, graying beard and then his balding head. "Damn. If you can't get the girl to open up, no one can. I know the prosecutor's office hopes for something they can use to bring charges."

"Keith." Kelda heard pleading in her voice before she'd even stated her case. "I don't want these clients. I want to be with my uncle."

"Whoa," Keith said. He spent the next five minutes massaging her neck and shoulders, and convinced her to stick it out for another four weeks, until the groups were over.

"Five weeks," she said. "Keith, I can't take five more weeks of trying to pry something from Cameo. She's taken a victim's vow of silence."

"Well, four after this week. Okay, okay, I'll pay closer attention to Pap and his offspring."

"Hap. Damn it all to hell, Keith."

Keith laughed. "How's Ragnar doing? Eating better, I'll bet."

Kelda nodded. "I think I'm going to move permanently to the Landing. Will you check into agencies on the Kitsap Peninsula? Close to Poulsbo."

"Hmm, do you need a little therapy session of your own? Or a little marriage counseling?"

"Marriage counseling from you?"

"Sure. Three marriages tell you I know something about both the down side and the up side of the institution."

"No marriage counseling." She didn't have the energy to get Arne into therapy. "Just a real leave-of-absence. Maybe a letter of reference in time."

"Oh, Kelda, don't threaten me like that. If you leave me, I can't bid for all these court cases. They're my bread and butter."

"Well, this bread's moldy and the butter's getting rancid."

"Okay, okay, I'll do whatever you need me to do to help you get through these four weeks." His hands flew up when she started to protest. "Five weeks minus, a few hours. Right now, I'm taking you out for something to eat and a glass of wine. I know you didn't think to bring some of your good cooking here." He looked at his watch. "You've got over an hour before your group arrives. And don't tell me you need time to prepare. I know better."

*An idea, like a ghost, must be spoken to a little before it will explain itself.* – Charles Dickens, 1812-1870.

*English Writer, social critic, creator of some of fiction's best-known characters.*

# 11

## Ragnar

Ragnar had heard plenty of times what a heart attack felt like to be prit-near certain his chest pains weren't one. Damn it all to hell, that would be a good way to go. Easier than taking to his bed and waiting. But now, with Kelda mostly back home, he wasn't in so big a hurry. Could be just trying to keep up with Walkingstick, work-wise, he'd strained something.

Could be *magesmerte*, way he'd been eating since Kelda took over the kitchen, serving him food and love on the same plate, him stuffing in heaps.

That cottage Walkingstick was renting would suit a man just fine, once the bathroom floor and walls were done. Maybe a little floor work in the kitchen. Been suiting for a hundred years, the cottage. Suited him and Ruth. Trouble was, their ghosts watched him work with Walkingstick—his wife Ruthie's and their baby Gunnar's. He and Ruth ought not have taken that name for the *lite barn*, what with not knowing where the first Gunnar let go his spirit. Ragnar had been ten when his older brother left for Europe. Only time he'd seen their mother more undone than at Gunnar's leaving was news of Gunnar's death. She wore his dog tags right to her own death. Said it was the only thing her adopted land ever sent back of her third born son. They'd sent back some of his uniform. Karli had packed that away, but Magna saw that as anonymous. The tags said his name, carried his spirit, she said.

Funny, odd funny, what names can do. Gunnar meaning fighter, and his and Ruth's *lite* Gunnar unable to fight enough to fill his lungs. Died suckling at his mother's breast.

Here he was, eighty and some odd years old, and worrying backward fifty and some odd years. Him the one always telling Kelda, "No sense trying to reweave that blanket." Kelda studied up on SIDS death and explained it to him. Made sense, a woman not so healthy would have trouble bringing a healthy life to bear. He ought not have done that, given Ruth seed for a baby, knowing about her health. Ought not have married her, him still in love with Lydia. That was his transgression.

Lydia. Talking in his head, going on about the inlet being called *The Indians* all the years she'd been a Hansen, getting him thinking maybe he should have let Walkingstick rent Karli's old workshop like he'd first asked. Might be Lydia wanted him to turn over a chunk of that land out there to Walkingstick, but if that was her thought she needed to quit sending him messages about Indian Joe. Course maybe she wanted him to go looking for Indian Joe's next of kin. Far as he knew there weren't any. Karli would know more about that, but he wasn't the one sending messages back to the Landing.

Might be it wasn't Lydia at all, putting those thoughts in his head. Might be just his old man's way of conjuring up help for Kelda with those taxes in years to come. That could explain the other message coming in, the one he argued with Lydia about. *Let her read that last journal, Ragnar,* Lydia said in his head. Damn it all to hell, she was the one told him to lock it away just before she died. He'd put that last journal in Karli's trunk and soldered the lock, and that's where he'd leave it until he had some proof Lydia's voice wasn't just himself getting senile.

Ragnar struggled himself all the way awake and saw the cribbage board and cards on the table. Here he'd gone and dozed off right in the middle of a game. Then he saw Walkingstick, eyes closed, mouth open, snoring some in the chair other side of the table. And him a young man, not yet sixty. Well, he'd worked hard on the cottage, like a man half his age. Ragnar knew the man's hip and leg were hurting while he worked. A groan would escape and Walkingstick would stop to rub or stretch out a kink. Now Walkingstick's eyes shot open, the way a man's will when he hadn't meant to close 'em in the first place.

"She home yet?"

Ragnar chortled, then clutched the left side of his chest with his right hand. He saw Walkingstick watching him, and shook his head, or nodded it, he wasn't sure which.

"You feeling okay?"

"*Ja.* Ate too much, maybe."

Walkingstick nodded for certain, and almost smiled. "What is it with men? Eat more than we can hold because something's good. Like we fear it may be our last meal."

They heard the great room door open and close, and both sat straighter, listening.

"Look at us, like a couple of animals, ears perk up at a sound," Walkingstick said. "Of course, we're closer to our animal spirits when we first waken."

Ragnar wanted to ponder that one, animal spirits, but here came Kelda, a worry on her face. One of them headaches, he'd bet. He scooted forward, wanting to stand for a hug.

"Uncle?" Kelda came straight to him, dropped to her knees by his chair.

"Help me out of this chair. Damn thing consumes a man my age."

"Are you feeling all right, Uncle Ragnar?"

"A little *magesmerte*, I think, from that Norwegian spaghetti you left us for lunch and we held over for dinner. Raymond drove out and got us sandwiches for lunch."

"Raymond?" Kelda said, and Ragnar knew she was seeking a second opinion.

"We ate like the three little pigs. Emma too," Raymond said.

Ragnar felt a burp coming, building somewhere deep inside, working its way up and out. "Ah, with that out and you home safe, I'm thinking I can get a little sleep." He was glad Kelda was giving him hugs and patting his shoulder, blind to the smile crinkling up Walkingstick's eyes. So, the man could smile. Could keep quiet, too.

Kelda was up, coffee made, fingers pressed to her temples, when Ragnar made it down to the kitchen the next morning. He liked having her there of a morning. Might be Lydia sent her home to see to it he got things said that needed saying. But not now, with her hands on her head. "Oh, *kär a*, is it the migraine?"

"Unnh," she said. "Yesterday morning, when I said April is the cruelest month, I think it was already May."

"*Ja.*" Ragnar put ice cubes in a plastic bag, wrapped a towel around them, and held them above her left eye, where the headache always started. Had done all the years he could remember, since her mother's death.

"I haven't done anything about the celebration." Kelda dabbed at her watering eyes and running nose.

"Not too many folks left for celebrating." He hadn't planned to be here himself. Four years back, when they had the one-hundred-year reunion, relatives he didn't recognize showed up. Nephews twenty and some odd years older than Kelda came with their own children and grandchildren, but likely wouldn't make the trip from where they'd scattered across the country. They were sons of Arvid and Erland, first and second Hansen sons, who went off to their own lives back before Gunnar went off to his death. Left Rolf, Karli, himself, and Olav to the Landing and the business.

"I know. They have their own lives. Still, we need to do something, Uncle. Saturday or Sunday."

"Saturday or Sunday would be right on time. We're not knowing for sure what day Old Helgar crossed the bay from Poulsbo."

"That's true." She smiled through her headache and patted his hand like he was the one needed comforting. "We'll have to start planning our menu."

"That's easy enough, the planning part, it's the cooking part that's a burden for you, *kär a*, that's why I'm thinking we might just as well let it go by."

She took the ice from her head and gave him a look that he felt clear down to his toes. "We'll have our celebration, Uncle. Norwegian meatballs and noodles, fresh salmon, crab salad, lefse, pickled herring, lots of flat *brød*, maybe some *fattigman*, just like always. Liem and Leah

80

Kerry will come, and Emma of course, even if Hansens don't. Lauren and Reva, too."

"*Ja*, and Walkingstick, I'm betting. Might be we should buy the flat *brød* and *fattigman*. Sluys' Bakery makes both, you'd not be having time."

Darned if she didn't laugh right out loud. Her eyes puddled and spilled, and she dropped the ice to grasp her head. "Uncle Ragnar, you say that every year, and every year I say, 'You like our own homemade better.' And then we make our own."

"*Ja*," he nodded, "but we buy the noodles these last years. Now, it would be my turn to do some cooking, I'm going to scramble up eggs and make your toast, then go give Walkingstick a hand. You think you'd be ready for some scrambled eggs?"

"*Ja*," she said, echoing him, giving a nod to go along with it.

That kept him grinning right on through the egg scrambling.

*Anger as soon as fed is dead - 'Tis starving makes it fat. - Emily Dickinson, 1830-1886.*
*American poet, lived much of her life in reclusive isolation.*

# 12
# Kelda

Kelda tried to remember when certain aspects of her job started triggering headaches. She'd counseled difficult people for over twenty years. Lately she'd yearned for the classroom of her early career, certain it had to be easier than the therapy room, though in truth, her groups were more educational than therapeutic, and they drained her energy too. With groups, she had to teach concepts *and* read cases. Her recently noted impatience with misbehaving youth spread to growing irritation with victims and absolute intolerance of abusers.

She ate the breakfast Ragnar prepared, grinning in spite of her headache, took ibuprofen with a last cup of coffee, and accompanied him out to the cottage to see how things were coming along. Sun flirted with the day from behind a thin cloud layer; the bay was a smooth soft silver, and the Landing shiny green with yesterday's moisture clinging to grass, evergreen needles and leaves.

They took the long way to the cottage, stopped to sniff opening lilacs, and wandered through the rhododendrons to see which were blooming. Kelda plucked three florets from a rose-blushed cream rhodie and poked them into the buttonhole on Ragnar's shirt pocket, picked another floret and put it in her denim shirt front, its sticky stem caught between her breasts.

"Oh, look," Kelda said, pointing at Jean Marie de Montague's scarlet blossoms. She remembered her mother saying. *There are many things I'd do without for this beauty.'*

"Lydia's most favorite," Ragnar said.

He took her hand, and she thought again how right the roughness felt. Not an old man's hand; a working man's. Her eyes glistened. She stole a glance at her uncle and saw his did, too.

"This place looks like a park. The Old-ones left us with a lovely park. Of course, you younger ones, you and Mother especially, expanded it." Her blood-engorged brain couldn't quite grasp the thought that was growing. Something to do with making the Landing a park. Could that be a possibility?

Ragnar loved the rhodies almost as much as Lydia had, all sixty or so of them, planted amidst cedar, hemlock, Pacific dogwood and sword ferns. He pruned them annually, moved one or two occasionally, so there were winding paths from gravel drive to lawn, to beach. Mulched clippings protected their feet. Violets, snow-on-the-mountain, assorted sedums and ornamental mosses grew atop the mulch. Here and there Kelda spotted fir seedlings held straight with wood stakes not yet weathered.

"Just getting a start here, those firs. Don't be worrying. Walkingstick knows to move 'em 'fore they get too big. He'll be potting them up and selling them, like as not."

"Raymond," she said, uncertain how she felt about his involvement in planting the little seedlings, his right to pot them up, as Ragnar said. A power saw hummed and stopped, hummed again. Fresh-cut lumber scented the air and sawdust accumulated on the drop cloth covered patio of the big cottage. She wasn't yet sure how she felt about his remodeling either, though it was more repair than remodel.

"I need to be giving him a hand," Ragnar said, a skip in his step and in his voice.

Kelda watched him move to the cottage, his white hair lifting with the breeze. He'd tucked his wool plaid shirt into khaki work pants that gathered up under his belt and sagged in the seat. Even from behind him, she knew he smiled.

She walked through the cottage, commented on the progress, watched her uncle decide where to work and to become absorbed. To Raymond, who'd stepped back to study his progress, she said, "His infant son died in this cottage. I worry that it makes him sad to be out here, but maybe it's the opposite."

"Ah. I felt something here. Thank you for telling me."

Felt something. She pondered that. "Has he talked about that?"

"He's fine, Kelda. I need him for the expertise. Let him be."

His dark eyes said more than his words, a message about men and their needs. She returned to the house, to her own tasks. She had an afternoon appointment with the bank trust officer to go over her funds, session notes to write up from last night's group, and calls to make about the Hansen celebration. She and her uncle had decided on Sunday. She called Arne first, lest she forget him completely in her focus on food preparation. When he balked at giving up another weekend, she just held her aching head and calmly said, "Do as you wish." He called back five minutes later to ask if he could bring Gerda. She hesitated a moment too long, then said, "Of course, if she wishes to come."

She left messages on both girl's answering machines telling rather than asking them to come, to arrive by two in the afternoon to give her a hand. Then she called Erik. The pounding in her head increased as she dialed, increased more when his wife answered.

"We wondered if you were going to bother this year," Patty said.

"Why wouldn't we?"

"Well, things have changed."

"Yes, they have, Patty, and I'd like to talk to Erik about that."

"He's so busy. I doubt our boys will be able to make it. We're trying to get ready for a trip."

"Is Erik there? I'd like to talk to him about my trust. I need some investment advice." She could hear Patty talking, pictured her hand over the mouthpiece whispering. Then Erik came on the line.

"Hi, little sister, what's happening?"

Erik, in his big brother mode, annoyed her, but she did respect his financial sense. "You know what's happening. Things are a bit tight, with just two of us covering the taxes on the Landing. I need advice."

She heard him take in a deep breath, and braced her head. "Kel, the place is way too expensive to maintain as single-family ownership. No amount of senior tax breaks and credits for timber holdings

Ragnar has coming will make it manageable. I know it's tough, but you're going to have to catch up with the times one of these days."

"Stop," she said. "Stop right there, Erik. I called for investment advice, not the 'let Arne develop the place for God's sake' lecture. I'm keeping the place for Ragnar, for as long as he's alive, just as we've talked of doing over the years. Give me some suggestions about what to do with the money still in my trust, and reasonable proposals short of selling the place." She made notes while he talked. Balance growth and income. Diversify. Consider selling a tree or two, some were worth more than a thousand each. Short-plat and sell five or ten acres. The land along the inlet was especially valuable because of the old growth fir on it, but it might be difficult to sell land without timber rights.

She set down her pen, pressed her left eye where the pain centered. "Erik, could we donate the Landing to the state for a park? Effective after Uncle Ragnar's death? Or put it into some kind of conservancy?" She glanced at the Old-ones' picture above the desk where she sat, hoping they'd give her a sign about that notion.

"Hmm. You mean like the Bloedel Reserve, here on Bainbridge?"

"Yeah, with the house as a visitor center, and the grounds kept as they are."

"And the trees untouched? I don't know, Kel. I think the Bloedels left a huge trust fund for upkeep."

"Oh." A long oh, like air out of a balloon. "Will you look into it for me? You and Patty know people I've only heard of. I haven't even talked to Ragnar."

"Hey, look, Kel, I'm sorry if you're bummed about Greg and me selling out, but the old place is a drain. It really is. Even Ragnar knows it. You're stuck in the Fifties."

She swallowed her anger. "Erik? Are you listening? Because I'm asking some favors. First, check on the park idea. Second, help me invest what's left of my trust so it earns more interest. And last, don't ever again say anything negative about the Landing."

She hung up, recited her Hansens' Don't Cry mantra, and pictured herself growing old at the Landing, her grandchildren visiting. There would be picnics on the beach, and bonfires, and walks in the woods looking for Johnny jump-ups and trilliums. They'd make pretend boats of bark and twigs, and have races on the creek. They'd collect shells and rocks, and put them in fruit jars with the collector's name on a canning label. They'd plant seeds and watch things grow. When she died, at a very old age, they'd have her cremated and scatter her ashes in Magna's Cedar Grove. By then, they'd be telling the next generation about the Old-ones, the hopes and dreams, the Hansens of America. She'd just skip her generation, and her daughters, and pin her hopes on the cloudy future.

The great room door opened. Raymond called, "Kelda?"

She jumped, knocked papers askew. "Oh no, oh my god."

Raymond stepped in, frowned, closed the door. "Ragnar's fine. Are you all right?" He put a hand powdered with fine sawdust on her arm. Traces of sawdust clung to his shirt and clouded his glasses.

"If Ragnar's fine then I'm fine too."

Raymond's frown deepened. "Have you been crying, Kelda?" He brushed her cheek with his fingers.

"Couldn't be. Hansens don't cry." She forced a smile. "Tell me what emergency we're having now. There is one, isn't there?"

"I'm not sure. There are some men here saying they're looking the place over for a golf course."

"A golf course?" Heat surged through her body, leaving her heart a bloodless lump in her chest. "Tell them to get the hell out of here. No, wait, I want to tell them myself. You'd probably be too diplomatic. Tell them I'll join them in a moment."

She dashed upstairs to put on lipstick and brush her hair. "Golf course?" she said to the mirror. "Whose idea is that?"

Kelda smelled cigar the minute she opened the door. A late model white van, Taglia Brothers, Ltd., in blue script on its side, sat in the circle drive. Two dark haired men in navy suits and one balding man in pin stripes stood with Ragnar and Raymond. One of the dark-haired men had the cigar clamped in his teeth.

She squared her shoulders, stared at the smoker, said. "Extinguish the cigar, please."

The three men glanced about. Behind them the bulk of the Landing's forty acres stretched green and lush all the way to the Kerry farm and the abandoned apple orchard. She knew Arne entertained ideas of getting his hands on both those parcels along with the Landing, and she'd bet these men did too.

"Ms. Hansen." The other dark-haired man moved toward her.

She looked past the advancing man at the cigar smoker. "Not on our drive. We don't want your garbage dropped on our property. Use the ashtray in your van."

"Ms. Hansen, I'm George Taglia, the smoker's my brother, Alfred, how are you?" He started to extend his hand, then waved it toward the others when she kept hers at her side. "And our attorney, Cal Callari."

It looked like someone sent the Mafia. She was getting as bad as Arne.

"Pleased to meet you," Cal Callari said.

"Cal," she said. "George. Alfred. Are you aware you've driven down a private road and parked in a private drive? I assume you've come at someone's suggestion."

The three men looked at each other, at their shoes, at Ragnar. George spoke. "We've come with the understanding that this, uh, parcel, may soon be on the market, and we'd like to sit down with uh, Mr. Hansen, and you, uh, the niece, is it? The two of you. You own the place together, am I right? Uh, sit down and talk. Just talk."

Kelda raised her eyebrows and strained not to wince at the pain. She stood with legs slightly apart, weight on her left foot, right ready to kick rocks. "We can talk here, standing."

George Taglia nodded, kept nodding like the on-off switch was stuck. "Uh, we develop golf courses. And Mr. Walkingstick is involved how?"

"Mr. Walkingstick is a close personal friend and one of our attorneys. Frankly, George, if this parcel were to go on the market, it would not be for a golf course. The runoff from fertilizers would negatively impact the bay. Local environmentalists, with support from local Native Americans, would never let that happen." She saw Ragnar smile, and Raymond's eyebrows lift. "George, Alfred, Cal, who sent you?"

"Uh," George started.

"George, let me handle this." Cal Callari pulled a lizard skin card case from an inside pocket. "Actually, Ms. Hansen, no one sent us. Word gets around a small town like Poulsbo. We're investors, we check out opportunities when we hear about them."

"Uncle, you've been around Poulsbo over eighty years now. Do you know this name? Taglia?"

"Know there's some Italian place on the waterfront. Ristorante something. Might well be Tag whatever. Got no need to eat there, myself, what with you cooking up Norwegian spaghetti like you do."

She rolled her shoulders a little to keep from smiling. "Gentlemen, your investment group is on the wrong track, and definitely on the wrong property." She moved to stand between Ragnar and Raymond, and put an arm across each man's back.

The three visitors coughed and turned toward the van.

"Have a nice day," she said to their backs.

When they were out of view, she clenched her fists and stomped about. "If Arne sent them, I'll kill him."

"Now, *kär a*, it's okay, they've gone, they won't be coming back soon. I'll run in the house, get you a little nip of the raspberry wine."

She saw Ragnar was still grinning, and suspected he went off for wine to keep her from seeing how much he enjoyed her performance. That's what it was. False bravado. Sell a few trees, sell a few acres, sell sell sell. There wasn't any other way.

Raymond had both hands on his cane, which he had poked out at an odd angle. He'd stood stock still and used the cane to point down the lane while she talked to the Taglia Brothers and Cal Callari. A silent usher, showing the visitors the exit. He watched her as he spoke, and she saw lawyer intimidation in his eyes.

He said, "Killing Arne probably wouldn't be defensible."

"Well that sucks, as my clients would say." She looked at his thick silver hair, braided and sprinkled with sawdust, his chiseled face and dark eyes, his flannel shirt and jeans, his rigid posture. "What kind of law did you practice?"

"Business and corporate. Some civil litigation."

"So, you don't have much experience defending murderers?"

"You are quick of wit and tongue. Perhaps you could defend yourself." His eyes held the light of a smile he didn't let his mouth know about.

"Too quick of tongue, for one who's trained to listen. I should have let them state their case so we'd know who sent them."

Raymond shrugged. "I suspect you will find that out. Thank you for elevating me to the status of friend. And attorney, as well."

"Does that mean you'll be submitting a bill?"

"No bill. Perhaps a question or two, if I may, about Hansen's Landing."

Kelda's mouth opened and closed. She pressed her fingers to her temples to hold in the awareness sliding into place in her brain. Bits and pieces of Ragnar's conversations lined up before her mind's eye like they'd been cut and pasted on a computer screen. Indian land. Karli's old shop. Raymond getting the fir seedlings, helping plant them, likely to sell some. Raymond and her uncle were plotting something.

"Here's wine and a cracker with it," Ragnar said, glasses clinking on the tray in his not quite steady hands.

"That's twice today you've served me." Kelda helped get the tray onto the porch table, and gave her uncle a hug and a bit of a shake. "Now, you two tell me what you've been planning for the Landing."

"Raymond, you give the talk." Ragnar wiped off chair seats with a dish towel.

Emma would flip. Kelda waited for one of them to speak, waited for her heart to settle into its normal rhythm.

Raymond hooked his cane over his arm and stood facing her, feet spread a bit for balance. "Kelda, I'd like to lease some of your land to collect and grow native plants. That's all I sell at my nursery."

"Little plants? Shrubs? Trees?"

"Yes, all those. Any and every specie of plant commonly found along the Pacific coast and Puget Sound basin."

There was a certain tension in both men that told her it went beyond growing native plants. "Don't tell me you want to log off the timber to make growing room."

"No, though I may ask to plough some cleared areas and experiment with some small plants in the midst of the oldest trees. The soil is undisturbed there, which makes it ideal for some natives."

"And what else? What's the downside?"

"I'd need to bring some hired help onto your land."

"What are we talking here? Prison inmates on work release?"

"Would that worry you?"

Kelda reached up, grabbed Raymond's shoulders and tried to shake him. "Look, one stingy-with-words man is all I can handle. Just tell me what you have in mind, and then let me think about it."

Raymond allowed his eyes to spark for a second, but his face didn't relax into a smile. "Glad I didn't have you as an adversary in my lawyering days. You can see right through me. I'd like to hire Indian kids that have gotten into trouble with the law, or with alcohol and drugs. Suquamish kids, because they're my people. Two or three at a time, carefully supervised."

"Oh boy. Troubled adolescents, angry at the world and willing to show it with all sorts of inappropriate behavior. Armed with tools."

She felt the men watch her. Time, motion, sound all seemed suspended. Neither knew of the anger building in her, especially anger at adolescents in trouble. Of late she'd been dwelling on her own teen years and all she'd done to help keep the Landing going. But it wasn't all the work over the years, the struggle in her own youth, that fanned her anger. It was fear, pure and simple. Anger born of fear she'd lose her uncle, the land, the Hansen history, her very identity.

For a moment, she considered throwing the wine glass for the sheer joy of hearing it break. She took a deep breath to center herself. Sipping wine before driving into Poulsbo for a meeting was not a wise choice. She ate a couple crackers and went inside to brush her teeth and swish some mouthwash. She needed to soften her sharp tongue before her meeting about Hansen finances.

*The eternal quest of the individual human being is to shatter his loneliness. - Norman Cousins, 1915-1990.*

*American political journalist, author, progressive and world peace advocate.*

# 13
# Raymond

Raymond remained with Ragnar on the great room porch, the two of them sipping wine, both uncertain what to say. Maybe uncertain what to think while they waited for Kelda's return. They both stood when she came through the door. She'd changed out of the jeans and denim shirt she'd been wearing when she stared down the Taglias and their attorney. He noticed her jacket, the color of an emerald, set off her blue eyes. He'd watched those eyes darken when she issued the directive to extinguish the cigar. Darkened by a powerful anger. The cigar trumped the insult of arriving unwanted on Hansen land. He understood insult, knew first-hand that injury heals faster.

She kissed her uncle, squeezed his hand, didn't protest when Raymond said he'd walk her to her car. "I fear I've trod on your hospitality, Kelda. Bringing troubled kids onto your property . . ." He stopped, tongue tied at the pain he saw in her eyes.

"Headache," she said.

He watched her drive away, then returned to the porch. "That vehicle does not fit that woman," he said to Ragnar, and wondered at the thought. When had he ever paid attention to who drove what? Or what clothes a woman wore?

"*Nei*, it surely do not. One of Arne's from the Hedstrom Construction, that thing. Two-hundred thousand miles, maybe. One of their girls drove off with Kelda's car. Took it back to school after wrecking her own. Damn it all to hell, we all are all the time taking from Kelda. It's no wonder she gets the migraines."

Raymond nodded, giving himself time to find the right comment. "The headache . . . does she take anything?" He thought about native plant remedies—black cohosh, white willow bark, others he'd read about.

"*Ja*, an ibuprofen. Maybe two, but it's not enough for what's bothering her. It's the worry about this place." Ragnar tipped his head back and swallowed a healthy portion of raspberry wine. "Fussing with feeding me. Won't go off to her bank meeting without asking what I'm wanting for dinner."

Raymond heard the pride and love in the man's voice, and felt a moment's envy. He couldn't recall ever being fussed over like that, and had no reason to expect he ever would be. Maybe his mother had been loving during the time they stayed in Karli's shop. Maybe that's why he harbored such pleasant memories of the place. Once they returned to the tribe, his mother started drinking. It seemed to him she'd stayed drunk until she died and wondered now if it was all due to loss of her husband, Raymond Morse.

"I spoke too soon about leasing the land. The part about hiring tribal kids in trouble with alcohol and drugs. Spoke before I thought it out." Raymond dug in his shirt pocket like a man digs for a cigarette, and pulled out a piece of wood. He had an apple box filled with small driftwood he'd collected along the inlet each time he'd come to help Ragnar plant fir seedlings. In his imagination, they were trapped animals or fish or birds waiting for his knife and imagination to free them. This morning he'd selected one from the box, and started whittling while he drank his morning coffee. He visualized a salmon swimming free. He opened his knife, selected a blade, eased away a sliver of wood.

"*Ja*. Kelda does that to a man. Draws words right out of him, things he never intended. Sometimes things he didn't know he knew." Ragnar chuckled. "She's trained. But she could do that back when, 'fore she ever went to college."

"I remember. From that summer when I got back from Korea." He'd been aware of Kelda's intuition then, too, and suspected now that they must have spirits in common. Perhaps, in time, he could ask her if she dreamed about animals, determine if their dreams carried them to similar places. That summer, thirty-five years ago, he wasn't thinking about animal spirits when he looked at her.

"*Ja*, that summer."

Raymond waited, but Ragnar just shook his head. "Well, at least I know leasing the land's not the biggest concern."

"It would be the troubled kids. I think folks with troubles are about to wear her down. And me, I'm the biggest trouble of all."

"No, that's not true. Kelda doesn't see you as trouble. More as her ballast." Raymond had prided himself all his professional career that he could read others without disclosing himself. He could stand silent and unflinching longer than any attorney he'd met, even after his injury that still sent knife-sharp pains through his body. He wasn't accustomed to being second-guessed.

When Ragnar didn't speak, Raymond went on. "Amazed me she suspected I had kids with criminal backgrounds in mind." Perhaps he should rethink that. Perhaps he wasn't ready to be around alcohol and drug abusers, and Kelda sensed that. For a very long time he'd been consumed with rage at those he loved because they lived to drink. Alcohol made a mess of their lives and the lives of all those around them. First his mother. Dead. Then his sister Lucy. Dead. All the wasted men Lucy dragged home like they were stray animals and she ran a shelter. Finally, his wife. Dead. Addicted before he met her, clean and sober for a time. An advocate for Indian rights, though only half Native American herself. Radiant during pregnancy. Started drinking soon after their son was born. Bored with mothering. Bored with marriage. Maybe he should have noticed her more; her clothes, her needs.

Now, remembering, he realized he had noticed some of the clothes, those worn to attract other men, but he'd made the wrong comments. He hadn't understood either of her addictions; men or alcohol. He hadn't understood that the work he did to keep corporations out of litigation, which provided well for a family, meant nothing to her. She saw it as one more way he bought into the white world she professed to hate. She suspected, as he had most of his life, that his biological father could have been a white man. Urban Indian, she called him, living his white half as an attorney, representing his

Indian half as superior to his Native clients. And, when drunk, she said he'd given his soul to that white woman named Lydia.

His anger at his wife sprouted long before she died. He buried it deep within, let it fester, let it poison him and their relationship. He'd taken her whiskey away from her that dismal night, and held her off while he poured it in the sink. She was already filled with it.

She stormed off to their bedroom and locked the door. He stewed in his study, unhearing until it was too late. Heard her say, "Shh," when their son called, "Daddy." Fear in his voice. Raymond tried to stop her from leaving. Tried to stop her from taking their son. Tried to stop her vehicle with physical strength. She steered at him, drove into him, a deliberate act. Fractured his pelvis, injured his left leg. She made it far enough that he wouldn't have heard the crash even if he'd been conscious. His son, his only child. Edward. He'd chosen the name for the child Lydia Hansen had rescued. Dead.

All his blood connections, his spirit, his soul. Dead. Maybe his wife had been right—maybe he'd given his soul to Lydia, and she was in the process of helping him reclaim it.

Raymond trimmed the carved salmon's tail. Spirits forgive him, he'd wallowed in anger, hated his wife for killing his son and herself, and needed the hate to deal with the sorrow. He spent the better part of a year, after hospitals and surgeries, strengthening his leg, making it let him walk. Hatred, bitterness and self-pity fired his determination. During the most intense pain, his mind carried him back to a rocky beach at the edge of a forest, and to a child who knew how to weave cedar bark.

While still in rehab, he took his first *pro bono* case as legal counsel for a grass roots group fighting a timber firm over forest practices. A physical therapist urged him to take the case as a new focus for his energy. Thus began his journey back to his spiritual self. That's when he became Walkingstick.

He heard the sound of a car coming down Hansen Lane, and noted that Ragner heard it too, maybe a few seconds later. "Emma," Ragnar said. "Good time to skedaddle back to the cottage 'fore she sees the wine glasses, starts on a tirade 'bout drinking in the middle of the day."

"You put the wine away, I'll wash up the glasses." Raymond liked an excuse to enter the house, especially the great room. He wondered if Emma's vacuuming and dusting pleased or irritated the spirits that lingered.

He was drying the last wine glass when he heard the door close, the footsteps he recognized as Emma's. She said exactly what he knew she'd say.

"What's a man doing messing in the kitchen? You done with that cottage?"

"Long way from done, Emma."

"Then you better get. And don't be wearing out Ragnar, giving Kelda more worry than she's got already." Emma had hot water running in the sink, the dish towel Raymond had been using draped over her shoulder, a dirty saucepan in her hands. "Looks like you done in any leftovers from whatever Kelda put together for lunch."

"Actually, I believe Kelda left a little something for you in the refrigerator."

Emma opened it, poked around. "This little dab? Might as well warm it, wash out the container."

"Come on, Walkingstick," Ragnar called from the utility room. "Leave Emma to her cleaning out the fridge." And then he winked, and Raymond learned another lesson about love.

*A friend is one before whom I may think aloud - Ralph Waldo Emerson, 1803-1882*
*American essayist, lecturer and poet.*

# 14
# Kelda

Kelda couldn't remember when Poulsbo transformed from a small fishing community to a historic Norwegian village, but she liked it. Liked the landfill that created the Marina, and the restoration that made old buildings attractive. Liked it all, except the parking. Some days, every slot on the narrow winding streets was filled. The Sons of Norway Lodge lot overflowed. She didn't mind walking, but hated being late for a meeting. She circled the public parking lot on the waterfront, saw reverse lights on a car, and sped up to be there before someone else came along.

She arrived at the bank a little out of breath, a little bewildered. Bank managers and trust officers changed frequently at small branch banks, but she expected to see someone that had been there the last time she'd been in, whenever that may have been. The current trust officer, a woman, admitted an unfamiliarity with the trust, though she'd authorized a disbursement twice the amount of the previous years to cover taxes.

Over the next twenty minutes, they reviewed the trust history. Lydia set it up before she died, the trust officer marked it for conservative growth with disbursement on request to Ivar Jonasson, Accountant, receipt acknowledgment to the trust manager. Those disbursements had been made twice annually. Ten years ago, a large piece of the trust monies had gone to Hedstrom Construction as a loan; it remained outstanding.

Kelda looked at the investment summary. It had worked well enough until property values escalated with the Kitsap Peninsula's growth; it would have worked better without the Hedstrom Construction withdrawal. Did it matter which account money was in? It did now, with the balance so low and the need so great.

"Would you like to make an appointment with the bank's investment counselor?" the trust officer asked.

"Not right now. I'll call for an appointment." She needed to get over her headache, think about leasing land to Raymond Walkingstick for nursery stock, troubled adolescents on the property, and collecting the debt plus interest owed her trust by Arne's company.

She walked along Front Street where tourists meandered in and out of shops with exterior walls, doors, and shutters decorated with rosemaling. The bright folk-art designs danced and blurred in her headachy aura. She turned down the Have Veien walkway on her way to the parking lot and waterfront. The pungent odor of a burning cigar wafted her way. A moment later four men in business suits came into view: the Taglia brothers, their attorney Cal Callari, and the Landing's former accountant, Tony Petrulli, who was Ivar Jonasson's son-in-law. The man she'd just fired.

She stopped in the center of the walk, pressed fingers to her temples, and waited.

"Kelda," Tony Petrulli said. "Heh, heh, heh, how are you?"

"Hello, Tony. George, Alfred, and Cal, right?" Alfred tucked the cigar behind his back. "Let me guess—a late lunch?"

While Tony Petrulli laughed again, Cal Callari told Alfred to lose the cigar. He stepped into a blocking position. "Ms. Hansen, could we interest you in a drink? Or coffee, perhaps." He gestured toward the coffee shop in the center of the Have Veien. "A latte or cappuccino?"

Tony Petrulli and that trio. She'd wrongly suspected Arne's involvement. "*En svart kaffe,*" she said. "This is Poulsbo, after all. I don't like my coffee contaminated, and I would like a moment to talk with Tony."

"Black coffee," Tony Petrulli said. "She said, 'a black coffee.' Uh, heh, heh, let's all step inside." He pulled back his coat and shirt sleeve and looked at his watch.

Kelda felt four pairs of eyes on her back and one pair on her face as she stepped up into the shop. The woman behind the counter, watching so intently, looked familiar.

"Kelda. Kelda Hansen, what are you doing in town? Have you moved back, too? Joyce Lindquist. I can see you're searching to remember."

"Joyce. Hello, I recognize the smile." It was warm and real, but it was Joyce's hands moving, punctuating as she spoke, that Kelda remembered.

"A regular black coffee for the lady," Cal Callari said. "Anyone else?" The other three men shook their heads.

"Americana. For here or to go?" Joyce frowned for a second, then tended to business.

"I'll take it outside."

Joyce poured steaming, fragrant brew into a paper cup. "Are you going to be in town for a while? I'd love to visit, if you have some time." This time her hands stayed put on the counter, but her eyes asked other questions.

"I'll pop back in before I leave," Kelda said, and watched Cal pull a twenty from a gold money clip. He had a pinky ring with five nice diamonds set in its brushed surface, and a heavy gold bracelet on one wrist. She stepped back out into mottled sunshine. The square cement tiles of the Have Veien were etched with names and greetings, dates of births, weddings, and deaths. One noted the visit of King Olav in 1975. 'Velkommen til Poulsbo.'

Tulips and daffodils bloomed in whiskey barrel planters. Liquid amber trees, planted in a pattern reminiscent of hopscotch squares, wore spring green maple-like leaves. Kelda sat on one of the benches that lined the walkway, and ran a finger over the rosemaling on the backrest.

"Please join me, Tony. Tell me about these men."

Tony Petrulli again consulted his watch as he sat. George and Alfred stood a distance away. George studied his well-shined shoes. Alfred held his dead cigar. Cal Callari came out of the coffee shop and hunkered down in front of Kelda.

"I'll handle this, Tony. Look, Ms. Hansen, we're a group of investors, currently looking to site a golf course somewhere in the area. We had reason to believe you, and others on that land finger, were amenable to discuss our venture. If we were premature in stopping by your place, we apologize."

"Premature would suggest the Landing might be available sometime later. Like when Uncle Ragnar is dead." The Kerrys and whomever owned the old orchard were the others on the land finger. She couldn't believe Liam and Leah would sell their land for a golf course.

"Uh, well, perhaps I chose the wrong word."

Kelda looked from Callari to Tony. "Is Cal your attorney, Tony?"

Before Tony could answer Cal said, "No, no, we're just business acquaintances."

"Apparently, I'm to speak to and through you, Mr. Callari. Until very recently, Mr. Petrulli served as my Uncle Ragnar's personal accountant. He also did the books for the family group which owns the Landing. The 'parcel,' as you called it. Mr. Petrulli knew before I did that the Landing's ownership group was reduced from four persons to two, and that the financial picture had changed rather dramatically. If he sent you to the Landing, I consider it an unethical act."

Tony pinched the crease in his pants. Cal cleared his throat.

"Mr. Petrulli's deceased father-in-law and my uncle were close personal friends from childhood until Ivar Jonasson's death. Almost eighty years. In my opinion, that makes it immoral as well." Her head pounded. The tiles of the Have Veien danced. Her stomach lurched.

"Kelda, I assure you, I haven't mentioned the change of ownership of the Landing to anyone."

Cal said, "Tony, I'll handle it. Ms. Hansen, Kelda, if I may, again we offer our apologies. It's clearly a misunderstanding. Mr. Petrulli is merely part of our investment group. The source of information, merely an interested party, obviously made an error. There's nothing unethical about it."

"An interested party?"

She waited, but no name was offered. It wouldn't make sense for Arne to send them. He wanted all that land himself. "Apologies accepted. I'd like one minute with Tony."

Cal stood, gestured with his head. The Taglia brothers followed him to study the window display at a book shop.

"Is Arne the source, Tony?"

Tony shook his head. "No, not at all. I know you and Arne hold different views on the best resolution for the Landing. Frankly, I was surprised when the group tendered the suggestion. They didn't mention the source."

"Thanks, Tony. You needn't say more." She turned and called, "Cal, thanks for the coffee."

Male laughter, forced, followed her back into the coffee shop. "May I have a glass of water, Joyce? I'll just sit until those four men are gone."

Joyce poured water from an iced pitcher, brought it, looked out the door. "They're gone. Are you feeling all right?"

"I just performed my don't-mess-with-me act for those four men in suits, and it escalated a migraine that started last night."

"Can I get you aspirin? Or Advil?"

"The water will do. I need to get back to the Landing."

"So, are you back home, so to speak?" Joyce sat across from her. "Downsized, like I was, and deported from the big city to the place we couldn't wait to leave thirty years ago?"

"I think so. Back home. Maybe. I don't know." She shook her head. "Actually, I'm not sure I ever wanted to leave."

"Well I did, but then I didn't live in a mansion like you. And I didn't want to come back. I'm living at my parents' place. House sitting while they're in Arizona. They spend six months there. But they're due back, and I'm going to have to live in their motor home and beg table scraps."

Joyce talked as much with her hands and facial expressions as with words. Kelda could see the hurt, and reached across the table to squeeze Joyce's hand. They'd been friends during high school, lost touch after, then seen one another two or three times in the last ten years. Joyce could pick up a conversation where it left off years before and bring it up-to-date. And she sounded cheerful in spite of her troubles.

"Joyce, the old house at the Landing is not a mansion. It's just a big old house. And you have an MBA."

"The house seemed like a mansion when we were kids." Joyce made circles on the table top with her water glass. "I have an MBA and two part-time jobs in Historic Downtown Poulsbo. My career somehow ended in a buy-out and realignment. I thought about a lawsuit, discrimination of some sort, but my male cohorts got the same treatment. It's been fifteen months. I can't find a real job. You know the story: overqualified, too expensive. Too many new college graduates comfortable with the newest technology."

"What about your husband?"

"Divorced. When I said 'Joyce Lindquist,' I meant it. I took my maiden name back. The only kind thing I have to say about my ex is that he's helping with our son's college costs. Our daughter graduated a year ago, so she's on her own. I have a condo in Bellevue, but the market's bad, so it's rented. I make enough on the rent to pay the mortgage and send my son a little money. I'm trying to live on severance pay and retirement, and figure out what to do with my life. One good thing, I can get a cup of coffee, no charge, even days I don't work here." Joyce laughed, her hands saying it's not all bad.

Kelda smiled. "You haven't changed. You can always find the bright side. And you can talk more than any Norwegian I know."

"Well don't tell anyone in town, but that's because I'm half Swedish." And she laughed harder.

"Mixed blood." Kelda laughed too, then glanced up at the clock. "I've got to go, Joyce. Uncle Ragnar's been having some health problems."

"I wondered. He must be in his eighties because my folks are in their seventies. It's funny; I was thinking about you today, and the Hansens and the Landing. I drove in along Fjord Drive, and looked across the bay. It's so green."

A man breezed into the coffee shop, humming, smiling. He sang, "Hello oh," and patted Joyce on the shoulder as he moved behind the counter.

"Good, you're back." Joyce made introductions and said, "I'm walking Kelda to her car."

As they walked, Kelda talked of Ragnar's health, her job, her fear of losing the Landing

"No wonder you're upset. The taxes must be horrible. It's none of my business, but can you afford them? Sorry, I'm really nosing in, but I'm so hung up on the expense of everything right now."

"The taxes are worse than horrible, but there's one possible ray of sunshine. We have a new tenant moving into the big cottage, and he's interested in leasing some of our land to grow nursery stock. Native plants."

"Let me guess. Walkingstick Nursery."

"You know him?"

"No, but the paper did a nice write up supporting the idea of landscaping with native vegetation, things that don't require so much water during the summer, you know the kind of press I mean. A business gets a little notice, but the real story is something else." Joyce's hands worked the air. "So, are you going to do it? Lease him some land?"

"It's one option. Fixing up the three small cottages is another, but I doubt they'd bring much rent. They're so old, they all need new roofs and windows."

Joyce stopped walking. "You still have the cottages? The beach ones your mother let us play in sometimes when they weren't rented?"

"Those are the ones. Less than nine hundred square feet, worn floors, old slat blinds."

"On the water. On the beach."

"The cove beach, which is rocks and seaweed at low tide." They'd reached the old Bronco.

"The tide comes back in."

"Old stone fireplaces that suck all the heat up the chimney."

"Fireplaces can be blocked off when they're not used. So, how are they heated?"

"We put in electric baseboard back in the Sixties. Expensive and inefficient, but the wiring all checks out as good. We've talked about electric wall heaters, and we've got decorative inserts in the fireplace openings."

"How expensive is the heating? I mean, for nine hundred square feet?"

Kelda shrugged. "We keep the thermostats low. Uncle Ragnar added insulation under the floors, but they're bare. The bedroom's small, the bathroom has an old pedestal sink with a stingy shelf and an old medicine cabinet."

"Let me guess, Kelda. You've been living in upscale homes built by Arne Hedstrom in his gated communities. Big rooms, lots of baths, gas-log fireplaces in every room. You don't know about the Kitsap housing market. Rents are higher here than in much of the greater Seattle area."

"There's only one washer and dryer for all four cottages, and they're in a poorly insulated room at the end of the carport between the second and third cottage. No dishwashers."

"No dishwasher is a serious problem." Joyce rolled her eyes and waved her arms. "I'll offer you three-fifty a month for one of them, sight-unseen, if you promise not to raise the rent for a year. To make up for the difference in what you should charge, I'll do anything I can to help with maintenance and repairs. I can scrub and paint. Mow lawns, pull weeds, maybe look after your uncle when you're gone."

"Joyce, that's way too generous."

"I'll get my dad to help. He likes to putter. Mom might pay me something just to get him out of the house."

"You mean it, don't you?" Kelda held her temples and looked at Joyce. "I've got to pick up something for dinner, and finish my case-notes. Tomorrow's a work-day, so I'll be gone until late."

"Quit stressing. Grab some TV dinners."

They both laughed at the notion of old Norwegians eating such things. "Call me, Joyce. It's the only Ragnar Hansen in the book." Kelda climbed up into the Bronco, turned the key, put down the window. "If you're serious, we can talk about updating the place."

She kept the window open as she drove to the Landing from the market, thinking about generating money from renting cottages and leasing land. It would help, but not enough. If Arne moved to the Landing, they could sell the Edmonds house, get rid of that huge mortgage and make enough to pay off the Hedstrom Construction lien on her trust. Her headache subsided to brain dullness. The strong coffee had helped.

As she approached the Kerrys, Leah waved and ran toward the car. Her long, gathered skirt threatened to trip her. Kelda pressed the brake and prayed, Please, not Uncle Ragnar.

"Kelda, tell me you're not selling the Landing to some . . . some golf course investors."

One of Kelda's hands pressed an ache in her chest. "I'm not selling; I'd rather give it to the state."

"Oh, thank God." Leah took in a deep breath. Her hand, too, pressed her chest. "Look at this." She thrust a brochure through Kelda's window. Before Kelda had more than a glimpse at the color photos, Leah said, "And this," and handed in a business card. Taglia Brothers, Ltd., in raised blue letters on expensive stock. "The back," Leah said. Kelda turned the card over.

*We're negotiating for the Hansen property and the old orchard across the road, and would like to discuss including your parcel in the deal. Prepared to offer above assessed value. George & Alfred Taglia.*

"I found it tucked into the door. I tell you, it made my heart stop and then leap. I called the Landing. Emma said you went to the bank. I've been at the window, hoping you'd get back before Liam gets home."

"Oh, Leah, I'm sorry." The headache tightened around her eyes again. "This all started because Uncle Ragnar bought back Erik and Greg's shares of the Landing. Things are a little tight, financially."

Leah's mouth fell open and her hand flew up to cover it.

"I guess he didn't tell you. He didn't tell me either, until last week." Tears sprang so fast Kelda didn't feel them coming. "Seems like a year. But it's going to be okay. We are not selling, and we're going to have our annual Hansen's Landing celebration on Sunday, and we want you and Liam to join us." She fished around, found a tissue, swiped her face.

"Your *fattigman* and pickled herring, and all that?"

"All that, and some time to visit." She blew her nose, heard a vehicle, the sound of gravel crunching under tires. Arne's big truck coasted to a stop. One more for the dinner she'd planned to serve tonight and its leftovers for tomorrow's lunch for Ragnar and Raymond. And Emma too, it seemed, and rightly so. Emma deserved every bite of food she got at the Landing.

# 15
# Arne

Arne couldn't believe it. Tony Petrulli sent a bunch of Pope-lovers to the Landing to play Let's Make a Deal. Least he guessed it was Tony. If not him, then who? Not that Arne had anything against the Pope, or Catholics either. Lots of good Catholic deal-makers. Screw somebody a little on a deal, go to confession, it's all okay.

The part about negotiating for the old orchard across from the Kerry farm threw him. He'd looked into that. Some chowder head Norwegian had left that tied up so it was near impossible to develop. Then, when he was telling Kelda she did right to fire the Wop if that's what he's up to, he got the bigot lecture and another lesson in How Kelda Thinks.

"I fired him because he told me to stick with head-cases, leave finances to someone who understands," she said. Shit. Man expects a guy with his fingers on the financial pulse of forty acres, waterfront on three sides, to figure it out.

Next thing, Kelda's dragging him through the old beach cabins, talking about fixing them up to rent. "Shit, Kelda, call the goddamn fire department, they'll burn them as training, clean up the mess after."

"Shit, Arne, I don't want them burned, I want new roofing, and I'm calling in my chits, not the goddamn fire department."

"What chits?" he asked, and damned if she didn't start ticking off things like she carried some computer disk around in her brain.

"First, for my Hansen trust money tied up in the construction business. That has to be repaid, Arne. Second, for all the times I gave in and moved to your newest development, your upscale homes with low maintenance yards where I couldn't plant daffodils because the leaves are unattractive when they ripen down. Third, for not ever setting Gerda straight about Knut and Uncle Karli's boat building business that never materialized, and about their drinking problems. 'Thanks, Kel, I owe you big time.' How many times did you make me move, Arne, when I told you all I ever wanted was a house I could make into a home? How many times did you say you owed me big time when I wanted to buy something but there wasn't money because Gerda just spent another wad? Well, I'm collecting."

And then she for crissakes cried. Shit. Man gets a message to call his wife immediately, ends up talking to Emma who's taken a hysterical call from Leah Kerry about a golf course at the Landing. 'You better come see for yourself what's going on. Kelda's meeting with the bankers right now.' Man drops everything, look what he gets.

"Fire Emma's ass, save yourself that much money for your Hansen taxes," Arne said to Kelda once the whole sorry mess got straightened out. But no, not Kelda Ronalda Hansen. She hugged the old woman, patted her on the back, invited her to stay for dinner. Talked Walkingstick into joining them too, not that it took much talking. One pork loin for five of them. Damn, it was good. Could have eaten the whole thing himself.

And the Almond Roca cookies. Arne figured Kelda had whipped those up for him, kind of make up for his missing one ferry, waiting in line for the next one, dealing with the cottages and the tears. Not like Kelda to cry. He went into the kitchen, cut himself a few more cookies while the others still sipped decaf coffee. And then Emma, kitchen policewoman of the century, came along, wrestled the knife right out of his hand, started in about calories and fat grams. Didn't even give him time to find a little ice cream to go with them. Damn, that woman could irritate worse than sand in your shorts.

Later, while Kelda was in the great room writing up cases, he and Walkingstick partnered against Ragnar and Emma in a little pinochle.

Out of the blue, old Ragnar got a burr up his butt about the old Bronco. "Damn it all to hell, Arne, she shouldn't ought to be relying on that worn-out wreck. There's a lot of waiting for the ferry and a lot of driving on lonely roads 'fore she makes it here eleven-thirty at night."

Well, for crissakes, he'd thought about that too, told her she was nuts to be staying at the Landing. Told her if she wanted to live out her life at the Landing she could have a nice new home. Told her about the resort inn idea, hell, she could have a nice new home right alongside the resort. Or they could build one of those new central-living communities, no roads in the middle, forget the inn. She'd given him her Kelda-look. "We'll sell only to Norwegians approved by the Sons of Norway," he said, and got another Kelda lesson. He couldn't remember all of it now, but it had to do with form follows function, and Norwegians not investing in wasted space.

So, while Ragnar and Emma chortled about winning, and Walkingstick carried wine glasses to the kitchen, Arne slipped into the great room. Figured it was time for bed, Kelda might want to reward him for agreeing to the cottage repairs. She'd finished writing her cases and curled up in a chair, reading those goddamn journals she must know by heart, she helped translate them for crissakes.

"I'm looking for the part about the cottages, but listen to this."

So, wanting to show he cared about the Old-ones, not just the land, he sat on the sofa to listen. Next thing he knew, Walkingstick came in to say goodnight, ended up sitting down beside him. Emma, wearing two or three sweaters against the night air, perched on the arm of the chair old Ragnar had just lowered himself into. And Kelda read.

Before he dozed off he'd heard enough to know that while Helgar made good money with his logging enterprise, it was Magna that invested it. Invested in the house, had those cottages for summer guests built, and bought up gold. Bought up gold and put it back against bad times so they wouldn't lose the Landing. Damn, Hansens had a thing about land, this land, the land he needed to get his hands on so he could get Gerda off his back.

Arne woke up, nice pillow under his head, shirt unbuttoned, belt loosened, shoes off, one of Magna's quilts over him. He heard kitchen sounds, smelled coffee. For some goddamn reason, he'd been dreaming about an old treadle sewing machine that Magna used to keep old Helgar and her seven sons dressed like princes, and a rowboat Helgar built her so she could row out for visits and trips to Poulsbo at her leisure.

Leisure, now that's something he wouldn't be having much of with Kelda on his case to fix those cottage roofs, add insulation, new wall heaters, whatever.

Even with the heavy drapes darkening the great room, he knew the sun was up and he'd be late meeting Maria at the office.

"Why didn't you wake me, tell me it was time to go to bed?" he asked Kelda. "Any orange juice in this fridge? Mouth tastes like a cat pissed in it."

"That's certainly visual, Arne. Maybe you should be a writer. I tried to waken you, but Uncle Ragnar's wine works better than a sleeping pill. You were out, and even though Uncle Ragnar thinks he can do prit-near anything he sets his mind to, his mind and my strength weren't enough to get you off that sofa."

Arne looked at the clock. "Seven-thirty? What time's the next goddamn ferry? I'm supposed to meet Maria in the office at eight."

"I think there's one at seven-fifty."

"Now how in hell am I supposed to make the seven-fifty, it takes half-an-hour to get there?"

Telling Maria about his afternoon, evening, and morning at the Landing got her laughing so hard she didn't notice him start on another cinnamon roll she'd picked up at the bakery. She'd even hugged him once, sent little electric shocks through him. Damn, for a smart woman she didn't have a clue.

"Now the rest isn't funny," he said, setting Maria up to feel sorry for him. "Kelda told me over breakfast that she wants to sell the house."

"The Landing house?"

"No, for crissakes." The woman was slow this morning. "The Shore Pine Point house. Our new house, not that old 'historical landmark.' I didn't tell you that part, that's what she's calling it now."

"Well it is, Arne. And I'd think you'd be glad she's willing to sell your house here. You included it and the boat and mooring in the proposal you wrote up to buy that whole town up on the pass."

"That's just a proposal for crissakes. Doesn't mean it's going to happen." Shit, he'd forgotten he left that proposal on her desk. She was a sharp little woman, this partner of his. Stayed right on top of things, kept them out of trouble more than once.

"You didn't think I'd read that one, did you? And, it's a fair guess that you haven't talked to Kelda about it. How many houses did you say she counted off that you'd moved her out of over the years?"

"Geez, whose side you on?"

"Kelda's. I've always been on her side."

"Oh, that's great."

"That doesn't mean I don't love you, Arne."

She moved so fast he wasn't prepared, took his head between her hands, planted a kiss on his forehead and had the cinnamon roll box closed and in the refrigerator before he blinked.

"If only that were true," he said, but she was in the restroom by then. He looked at his watch. Shit, now he was late for his next meeting.

*Historic continuity with the past is not a duty, it is only a necessity. - Oliver Wendell Holmes, Jr., 1841-1935.*

*Legal scholar and judge; American justice-Supreme Court, Acting Chief Justice, fought in the Civil War.*

## 16
## Kelda / Raymond / Ragnar

Kelda had read the Old-one's journals late into the night, long after Arne fell asleep, Raymond and Emma left, and Ragnar went up to bed. She came from a family that worked hard and ate well, traditions she followed. Good food mattered, and so did sharing it with family and friends. She recognized that having Raymond and Emma eating with him were vitally important to Ragnar's improved health, and that meant starting something the three could eat that evening while she dealt with her clients.

She dug in the freezer, found chicken breasts, quick thawed and browned them, and simmered them with a Dijon mustard sauce. While they cooked, she prepared rice pilaf and a salad, and left a note for Emma to cook some of Ragnar's frozen green beans. "There's plenty for you three," she wrote, and went off to catch the ferry without disturbing the men at work on the cottage.

Shawndra came to the agency from school, and was late, so Kelda started with Mandy alone. The woman relaxed, even smiled, without her daughter there, then tensed when the therapy room door flew open and Shawndra stomped in, over-painted lips in full pout.

"You're late, Shawndra," Mandy said.

"Like I even want to be here. Fuck."

Kelda blinked, thought about troubled teens working under Raymond Walkingstick's supervision at the Landing, thought about her own teen years, and decided she'd had enough of troubled teens sometime back.

"Mandy, if I abort these sessions, Shawndra will go directly into the juvenile justice system. Will that create serious problems for your sons' care while you work?"

Before Mandy could answer, Shawndra said, "So you're gonna have the police come pick me up. This is fucked up."

"*Hold kæft,*" Kelda said, calm as the sea before a storm. "That's Norwegian for 'shut your mouth.' I mean just exactly that. Do not say another word or you'll have your next meal at the juvenile corrections facility." She concentrated on remaining calm, breathing in deep breaths and breathing out her impatience. Her chest ached where her heart was beating too fast.

Sheawdra turned to face the door, like she might risk running.

Mandy looked relieved. "I can manage the boys somehow."

"Good. Now, Shawndra, it's up to you. If you want your deferred sentence to remain deferred, sit down and listen."

Shawndra sat.

"Mandy, please relax as much as possible. We have work to do." Kelda willed the tension in her upper body to ease, not develop into a heart problem like her mother's. She really wanted to talk to her uncle one more time before this job killed her. And to Raymond, though why him and not her girls she couldn't imagine and didn't have time to ponder.

In the next forty-five minutes Kelda poured every ounce of her training, experience and common sense into setting Mandy and Shawndra on a course that could lead them to resolution of their conflict. She watched Mandy accept the privileges of her role, assert her power, make eye contact.

"Did I see a change in postures?" Rachelle asked, when mother and daughter left. "You have only twenty minutes before the Smith's. I've got a frozen entree heating in the microwave, since I didn't see you bring in anything that resembled lunch."

"No, I didn't have time after I prepared Ragnar's dinner, and I don't really have time right now. I need to talk to Keith, and then to Raymond about his troubled kids from the tribe. Leasing the land isn't going to bring in enough money to make it worth having troubled teens around."

Rachelle frowned, pulled food from the microwave. "You lost me there somewhere after the Smiths. Who's Raymond? And Keith isn't here, he hasn't come back from lunch, so you do have time to eat. Just barely."

"Oh. Sorry. My mind seems to be at the Landing. Raymond's the man renting the large cottage. As for heating food for me, thank you. That makes me feel good."

"Ha," Rachelle said, "you were about to say it wasn't necessary, weren't you? It's okay for you to fuss and fret over your uncle, and your husband and daughters, and your clients, but no one's supposed to fuss over you."

The Smiths consumed the rest of Kelda's Wednesday afternoon, and absolutely nothing changed from where they'd left off Monday. She grabbed a case management form, wrote NO PROGRESS on it, and folded it into a paper airplane. When Keith said, "Come," to her knock, she opened the door and sailed the paper at him. It looped once, crashed against his chest and back-flipped onto his desk.

He picked it up, tried to hide a smirk that suggested he'd had a very nice three-hour lunch. "What do you want me to do, Kelda? This is one of those sticky cases. The court won't take it back unless we have new information to report."

"Meaning what the court wants is for me to wring the offender's identity from Cameo, and then violate therapist-client privilege by telling."

"There's no 'privilege' in child offenses. Especially in child sex offenses. You know that."

Of course she knew. She also knew some prosecutors would sacrifice Cameo to get to her offender, to make a case.

"Take me off the case. Let another therapist try. For all I'm accomplishing, we could video tape a session and replay it twice a week. Nothing changes."

"Now, Kelda," Keith started, and then consumed most of her hour-break trying to appease her. She let him wear down her resolve, but only after she extracted his promise to sit in with her on the Monday session with Hap Smith and his children.

Rachelle stuck her head into Keith's office. "Kelda, a man from your group is here. He'd like a private minute. I put him in the therapy room."

"Don't let him use up all your break," Keith said. Then he looked at his watch, shrugged. "Damn. Sorry, Kel. Monday things will be different. I promise."

"Sure, uh huh." Keith's promises were made to be broken. Like Arne's. Maybe all men were the same. Except her uncle. And Raymond Walkingstick. He seemed to be on her mind.

The man from the group stood waiting, baseball cap clutched in grease-stained hands. Gasoline and tire smells, and male sweat, had drifted from his body and filled the room. Kelda could taste it.

"Ms. Hansen, I'm Lenny from the group, I been thinking about something you said, the thing about abuse being a learned pattern of behavior and we have to learn a new way of relating. Well, I guess you're right, I finally figured it out, my dad hit on my mom and all us kids. I guess that's the learned part, right? And I was doing the same thing, and, Ms. Hansen, I really want my wife and family back."

He fought it, but a tear escaped and rolled down his cheek. It left a clean path in the working-man grit.

"Would you like to sit down and have a cup of coffee?"

"Yeah." He swiped the tear with the dirty cap and looked at the furniture. "You got something I can put down first? I should bring you some of them papers we put in cars when we have to get inside."

"Let's go into my office. I'll get the coffee."

The rest of the group was restless by the time Kelda and Lenny joined them. "It's my fault, I came early and took up her time," Lenny said. His breakthrough led to a good group discussion, and a quick three hours. Two men lingered past the nine o'clock session end, so she just made the ten-thirty ferry. She took the Smith case forms with her, though she couldn't think what she could write on them beyond what she'd already written. No progress.

She stopped at a market for flour and a few other items, and arrived at the Landing just before midnight. Raymond Walkingstick stood in the light of the long porch. Her heart lurched when she first saw him, settled when he waved and ambled toward her car. He leaned heavily on his cane.

"Need help carrying anything?"

"No, I can get it. Just a couple bags of groceries." She pushed the unlock button. Raymond opened the back door and hefted the bag with ten pounds of flour. "Raymond, I can manage. It looks like your leg is bothering you tonight."

"That's just for show; my sympathy catcher. Good thing your uncle dozed off in his chair. He's been kicking up a fuss for hours."

Kelda heard him groan as he turned. She fought her instinct to take the bag from him. Something in his look stopped her. "I should have called during my last break to say I might stop at the store."

"Worrying started a lot earlier than half-an-hour ago. He says this is the night you're alone at your agency with twelve men court-ordered to take anger management. That true?"

"More or less. And I'll bet he also said, 'Damn it all to hell, someone ought to line 'em up and shoot 'em in the balls, assuming they've got any. Man beats a woman has a nerve calling himself a man.'" She heard Raymond chuckle before he spoke.

"I tend to agree with him," he said. After a pause, he added, "It's not wise to be alone in the building with such a group."

"There's safety in numbers. One angry man alone is more likely to act out. Tonight, I had one guy come in early. He'd had an epiphany and was struggling with his guilt burden. He was a good catalyst for the group. I might be able to sign off on them."

"Kelda, what led you into such a career?"

"That's easy." After saying that, she wondered what to tell him, and decided on the truth. "Family therapists almost always come from complex families. We understand that family patterns and dynamics shape individuals, but we need to know just exactly how. I may be working with other families, but I'm always sorting Hansens. And Hedstroms."

"*Kär a*," Ragnar said, opening the great room door. "Here, I am, dozing off, you're still at it, working all hours."

She let him take the bag she carried.

115

"We'll be working all hours the next few days, Uncle. Crushing cardamom, rolling flat *brød*, shaping meat balls." She and her uncle named off foods and preparations as they stored groceries. "Raymond's going to have to share you." Then she called, "Night, Raymond," when she realized he was leaving. She watched his flashlight beam lead him past the rhodies and lilacs, and along the road to the cottages, and knew he was in pain. He shouldn't be sitting up late with Ragnar. She made a mental note to thank him, hoping he'd continue doing so until she started her leave.

Raymond let himself into the cottage cluttered with the tools and debris that seemed to sprout and grow with repair tasks. He'd completed the bathroom subfloor and reinstalled the old bathtub. Bending over to start hot water for a bath brought a moan. How could a hip made up of nylon and titanium parts ache so? He poured Epsom salts into the rushing water, stirred them into dissolution, then limped to the kitchen to heat water for a cup of chamomile tea. If the bath and tea didn't reduce the pain to a manageable level, he'd resort to aspirin.

He set the mug of tea on the shelf someone had built over the faucets and grasped the clamp-on rail to steady his descent into the soothing water. As he sipped and soaked, he wondered about herbs his ancestors might have used to ease pain from arthritic joints. He had some memories of things heating in baskets woven tightly enough to hold water, of salves and ointments being rubbed on young skin by leathery hands, of smelly tonics being urged into reluctant mouths. He remembered a white-haired man and woman with face wrinkles so deep they looked like furrowed ground. Whatever they'd dripped past his lips in his earliest years must have been offered with love—his mind's picture of them always relaxed his face muscles, reminding him what it felt like to smile.

With the help of the couple who lived in a mobile home on his nursery grounds, he was acquiring information about how his people used native plants. Those two knew more about it than he'd ever be able to learn, but they could only pass along their knowledge when he knew what to ask. Neither ever pointed to a plant and said how its roots, bark, leaves, or flowers had once been used. Neither understood what he was talking about when he said he was studying ethnobotany. Still, they knew things he wanted to learn. Sometimes he wanted to weep at the wisdom that dissolved into dust as the elders died. Or rotted away as they swamped their brains with alcohol. The tribe combated that now, worked to bring pride back to his people. But more than one generation had been lost in the interim.

He took a swallow of tea and leaned his head against the tub's high back. He was comfortable here, in this tub, in this cottage, on this land. He'd like to live on the other side of this narrow peninsula, about a half-mile from where he now tried to ready his body for sleep, but it was too soon.

Too soon to offer Kelda whatever he had to help with her struggles. He saw determination and pride in her, and admired it, though he missed the enchanting girl-woman of fifteen, who'd revealed a love of life even in the wake of her mother's death. Her marriage puzzled him; her delight in her uncle charmed him; her love of Hansen history fascinated him. Especially in light of that gift of herself she'd given him when she explained why she'd chosen her career. Just what about Hansens was she sorting? Was she communing with the Old-ones' spirits?

When the water grew cool, he pulled himself out of the tub and moved to his bed. He lay for a long time, willing his mind to rest, willing the pain to subside, pushing away conscious thought. He heard a scratching through the fuzziness, and rose to open the door to Seatlh, his ginger cat, who'd adapted to the move from city condo to country cottage as though born to it. Before he closed the door, he thought he saw someone moving out on the old dock. He blinked and squinted his eyes. Nothing. "Must be a dog out there. That why you came in, Sea?"

Sea jumped onto his bed and started his grooming ritual, and, finally, Raymond felt sleep coming to carry him away from the pain in his hip. As he drifted he wondered if Kelda liked cats.

Ragnar poured a mug of coffee and took it into morning sunshine where Kelda sat sipping on the flagstone patio, her shoulders draped in one of his tattered sweaters. For a moment, he thought it was Lydia, the sight carried him that far back.

"Good morning, Uncle," Kelda said, nearly sang, so his heart lifted right up and poked at his wool shirt. "No work for four days. Just a little cooking and pruning the wisteria and those scruffy shrubs along the old skid road and maybe cleaning these flagstones so we can have dessert out here Sunday."

"No work," Ragnar said. He looked across Liberty Bay and conjured a vision all the way to Norway, where a young man packed a steamer trunk with axes and woodworking tools, hand-sewn clothes, and layers of *flatbrød* meant to keep him alive in America. "No work, 'cept making *flatbrød*. It and a little water to drink, a man could survive a good long time."

They went to the basement together to carry Magna's *lefse* griddle up the stairs and plunk it on the stove. Best thing for baking the *flatbrød*. Round cast iron like the best frying pans, near 18 inches across and no good way to fit it on a burner on the electric stove. He managed to do the hefting and carrying, leaving Kelda to fetch the turning paddles Helgar had crafted.

"Seen where they have electric things for baking the *lefse* and *flatbrød* nowadays."

"Magna's recipe might not work on anything too fancy, Uncle Ragnar."

"Might not at that." He read the recipe, written by his mother, translated into English by Karli and himself all those years back for Lydia's use. About three-pounds graham flour, four or five cups white flour, one-cup or so shortening, one-quart buttermilk, one nice teaspoon soda dissolved in hot water, little salt. No mention of cutting the shortening into the flour or adding the buttermilk and dissolved soda and salt together, little at a time. No mention, neither, of rolling paper thin with the waffle-grooved rolling pin near long as his arm, or lifting it onto the griddle with the paddles and without poking a hole in the dough. Turn once, brown just so and set on the big flour sack towels spread out on the counter.

"You do the mixing, I'll help with the rolling," he said, trying to remember it was Kelda, not Lydia, with flour up to her elbows.

Kelda took a phone call while she worked the dough, told someone to come on out, have a look, put the phone back with dough bits and flour on it, it looked so right in this old kitchen he felt his eyes get all wet and had to turn away while she explained about a high school friend, Joyce Lindquist, on her way out to look at the cottages. Ah, the Lindquists, some years younger than him, lived in Poulsbo all their lives.

Joyce popped in, came through the great room saying, "Mmm, aromatherapy, food cooking and coffee brewing. It's so Norwegian. I'll take the second cottage, the one with the shared carport and handy to the laundry equipment."

"Are you certain?" Kelda asked. "You haven't seen what it looks like inside."

Joyce laughed, and Ragnar heard little chimes, like a distant church bell ringing in a new day. "Inside doesn't matter. It means I have more beach since the cottages on either side aren't occupied. I love rocks, and I can watch the water creeping in on them, changing them from plain to all sorts of colors."

Ragnar shook his head. The woman could talk, sip coffee, wash up and pitch right in on the kitchen work without so much as swish of a dog's tail, not that they had a dog's tail to swish. She'd said she didn't really remember him when Kelda did the introductions, but she remembered Kelda's mother, how Lydia loaned her all sorts of books and helped her more than once with a dilemma, and that was all it took. If they could find another woman or two like her, or another man or two like Walkingstick, they'd fill those cottages right up. Course that wouldn't be enough income, not even with leasing some land for those native plants, he could do the math even at eighty and some odd years. He still needed to get to getting, though maybe not quite so soon, maybe not by taking to his bed. He could just as soon keel over doing a little carpentry with Walkingstick, maybe fall off the roof.

No sooner did he have that thought than Arne Hedstrom pulled up with a couple trucks and a crew, said he'd come to do the roofing, s'posed he should start with the big cottage. Being Arne, he started by finding the butter dish, slathering butter on a piece of *flatbrød* big enough for his whole crew, eating it all himself, then looking for coffee to wash it down..

Ragnar nodded, a nod meant to say that's the first and last piece you'll be needing, not that Arne ever understood the Norwegian language. "*Ja*, Walkingstick's first, then Joyce's second, which would be the Number Two."

"We'll go take a look, Joyce," Kelda said. "You might change your mind. There's no curtains on the windows. I bought unbleached muslin and osnaburg to make new ones, and then we decided to quit renting."

"I think I can still sew curtains," Joyce said. "Mom has a sewing machine."

"Plenty machines right here," Ragnar said.

Kelda worked the turning stick under a piece of rolled dough, lifted it to the griddle. "Three. Magna's old treadle is my favorite. Sometimes I sew scraps of fabric together just to be treadling. Two electric ones. We could have a curtain-sewing bee."

"A treadle?" Joyce said, her voice all musical notes. "Wrought iron stand, carved oak drawers, black head with silver lettering? Or is it gold?"

The two went off to the sewing room to look at the treadle, then out to inspect the cottages, leaving Ragnar to get more dough rolled out for baking. Emma showed up, fussed at flour everywhere, and followed Kelda and Joyce. She gathered up a broom and dustpan, mop and bucket, rags and cleaning supplies.

"Shoot, might just as well start out there, no sense cleaning this kitchen while there's a man in it."

Next thing Erik popped in, said he'd start with mowing the lawn, then get on the pruning. Said Ragnar was right, selling out didn't mean he shouldn't be helping out, leaving it all to Kelda. He'd had a good life at the Landing.

"Damn it all to hell, Lydia," Ragnar said to the vision standing beside him in the Landing kitchen, "too many things going on all at once here. Could be I'll need to be keeping on for a time, but I'll be needing your help to get things on an even keel."

*If you don't believe in ghosts, you've never been to a family reunion. - Ashleigh Elwood Brilliant, 1933- ...*

*Author/artist & syndicated cartoonist, born in UK, living in southern California.*

# 17
# The Celebration

Kelda could hardly believe what they'd accomplished that day, with Arne's crew working on the cottage roofs, Emma and Joyce cleaning their interiors and Erik working on the landscaping. She dug around in the freezer, found several containers of little neck clams Ragnar had dug and frozen, and made up a huge pot of Hansen Clam Chowder for dinner. Arne and his crew ate their fill and headed back to Edmonds for the night. Emma fussed at the continuing kitchen mess as Kelda started dough for *fattigman*. Ragnar fell asleep after one game of cribbage, so Raymond came to the kitchen to offer help. She gave him the task of husking and grinding cardamom seeds.

"This an herb or a spice?" Raymond was taking his time crushing the tiny aromatic seeds in Magna's old hand crafted mortar.

"A spice. I need a generous teaspoonful, ground fine."

"That's going to take some time. How do you know it's a spice?" Raymond inspected the little black and brown seeds. "Could be the leaves of it are herbs."

"It's expensive, it comes from the tropics. It's like cinnamon—one of those things spice merchants sailed off to find back when."

"So, it can't be grown here. Does it have medicinal value?"

"I don't know, Raymond. I'll look it up, but right now I need you to grind."

He grinned. "Spell *fattigman*. And define it."

It was the first real smile she'd seen on his face. She spoke over the whir of the old electric mixer. "*Fattig* means poor. Poor man's cookie. They're our favorite. Ragnar's and mine."

"Poor. With that good brandy you're pouring in? Not to mention whipping cream, butter, half dozen eggs. And these little seeds. What did you say, twelve dollars for this three-quarter ounce packet, and ninety percent or more just husk. That would make it close to two-hundred dollars an ounce. More expensive than exotic perfume."

That surprised her; the quick math and his mentioning perfume. "Joyce Lindquist would call it aromatherapy, the fragrance of exotic baked goods."

"This kitchen always smells good. I like walking in here to fill my senses. Good food prepared with love. It lingers, the love of your first Hansens."

Goosebumps rose on her arms. The Old-ones and her mother Lydia were with her. "Literal translations don't always work. I think poor originated with use of ingredients on hand on a farm. The Old-ones fermented fruit juice for brandy. Ragnar says Magna collected juice from her canned fruits and put it in a crock. They did without things another family might have considered a necessity so they could have some of their traditional foods. It must have carried them home in spirit."

Raymond cocked his head. "Sometimes I think a memory of my earliest life, or maybe even pre-life, visits me. It lifts me to a place of love. It seems to be associated with aromas."

That startled Kelda so much she stuck a spoon into the old Kitchen Aid beater, interrupting the mood. The only men she'd known who admitted to such awareness were Ragnar and one former boyfriend, a Hawaiian who stayed in touch with his peoples' spirits. There had been a time when she'd considered herself in love with him and he with her, but both knew they belonged to the land of their origin.

When the *fattigman* dough was chilling in the refrigerator and Emma had cleaned her last and left, Kelda and Raymond went into the great room to look through the herbal medicine books Joyce had brought to the Landing. They included recipes to help almost any ailment. Kelda found a tea recipe that used cardamom, cinnamon, cloves, black pepper, and green tea. "Listen to this tea recipe, Raymond."

At the same moment, Raymond said, "This room is a sanctuary. I can feel the spirits. I feel honored to be here with Hansens, past and present."

The book with the recipe flipped closed. Her mouth dropped open.

"I'm sorry, I interrupted you," Raymond said.

"Interrupted? Oh, the tea recipe. I'll find it. It said cardamom soothes the intestines." She leafed through the pages. So, Raymond felt the Old-ones' spirits. Arne laughed when she or Ragnar mentioned them. Lauren and Reva rolled their eyes. Emma said she often felt their presence, it must be them always kicking up so much dust in the place.

"I'm studying the ethnobotany of the northwest coast," Raymond said. "One day I'd like to distribute that information with the plants I sell."

"I meant to ask you about that. About how you can run a business when you're here working on the cottage."

"An older couple live on the grounds and answer the phone. It's only a couple acres. I'm just getting started."

"Ethnobotany as in Natives' use of plants?"

"As in the relationship between plants and people. All people. The edible parts of plants that go to waste. Ceremonial uses, fermenting processes. Making tools, baskets, shelters."

She said his name, then shook her head. "Nothing. I don't know. Some idea flew past, but it moved too fast. Like an electrical shock. I'm just tired."

He grabbed his cane and pushed back his chair. "I'm keeping you up. Thanks for dinner, and for letting me help with the *fattigman*. I'll see you tomorrow."

He disappeared out the door before she got out of her chair. She wondered what she'd done to send him out into the night so suddenly. She wakened Ragnar, herded him to the stairs to head for bed, and warmed his heaters—gel packs, purchased from a health-care catalog, that could be popped into the microwave and then placed on aching joints. Ragnar said warmed beach sand would likely work as well. He was right, but he no longer protested the commercial ones.

The next morning Kelda sipped strong black coffee in sunlight that streamed through the kitchen window and thought about one-hundred-four years of Hansens at the Landing. In her mind, she saw the old wood burning kitchen range with its white enamel oven door, now tucked under one of those covers in the basement. She'd done her first cooking on it, her first bread baking in its oven. There were enough items stored in the basement to recreate an early 1900s kitchen.

She liked this 1950s kitchen, built in a U-shape for convenience, used for food preparation, not for reheating and storing items purchased at a deli or take-out counter. A dough board had been set into the black-edged apple-green tile counter, and black glass knobs and pulls added to white doors. The linoleum was an aged-white with black strips at the perimeter and a green square in the middle. Emma kept it waxed shiny. She wouldn't understand a no-wax vinyl floor and wouldn't believe wood or ceramic tiles belonged in a kitchen.

The appliances, including a dishwasher first added in the sixties, were white and of various vintages depending on when their predecessors gave out, and likely less energy efficient than new models.

One after another the others joined her in the kitchen, and she saw them as shifting particles in a kaleidoscope. She rolled and cut *fattigman* dough; Raymond looped and tied it; Ragnar dropped tied dough in oil, lifted golden *fattigman* out to drain on brown-bag paper. When they'd cooled, Kelda sprinkled on powdered sugar; sugar dust drifted like angel-dust in the sun's rays. Emma washed dishes and utensils, sending soap bubble rainbows dancing in the light.

Kelda baked all day Friday, prepared main dishes all day Saturday and set the table early Sunday morning. White on white damask cloth, rosebud china, heavy old sterling and crystal. She cut flowers and made a centerpiece of pink azaleas, tulips and bleeding heart, all the tints and shades of pink from pale to rose, with green leaves in linear, palmate and oval shapes. Then she filled Magna's crystal water pitcher with lilacs and set it on the sideboard.

"Shoot, Kelda, you should take up flower arranging or table design, you're that good, you could quit that therapy job," Emma said.

Kelda smiled, kept at her tasks, had everything ready on time: baked salmon, meatballs in cream sauce, noodles, crab salad, *flatbrød*, Hardanger *lefse*, pickled herring, spiced crab apples, dilly beans, pickles, olives, raspberry jam, all the desserts. She turned around once and found Erik in the kitchen, nibbling, turned around again and saw Arne in the kitchen drinking German beer, opening one for Raymond; Erik's wife Patty, one hand on Raymond's arm, her diamonds flashing rainbows. No prettier than soap bubble rainbows a couple days ago.

Gerda Hedstrom came into the kitchen, blue dress and blue hair. Lauren followed, a spun-gold blonde beauty, with Reva, hair more honey blonde and skin Hansen-freckled, in her wake.

Finally, Ragnar, Kelda's anchor, comb marks in white hair, pink scalp showing, and blue eyes shining.

And Emma in her best dress and dressy white apron. "Shoot, we might as well serve out here, seems this is the room they all like best."

The doorbell rang, Liam and Leah Kerry entered, and Emma swished her hands to move the kitchen crowd to the dining room. A pipe poked out of Liam's back pocket, a tissue wrapped bundle from under Leah's arm.

"I've brought a gift for the Hansens, for the Landing." Leah held up a wall-hanging, a fiber-art landscape of the bay and beach, the dock, the house and gardens. And in the background, the evergreen forest. Leah's work hung in the best galleries and commanded handsome prices.

Kelda's hand was at her throat, over her racing pulse. She swallowed to stop tears that wanted to flow, expressed her pleasure and listened to voices of praise.

"Now you know why I dragged you all over the Landing collecting bark and roots and flowers," Leah said. "The yarns all came from our sheep, the dyes from right here at Hansen's Landing."

Over continued ooh's and ah's, Raymond said, "Leah, will you teach me how to make the dyes? Not that I'll ever have a talent to use them as you do. I would just like to have jars filled with the colors. I'd label them and arrange them for view, perhaps in a north window where fading would be minimal. A reference to nature's offerings."

"I'd be delighted to teach you, and to give you wool lengths to dye, if you'd prefer that for display."

Champagne corks popped. Erik poured into flutes arranged on the sideboard. Lauren and Reva passed filled glasses to guests and family. Erik raised his glass. "To Ragnar Hansen, *Borgméster* of Hansen's Landing, our connection with the Old-ones."

Glasses clinked. Kelda blinked. If a tear did fall her smile would catch it.

"And to my sister, Kelda Ronalda Hansen, the *datter* of the Landing. May your dreams be realized."

Kelda dug in her pocket for a tissue, fought for composure, lifted her glass. "To Uncle Ragnar, the father of my heart."

Ragnar answered, "To Kelda, my *Kär a*. You make an old man proud."

"To the Hansens of Hansen's Landing. Fine neighbors, they are." Liam Kerry lifted his glass.

"To the Hansens." "The Hansens." "The Landing." "The Old-ones."

"To the cooks," Arne said. "Now, let's eat."

"Arne dear," Gerda said, "before you start could you remove those dreadful lilacs. That cloying scent is destroying my sinuses."

Kelda swallowed a barbed retort. "Reva, will you take them into the great-room? I think the Old-ones might enjoy them. Please, everyone sit. Reva and Lauren are handling the serving."

Somewhere in her professional training, Kelda had learned a math formula that held a key to the complexities of large families and gatherings. Sixty-six separate one-to-one relationships existed at their table of twelve persons. It accounted to some degree for the dissonance. While Gerda lamented the utter waste of dear Arne's time and talent fixing up the old shacks, Raymond hailed the historic value of the cottage he had the privilege of renting.

While Patty commented that such absolutely wonderful food came out of such an antiquated kitchen, Erik rebutted that new kitchens seemed too sterile to use.

"At least that's been the case with ours, hasn't it Patty?"

"Erik, pour yourself another glass of wine," Kelda said. "Patty, you work with the historical society. Could you help me set up a kitchen that represents the turn of the century? I think we'd find everything we need in the basement."

"Well, of course I could help, but good-god, why?"

"I'm not sure yet, but it would be part of something that's been teasing my brain lately. Something I see happening at the Landing."

"Mother," Reva said, "Mr. Walkingstick said I remind him of you when you were fifteen. Should I take that as a compliment?" Reva's eyes did a little roll on their way to touching Raymond's, but her smile showed his attention pleased her.

Raymond turned from Patty, who again had a hand on his arm. "It is meant as the highest compliment."

Ragnar nodded, one, two, three. "I think you do look a bit like Kelda, now I take notice. Count it as blessing and honor."

"It's a damn shame you can't cook like your mother," Arne said. "Kelda, you got some more meatballs hiding somewhere?"

Emma scowled at Arne. "No, she's not hiding them, I am. You know how much heavy cream she puts on them things?"

"Maybe Reva will take pictures of Mother's cooking and serve them, Daddy." Lauren was annoyed at being left out.

Arne grinned at his older daughter. "Lauren, honey, find me the meatballs. And the salmon, while you're at it."

"Everything is outstanding, as always," Leah said. "I'd love to have some of your recipes, Kelda. Remember, you were going to try to make sense of some of them for me. And teach me how to season things."

"I'll teach you what I can, if you'll teach me how to weave."

"Might be you should start a school out here," Ragnar said. "There's plenty you could be teaching, what with Leah and Liam's shearing sheep and spinning yarn, and Raymond's native plants. Kelda can teach prit-near anything, and now she's telling me what foods cause the arthritis."

"A school with a museum on the side," Patty said.

Gerda leaned forward and squinted at Kelda. "Oh, for heaven's sake, Kelda dear, why do you want to tie yourself down to this property? The buildings are falling down around you, and the taxes will only continue to go up."

"I don't think Old Helgar would much like you saying that about his building, Gerda Hedstrom. These buildings won't be falling down with anything less than ten points on that Richter scale. Your own husband Knut would be saying the same, if he was here."

The idea Kelda had been trying to catch circled closer. Not a school; not a museum either. Something that wouldn't change the Landing substantially, or threaten the trees, but that would bring in enough revenue to pay the taxes and provide for some basic comforts for Ragnar and herself. And Arne, if he chose. Something that gave her time to learn new things: yarn dying with plants, aromatherapy, herbal medicines. Maybe even time to write a story about Hansen's Landing.

There was a tap at the entry door, and then Joyce Lindquist's voice. "Am I just in time for dessert? That's the part I like best. I've brought an *Oslo Kringler*."

*We need to haunt the house of history and listen anew to the ancestors' wisdom. – Maya Angelou, 1928-2014*

*American poet & memoirist, civil activist.*

# 18
# Hansen Family History

With dinner over and the table cleared, Ragnar invited folks out to the flagstone patio to catch the late afternoon sun. Cumulus clouds intensified the sky's color, turning it almost sapphire to the north. The bay rippled in the breeze, its blue reflecting the sky. The air smelled clean, no other word for it.

He listened to their guests' mingled groans and regrets for not saving room for dessert. Still, crumbs built up like an ant trail between the patio and the breakfast room where Magna's crystal serving trays held Hansen *krum kaka* and *fattigman*, and Joyce's *Oslo kringler*. Might be they'd overeaten like they said, but he noticed most could nibble a little something with their *kaffe* or another glass of wine. Powdered sugar dust and pastry specks down dress and shirt fronts gave them away. Someone had even gotten into the blackberry pie.

Seemed like a dozen conversations going at once. Ragnar stayed out of them, even when he overheard Gerda Hedstrom say not so nice things about Hansens. She had the Kerry's attention, if not their interest. Instead of piping up, he put a piece of *kringler* in his mouth to keep it busy. He'd heard it before, and it wasn't his ear she aimed for. But ignoring her made him chew the soft pastry so hard his teeth ground. Gerda would not be caring to hear about how the Old-ones invested the essence of their love and plenty hard work in their land. And their courage and spirit, until their bodies wore down and only their souls remained. None of that would touch Gerda Hedstrom.

She'd gotten stuck in being upset with the Hansens back when. He kept his mouth clamped shut long past the last swallow of pastry, right up to the moment Gerda switched to talk about Wallace Taylor.

"He didn't drown, that's been clearly established," Gerda said, a look of triumph in her eyes. "He was murdered. The Hansens of Hansen's Landing might not act so high and mighty when that truth comes out."

"Damn it all to hell." The words slipped past Ragnar's mouth and floated in the air like the report of a shotgun. He looked around as conversations stopped. He'd meant it to be a thought that just sprung into his head. Could be that young reporter from the Poulsbo paper might have been encouraged by someone other than his editor to come snooping around.

"A respected businessman, Wallace Taylor," Gerda said, lips pursed like she'd sucked lemons rather than fed herself *fattigman*, one right after the other. "He owned the garage that serviced all the cars in this area in those years, so I've been told. Left a bereaved wife and children to run a business for which they lacked the needed skills."

That's when Ragnar gave up all intentions of remaining quiet. "Left a good deal more, much of it shameful, none of it talked about openly, most certainly not at a Hansen family celebration."

Arne had stepped into the fray, put his arm across his mother's back and escorted her and her evil tongue back into the house. Ragnar figured chances were good that Arne had overheard Karli Hansen and Knut Hedstrom speculating about Indians taking the matter of Wallace Taylor's tom-catting into their own hands. Likely heard it more than once, given how those two could rehash old-timers' stories while sipping Hansen's homemade beer. If the tribe had been involved in Wallace Taylor's demise, Karli might well have known, given he kept close company with those tribe members taking salmon at the Landing inlet.

Turned out Arne couldn't keep Gerda in the house. Time was he'd managed many an end-around play on the football field back in high school, but it would take more than that to silence his mother. They came back outside together, Arne carrying a crystal dessert tray filled with Norwegian treats. He saw Kelda's eyebrows lift and Reva respond faster than a blink to take the tray and set it in the middle of the patio table.

Kelda linked her arm with Ragnar's and said, "You can tell some of the Wallace Taylor story, Uncle. Illegal whiskey making and selling is part of the history of this area. Tell us what you know and let us surmise the rest."

Ragnar gave Kelda three nods meant to let her know she'd saved him from saying too much about Wallace Taylor's comings and goings in the dark of night by turning attention to the whiskey making and selling part of the story. He stood his straightest and kept his eyes on Emma, closest to him in age and knowing more than she'd let on about those times sixty and some odd years back.

"It was the whiskey what caused Wallace Taylor his troubles. Them were prohibition days, 1920 into the Thirties, with whiskey making a thriving business in a good many places in this country. Now, making a good product requires some talents that poor Wally never had. He was a businessman like Gerda said, but his garage pumped out more than gasoline, his automobile work helped many a customer hide a gallon of hootch. Them who did the distilling were called moonshiners; them who sold it bootleggers. Wally got himself a spot in the middle, bought from the shiners, sold to the leggers. All sorts of things can go bad in that business."

Walkingstick got himself some distance from Patty to stand alongside Ragnar, who gave the man a critical look. Skin a bit pale for a full-blown Suquamish, but eyes black as a night without stars.

"I can tell you about another chapter in Ragnar's story," Walkingstick said. "My people have a devastating history of alcohol abuse, and a canny ability to acquire alcohol regardless of laws. I'm not old enough to know where they did their buying and trading during Prohibition, but I'm wise enough to know they kept quiet about their sources. Ragnar told me that no whiskey making ever took place at the Landing. We're here to celebrate the Hansen's and the Landing, not to memorialize Mr. Taylor."

Erik said, "Hear, hear."

Emma said, "I'll make another pot of coffee to help you wash down what's still left of the desserts. We can thank Raymond for helping Kelda and Ragnar with the *fattigman*, and Joyce for the *kringler*."

Patty made her way to Walkingstick's side to pat his arm like she'd been the one who set him up to do the talking. Kelda, who'd kept her arm linked with Ragnar's in a way that made his old-man eyes get watery, gave an extra little squeeze. And then, to make matters worse, or better depending on how you saw the world, Reva came up along his other side and took his other arm. "Tell us the story about Mom being born to the Landing. That's my favorite."

"Ah," he said, "that's a long story, written in sorrows sprinkled with wisdom. The sorrows are the three daughters born to the Old-ones and dead within hours of birth. All three lie at rest under the cedar trees up the lane by the salty pond that fills when the tide runs high. The wisdom comes in the words Indian Joe spoke to Magna. He called cedar a woman's tree, for the smooth needles, and for the bark that can be woven into bowls and branches. A bit of cedar can kindle the fire. Its shavings serve as a perfume in closets. One tree can be hollowed out to serve as a protective womb for warriors going to sea. Magna wrote Indian Joe's most important words in her journals.

'*A girl-child called home before she knows the trees needs the cedars' roots to embrace her and keep her warm while her spirit waits to guide the female born to the land.*'"

Everyone remained quiet, even Gerda. Ragnar took a deep breath before telling the part Reva waited to hear.

"Helgar and Magna had seven living sons who gave life to seven sons. Arvid and Erland had two each. Gunnar died in World War One without marrying. Rolf and Karli never married neither. They were off in the logging camps for so many years, and then these parts seemed to run out of women. I married Ruth and she gave me *liten* Gunnar. Born sickly, he was, and died before he crawled. Olav married Lydia, and they had your uncles, Erik and Greg. That's the seven, if you're counting.

"Then finally comes Kelda, your mother, born to the land for certain, and she gives us you two girls to complete the picture. It was written as prophecy, and it came to be."

He couldn't remember when he'd said so much in one breath. Now that the cool breeze and spent words took the heat from his face, he could stop thinking on such serious matters. Folks should be having fun. "Erik," he called, "you find the croquet? And the bad mittens?"

That got them laughing, even Reva who'd cried a little. Ragnar knew badminton well enough, but Erik called the shuttlecocks mittens and batted them about when he could but toddle. They'd gone through many a set at the Landing since Lydia brought the first, back before she married Olav. Back when Ragnar still hoped he would be the brother she chose. Might be he should have spoken up, tried to change her mind. He could feel her hugging him now, right along with Kelda, who was born with too much to shoulder, truth be known.

Might just be that Reva would grow to give her mother a hand. Might be, too, that Walkingstick came along when he did to offer up some wisdom for the current Hansens of the Landing. Ragnar had a feeling that Lydia was trying to tell him what wisdom, but he couldn't grab hold of the connection, what with the hugs now including Lauren. That made the three of the prophecy right there with him.

*The great art of life is sensation, to feel that we exist, even in pain. - Lord Byron, 1788-1824.*
*English poet, peer, politician, playwright. Leading figure of Romantic movement.*
*Bisexual, alcohol issues.*

## 19

## The Landing

Kelda clamped her lips between her teeth to keep from interrupting her uncle. He needed to speak; her daughters needed to hear. There were times of late when she looked at her daughters and wanted to pull them back from young adulthood. She hadn't achieved all she'd hoped for as their mother. And then, this afternoon, she felt Reva return to her, not all at once, but gradually, like a new butterfly drying in the air before opening its wings.

It started when Reva repeated Raymond Walkingstick's remarks about their likeness, grew with Reva's quick glances that Kelda felt more than saw through dinner and when Ragnar spoke, and opened into a delicate being when Reva let tears fall when her Uncle Ragnar spoke of the wisdom of Indian Joe.

Something happened to Kelda at the same time, within or without she wasn't certain. The sun seemed warmer, the evening air more fragrant, the colors brighter when Ragnar spoke the old Indian's name. A message moved through her brain. *More blooms will come forth on the branches of this story.* She didn't know what it meant, just that it had something to do with Raymond. For a moment, less than a moment, she seemed to be looking through him as though he were Indian Joe, and would vaporize at the story's end. In that vision, he stood between Helgar and Magna, each with one arm around him and the other reaching toward her. In the wake of that vision, she stayed out of the fray, observing how the others interacted.

Patty caught Raymond in her web and kept him there. She claimed him as her partner against Erik and Reva, first in croquet, later in badminton. Patty, who usually spent her charm on Arne, let her hand linger on Raymond's arm at every opportunity.

Gerda played her my-dear-Arne game, and he went along, the attentive son. It gave Kelda pause; Arne had long played Gerda's game to keep a sense of peace between her and the Hansen family. A second message took root. *Arne knows something he's afraid to tell me.*

Lauren left the gathering to phone her current love-interest. Joyce drew pictures in the air to describe the cottage she would rent, and led Liam and Leah off to see it. Arne and Gerda followed, to admire the roof work.

Emma grabbed Kelda's hand and motioned for Ragnar to follow Joyce who called back that she'd paint, inside and out. Arne answered that he had extra fives of exterior white at the shop. Joyce unlocked the cottage door, her hands moving as she explained her love of rocks and the beach view. By the time Kelda reached the cabin, Leah was exclaiming over its charm and light, perfect for an artist's studio.

"And for drinking coffee and looking at agates I collect," Joyce said.

Kelda was in the middle of telling the cottages' history, all built in 1897, when she heard the Landing bell, and stopped mid-sentence. Ragnar was at her side, everyone was in view, either in the cottage or yard. But Lauren was calling, "Mother. Hurry!"

Kelda ran, certain she left a burner on, or perhaps a candle flame caught by a breeze, burning the area of the house not yet visible to her. Reva ran beside her, urging her to slow down, to breathe.

"Mother. It's your boss. Keith. An emergency, he said." Lauren pushed her golden hair away from her face.

Kelda looked at her beautiful daughter. "Please see to our guests, Lauren. Perhaps someone would like fresh coffee and a piece of pie."

"Me? Make coffee and cut pie?"

"Me?" Reva mocked. The two picked up their sister-act where they'd last left it.

Kelda turned her back to them and crossed to the phone. "Keith?"

"Kel, I'm sorry about this call. Your cell phone's not in service. I know it's your family celebration day, I hope it went well."

"Yes, very well. What happened?" She closed her eyes, certain she knew.

Keith lowered his voice to a strained whisper. "There's a detective here, I'm trying to keep to the facts." Then, voice normal, he said, "Hap Smith's been shot, and the son seems to be the suspect."

"Shot?" Fear clutched and twisted Kelda's insides, and sent prickles down her arms and legs. The fear she'd long had that something untoward would happen, something she could foresee but not prevent. Strong hands touched her shoulders and helped her find a chair. She sat, saw a pen in her hand, didn't know how it got there. "Shot?" she said again. "Shot dead?"

"Dead. Shot in the head. Rifle. Close range."

"Dead." She heard the word stretch in a low moan, and realized it came from her. Sorrow not for the dead, but for the living, for a boy and girl whose lives would be destroyed. The hands on her shoulders tightened, massaged while she listened to an explanation she'd already guessed; Tory caught Hap molesting Cameo.

She placed a hand on one of those rubbing her shoulders and looked up. Raymond Walkingstick. She'd thought it was Erik being big-brotherly. She'd known it wasn't Arne, who would have lashed out at her for her chosen profession. Perhaps he had been right all along.

An involuntary groan escaped as Raymond lowered his body into an aromatic bath. His leg and hip had started forecasting the now falling rain even before the croquet game. The delights of the day, and later Kelda's trauma, had acted as distractions from pain. Only now, alone with his tea and bath, did he acknowledge the deep ache in his bones. For a day like this one, he'd gladly endure this pain.

Tonight, he remembered what it meant to be a man.

Not an Indian man, not the half-breed his wife assumed him to be, acting more Indian than full-bloods, she often said. Not an attorney or native-plant nursery owner. Merely a man in a world of men and women.

He breathed in the scented water, giving himself up to the healing powers of the medicinal plants–cypress, juniper and lemon, guaranteed on the package to ease arthritis, gout, and other bone and joint pains. Until he could learn which natural plants to gather and how to use them, he would rely on what he could buy at the health-food store. He'd also purchased a package of dried slippery elm and cayenne barks to use as a poultice. If they worked, why not the inner bark of alder? He'd read that Natives used it for antibiotic needs, including skin sores. And today he'd learned Leah Kerry used it for dye for some of her red shades.

He kept the water hot, a degree or two hotter than he thought he could endure. He knew the scar tissue and crater on his injured leg would be an angry purple when he dried them.

Meeting Kelda's daughter Reva carried him back to a time before he'd let sorrow and anger consume him. Reva looked so much like the mind-picture he'd kept of Kelda that he had to remind himself not to stare. Patty's flirtatious charm provided a cover for his retreat into memory and to acceptance that he'd returned to the Landing for more than one reason. Thirty-five years ago, he'd punished himself for looking at Kelda with lust and desire. Now he knew that his spirit-ancestors had a relationship with hers. The attraction was no longer just physical. He'd been drawn back to the Landing for his lessons before dying. He must learn not just for himself, but for his mother and sister too, to ease their souls, to release them from the well of his sorrow.

For the second time he'd had the vision; he'd stood between the Old-ones, an apparition. The first time the vision visited him had been in the great-room the night he ground cardamom for Kelda, just as she'd said his name, and then dismissed it as an electrical shock. He'd felt it too, and caught a glimpse of himself with Kelda's grandparents, as if death were calling. The thought of his own death had never frightened him. For a time, it was something he and Ragnar seemed to have in common. A readiness, almost a desire, to leave behind all the struggles of their current lives. But now, for the first time in a very long while, Raymond felt inclined to live, and he'd seen the same inclination in Ragnar.

He'd had a sense of death, and wondered if it was to be his own, when Lauren rang the bell. He saw the fear in Kelda's face as she ran toward the house, and knew it wasn't only her uncle and her children that dwelled in her heart. Staying with her when she took the phone call seemed the natural thing to do, though others, by relationship, might have had more rights. But others were busy tending to one another, with Joyce, not Lauren, in charge. Kelda hadn't known who stood behind her, who felt the shock waves moving through her body, until after she'd released the dissonant energy in the sound that is no language and all languages.

She'd looked at him then, and though she didn't smile, her face changed. He'd watched her as he worked at the tension in her shoulders, his fingers noting each change in the conversation. She'd placed her hand on one of his. "They've taken a sixteen-year-old boy to Snohomish County Jail. A detective's coming on the line."

He listened to her brief responses, watched her head shake, saw her mouth open to speak, and then close again. Finally, she said, "Detective, I will be in my office tomorrow morning by nine. If going over there tonight would erase this nightmare for Tory and Cameo, I'd swim. As it won't change anything, I intend to see to my ailing octogenarian uncle and our guests. This is our day of celebration. I'm ringing off now." She broke the connection, placed the phone hand-piece in its cradle, and covered her throat with her hand.

He'd watched the pulse in her neck and felt he'd intruded, but she smiled, took both his hands in hers and kissed his fingers. First on his left hand, then the right. An intimate moment, but in the presence of others. Had they been alone, he would have pulled her into a hug.

He drifted into a sound sleep despite the change in barometric pressure, then jerked awake to Sea's scratching and mewling protests. Sea skittered in when Raymond opened the door, back arched, ears pinned, pointing like a dog toward the dock. Someone or something moved. An animal? No, a person. Wide awake now, Raymond pulled on his pants and watched, prepared to take action if it was an intruder. He found his cane and a denim jacket, and stepped out onto the porch with Sea following. While he watched, the dock prowler turned to walk toward the beach, stopped, leaned against the side-rail, then sat where the dock began. Kelda.

He slipped his arms into the jacket, left the door open enough for Sea to make a decision, in or out, and let his cane guide him to where Kelda sat. His leg felt strong, pain-free even in the rain. He knew she watched him approach, and he peered through the darkness for clues on her face. He stopped on the lawn at the dock's edge.

"Raymond?"

"Yes. Are you just having a restless night? Nothing else has happened?"

"You do worry about Ragnar, too." A sound, something between a laugh and sigh, rippled the night air. "I'm just cogitating, as all the uncles used to say. Ragnar had a bit of a bad time, but he's sleeping now. Reva's in the house. She knows I'm out here . . ."

Her words stopped, but not her thoughts. He read them, caught in the raindrops, and spoke with assurance. "It's not his time, so you can put that fear aside. The celebration wore him out. His body is responding to that and the worry about what you'll be facing tomorrow. Later today, actually."

"How do you know that? That it's not his time?"

"The spirits told me." He mustered up a posture that he hoped would convince her he had powers to see into the past and future in a single glance.

"Oh, Raymond, you're full of it. Are you sure you're not part Norwegian?"

"I speak the truth." He wasn't telling tales, though how he knew he couldn't say. It had something to do with his being called back to this place. From time to time, wisps drifted into his consciousness, but he'd never trained himself to listen. The signs were around him here; he had but to see. He knew from the time he'd spent with Ragnar, first planting trees, later working on the cottage, that the man worried not about death but about responsibilities to the living. He knew something haunted Ragnar, and that the man would remain earthbound at least until it was resolved.

"May I sit with you?"

"It's wet. Help me up and we'll walk." She extended a hand, though she needed little help. "It was a good day, up until that phone call." She spoke more to the mists than to him.

"Yes. One of the best in my memory." He watched her grin.

"I think you enjoyed Patty's flirting. She's very seductive."

"Even gimps can enjoy flirting. It's been a long time."

"Oh, Raymond, don't call yourself that." She stopped, cocked her head to the side. Her hand touched his, her eyes went serious. "I wasn't trying to seduce you, you know."

"I'm sorry to hear that."

"That summer I mean, when I knew you as Edward, when you'd just come back from Korea. Emma harped about that all summer. 'He might be older, but you're more mature. He's from the tribe, you have to be careful. There's differences, and you can't be ignoring them.' On and on, every day, reminding me to cover up and watch what I said. That's been on my mind today, maybe because you said Reva reminded you of me at that age."

"Oh. I see. I didn't know that, about Emma's concerns, but it wouldn't matter what you did or said; I was seduced the minute you answered the door. I'd have stumbled and stammered even if you hadn't given me the news of your mother's death." His words shocked him; he'd never known he could speak so honestly.

"Oh, Raymond, I'm sorry." One hand touched his again; the other wiped rain from her face. Or was it a tear?

"Why? I needed to feel alive, after the horrors of war. And I had enough sense about me to know you were young and vulnerable."

"You're wrong about the young part. I've never been young. I never learned how to be carefree and play. That part of me just didn't develop. But it will now. I plan to resign my position at the agency, even though it will create problems for some clients."

She held his hand. Like earlier, he felt energy flowing through her. He didn't think she realized she held his hand, and he hated to break the spell, but he wanted to help her through her latest crisis.

"I'd like to go with you when you meet with the detective." He'd offered before, when she'd told the others about the murder. Arne and Ragnar both liked the idea of an attorney being with her, but she'd refused.

Her head started moving from side to side. "No. But thanks."

"Why do you find it so difficult to accept favors?"

"I don't. Do I?"

"It seems to me you do." He could see her eyes, almost see their clear blue in the rainy darkness. The intensity in them pierced his heart.

"I do have a favor to ask. I intended to call you in the morning, before I left, but now will do. Please stay with Uncle Ragnar every minute while I'm gone."

"Of course. I'm honored to be asked." He'd rather accompany her, but he'd accept this as second best. She nodded, looked at the bay, took a few steps, came around on his right side and tucked her hand under his arm.

"Good, because you're bridging a gap for me. I'm so angry at myself. I promised Uncle Ragnar I'd take a leave and be here when he needed me, and then I let my boss talk me into staying part-time. Tomorrow, when Ragnar's worrying, you'll be here to speak for me. You can tell him it's our turn-around day. No more worrying backward."

"Worrying backward?"

"Just tell him. While you're at it, think about making it your turn-around day too. You worry backward just about as much as we do."

They walked together to his cottage where Seatlh still waited just outside the door. "Hello, kitty," Kelda said, and knelt to pet him. Sea hesitated just a moment, then put first one front paw and then the other on Kelda's legs, pulled himself up, and settled in her arms.

"Well, that answers one question," he said, but Kelda didn't seem to hear. She petted Sea and scratched his head and under his neck. He tucked his head up under her chin.

"What's his name?"

"Seattle." He pronounced it with the guttural undertones he thought the Salish language would have given the old chief's name.

"Oh? Spelled how?"

"S E A T L H . . . T before the L."

"Hmm. I saw it spelled that way once, but I can't remember where. Maybe a book about Washington's history."

She handed Sea over. He purred, content. Raymond watched Kelda walk to the house. "I know how you feel, old boy," he said to his cat.

*The deeper the sorrow, the less tongue it hath. –*

*The Talmud*

## 20
## Kelda

The great-room seemed all astir when Kelda returned from her stroll to the dock. She circled the oak table to look at the Old-ones' photo. Outside, the rain picked up, dripped from the downspout onto a gravel-covered drain that led back to the bay. She ran her fingers across the backs of the journals, then over the wire teeth of Magna's yarn cards. She'd given a similar pair to Leah, who used them to disentangle newly shorn wool before spinning. Her eyes settled on Helgar's hand-crafted wood-planes which served as bookends for the journals. She whispered, "What is it?" Her fingers traced small scars in the plane's heavy wood and tested the sharpness of the blade forged in Norway. A wind gust blew rain against the window.

*Take off another layer. Go a little deeper.*

"Yes, okay, I'm listening." But the room went still. Outside, the rain lessened. She went to bed, intending to ponder, to prepare for tomorrow, not sure she wanted to go any deeper in the Smith case. Her mind wandered, returned to the conversation with Raymond. She dozed, dreamed, wakened to sounds that seemed to have no source, or to disappear before she could identify them. About three o'clock, she heard retching, and stumbled to Ragnar's room before she'd completely wakened. She helped him like she would a child, got him settled in bed, brought a little soda-water to sip.

"*Magesmerte.* An old man shouldn't ought to eat so much rich food." He closed his eyes. She sat by his bed until soft snores assured her he'd fallen asleep.

At six-thirty she phoned Raymond. "Are you well? Your light came on early."

"Well as I've been in a long while. Sea needed to go out. I've been sipping coffee and whittling."

"Whittling?" She tried to picture him sitting alone, wondered what he thought about and wondered why she wondered.

"Little driftwood carvings. Driftwood from your beach."

"Oh." *Take off another layer. Go a little deeper.* "Can you come over about seven? Ragnar's been vomiting, but I think it's passed. Reva and I need to leave by seven-fifteen."

The mists cleared while the ferry chugged and churned across the Sound. They'd left late because Kelda had such a struggle leaving at all, and remained on the car deck where she scribbled notes and Reva read a textbook. Kelda wore a black pant suit, more somber than sophisticated. It fit her mood and forthcoming meeting. Forced concentration on her notes couldn't drive concern for Ragnar from her thoughts. Her cell phone rested on the seat beside her. From time to time she picked up the phone and ran her fingers over the key pad, like a child rubs the satin binding on a blanket, and for the same reason.

"Relax, mother. With Raymond and Emma both there, Ragnar will have more care than he wants."

Kelda sighed. "You're right. Sorry about missing the earlier ferry."

"It's okay, Mom. I can afford to miss a class. I don't very often."

Mom. Reva called her mom. She drove out of the ferry hold into brightness that called for sun glasses. Good for hiding conflicting emotions. And lack of sleep. She pulled up alongside Arne's car where he waited to pick up Reva.

"You sure you're going to be okay going alone, Kel?"

"Yes, Arne, I'll be okay." Kelda squeezed his arm, hugged her daughter, and drove away. Cloud puffs roamed the bright blue sky. In the distance a scud-cloud maneuvered over the drifting white,

144

searching a target. It zeroed in on Mid-Sound Mental Health like a heat-seeking missile and dumped its load a second after she locked her car door, several seconds before she reached the agency's entry. Inside, she shook her hair and brushed at raindrops on her jacket. Keith intercepted her before she reached her office door.

"You're forty-five minutes late. The detectives have been waiting. You should have worn a raincoat, your suit's all spotted."

"It's nice to see you too, Keith." But it wasn't. His tanning-bed color had drained out since she'd last seen him, and his eyes looked as bad as hers felt. The soft-light, soft-music reception room glared and screamed at Kelda's shot nerves. "I missed the seven-fifty ferry. I phoned."

"Things have been a little crazy, Kelda. I didn't get the message until too late to delay the detectives." He glowered at Rachelle who sat under a cloud as dark as the one that had just released its rain. Sun already made prisms of droplets clinging to the windows. In a lowered voice Keith said, "This doesn't look good for the agency. Come on. The detectives are waiting in my office."

"How many?" she asked, but Keith had already opened his door and started introductions. Detective Meehan, the man she'd spoken with on the phone, and Detective Pritchard. They rose. Both were six feet tall, beefy, middle-age white males; both wore suits with white shirts and knotted neckties. Meehan did the talking.

"Good morning, Kelda." He offered his hand, large and hair-backed. "We spoke on the phone. I may call you Kelda?"

She hadn't liked his voice last night, and she didn't care for his looks this morning. He exuded pomposity. "If we're using first names, I'll need to know yours." She delivered her words with a pleasant smile.

Meehan countered with a bone-crushing hand-shake. "Ms. Hansen," he said, settling the matter of names and titles. He had a melodic voice, one that seemed more suited to radio announcing than police work.

"Detective." She sat, opened her briefcase and looked at Keith who was having trouble getting comfortable in his executive chair. His jacket and tie made him look choked and irritated.

While Keith fidgeted, Meehan took the lead. "Obviously, you know why we're meeting. Now that we're face-to-face, I'd like to restate the particulars of the Smith case. Then we have some questions. Will that be acceptable?"

Kelda nodded, but Meehan hadn't waited for a response. She listened, back rigid, head high, hoping the words would bounce off such armor.

"Hap Smith was shot with a thirty-ought-six at close range. Private home, small bedroom. Two shots. One entered his upper torso at an angle that suggested he'd been in the process of turning; the other entered his head just above his right eye. The female with him, identified as his daughter, Cameo Smith, was spattered with her father's blood and tissue. The son, Tory Smith, called 911, and then allegedly comforted his sister.

Snohomish County deputies and Alderwood Manor's city officers both responded. I was called, as was the medical examiner from the county coroner's office. The victim was declared dead at the scene. He was clothed, though his trousers were unbuttoned and unzipped, and resting low on his hips. The female, Cameo, was dressed in a bathrobe when a female officer arrived. Cameo and the female officer were transported by ambulance to Manor General Hospital. The male suspect, who admitted to the shooting, was transported to Snohomish County Jail in Everett."

When Meehan paused, Kelda asked for an update on Cameo. The detectives looked at one-another. Pritchard shook his head; Meehan shrugged. Cameo was not the concern here. Detective Meehan opened a folder and pulled out several sheets of paper. "We need to go over the suspect's statement with you, uh, Ms. Hansen."

Detective Pritchard leaned forward, one hand extended toward Meehan. "Ms. Hansen, the suspect's statement is graphic. I don't know if Mr. Burgess or Detective Meehan briefed you. Unfortunately, because the suspect included your name in his statement, and because you are connected via your profession, we are revealing it to you in its entirety."

Keith squirmed; Kelda sat straighter. Detective Meehan gave them copies of Tory's statement and read aloud.

146

*I, Tory Smith, shot my father, Hap Smith. If anybody cares, here's why. I got home early from my job and found him with my little sister. He was trying to pull up his pants. They was in her bedroom. She usually goes to work with me, but she's got a cold. The restaurant manager don't like her hanging 'round when she's sick. Hap Smith is a piece of shit. Society don't need him to carry on the name. Now I've took care of that. He already made it so Cameo wouldn't never have no kids. Now he's dead, and I'll be in prison.*

There was more, much more, more graphic than Kelda expected. It would shock readers. It would likely keep Tory incarcerated for the rest of his life if it were admitted in court. Admission that he'd helped Cameo get an abortion, that Hap tried to kill Tory with his bare hands and Tory reciprocated by trying to kill his dad that time, that he regretted failing. He wrote that all three were sent to counseling, including some of the suggestive statements Hap had made regarding Kelda's looks.

At the end of his statement, Tory wrote,

*"Ms. Hansen's real nice. She tried to help us, but it was already too late."*

Though Kelda heard and saw every word her mind lifted her from the ugliness and carried her to the Landing. Her uncle's bad night came from this. She'd told him only that a client had been murdered, though she'd guessed the circumstances. Uncle Ragnar's antenna picked that up. He'd been doing that and getting sick to get her away from this work that nibbled at her spirit. She remembered Raymond's advice as he walked her to the car: answer the detective's questions matter-of-factly, and repeat what she'd recorded in the case notes.

The air in the room tasted rancid. Kelda knew at least one of the detectives smoked. Tory's pain bled from his statement and slouched in the room much as the boy slouched during sessions.

Detective Meehan shifted in his chair and adjusted his face. "Ms. Hansen, did Tory Smith, in your presence and hearing, threaten to kill Hap Smith?"

"That is recorded in the case notes, as is my response. I believe you have a copy of the notes."

Meehan narrowed his eyes. "Do you realize the gravity of Tory's statement?"

Kelda looked at Meehan's narrowed eyes. "Yes, I do. If memory serves me, I explained that to Tory. We don't joke in therapy sessions. Tory knew that comment . . . threat . . . would be recorded in my notes. Why don't you review them? I can't quote them verbatim."

Meehan's look suggested this process would be easier if she squirmed. "Tell me, just how do you view Tory's threat? Now, in hindsight."

"It makes the prosecutor's job easier. And yours, I would guess."

"Does that worry you, Ms. Hansen?"

She maintained her posture as she spoke. Her eyes wanted to narrow, shut even, so she lifted her brows. "It terrifies me, Detective Meehan. It makes my stomach lurch. It's taking all my reserve to avoid vomiting."

Meehan shifted in his chair. Pritchard smiled, but stopped himself by rotating his head and shoulders, and removing his glasses. He polished them with a handkerchief, held them to the light, nodded. Nods she could read.

"Mr. Burgess hasn't located a copy of your case notes from your most recent session with the Smiths. Last Wednesday's session, if I'm correct," Meehan said. His accusatory tone conveyed the weight of her neglect.

"That's because he hasn't received a printed copy. They're in my brief case. Actually, I reported 'no progress' before I left last Wednesday, but Mr. Burgess requested a more detailed write-up. I completed them after hours and sent them encrypted."

"Isn't that irregular? To leave before your case notes are written?"

"In Kelda's current situation, no," Keith said. "She's actually working only two days a week at this time, and her schedule is full. Too full, actually."

"May I have the notes, please?" Meehan asked.

Kelda looked at Keith as she spoke. "My responsibility is to deliver them to Mr. Burgess." Keith took the report and passed it to Meehan, who scanned it for highlights.

"Ms. Hansen, your notes repeat the words, 'flat affect,' in reference to Cameo Smith. Will you explain what you mean by that." Meehan smiled. "My psychology's a little rusty."

Like hell, she thought. "It means that she displayed no emotions, or almost no emotions. Once she did use tissues to wipe her eyes or nose. I've noted that."

"You mean her emotions were inappropriate for the events? The topics you were discussing?"

"No, I mean she displayed no emotions. I saw no anger, no sadness, no fear. Just flat affect. I've recorded the few words she ever spoke, and commented that she delivered them in a monotone."

"Ms. Hansen, did you see this coming? Did you suspect Tory would act on his threat to kill his father?"

"Now, wait a minute," Keith said, coming up out of his pseudo-relaxed position and looming over his desk. "That's out of line. That would indicate that Ms. Hansen, and thereby the agency, has some responsibility in this act, which she and we do not. I agreed to let you question Ms. Hansen without our attorney present on your assurance that you were just gathering background data. I suggest you review the report we received when this case was referred for therapy."

"Will you excuse me?" Kelda said, already on her feet. "I need to make a call." She took her briefcase, went into her office, closed the door and punched the Landing number on her cell phone. "Emma?"

"He's resting just fine now," Emma said without being asked. "Him and Raymond already had a game of cribbage. He took a little tea and toast. The way he complained about my toast, you'd know he's feeling better."

"Oh, Emma, I adore you. Will you heat some broth later? And rub the salt off the crackers? And let him have a little raspberry jam if he asks."

"Now you stop fretting. I can handle things."

"I know you can." Kelda sniffed and blinked. No need to go back to that group of men with her emotions showing. "And Emma, tell him I love him, and this is my last day here. I'm tendering my resignation effective the end of this workday. Will you tell him that?"

"Tendering, you say? That's for meat, I think. It's best you quit that job."

Kelda laughed, and looked up at a knock on the door. "I've got to go, Emma. I'll call again in an hour or so." She pressed 'end,' and said, "Come in."

Detective Pritchard stood in the doorway, his head tilted, his eyes questioning.

"Sorry, I'm a little giddy at the moment. My uncle is feeling well enough to complain to his housekeeper about the quality of the toast she served him. That's good news."

"I understand. May I?" Pritchard gestured toward a chair.

"Yes, Detective." She looked at his eyes, and judged him a decent man. "Did Mr. Burgess explain to you and Detective Meehan that I cut back my hours here to care for an uncle who's been unwell?"

"He mentioned that." Pritchard sat, put his left ankle on his right knee, and gave Kelda a long look. "Your receptionist is trying to reach someone at Manor General for me. We were remiss in not knowing how Cameo is faring."

"You're not playing 'good cop–bad cop' with me, are you?"

Pritchard chuckled. "No, no, there's no need. Meehan's a hard-nose. Loses track of the goal sometimes." He fiddled with his pant cuff. "Uh, Ms. Hansen, this may sound invasive, given your professionalism, but I'd suggest you avoid trying to visit Cameo or Tory until the prosecutor files and attorneys have been named for each of them.

"I don't believe I mentioned visiting either of them."

"You didn't, but I suspect you intend to. And there's nothing wrong with that. In fact, you will certainly be contacted by the boy's attorney, once someone is appointed. I'm just suggesting you wait. If I may, I'll stay in touch with you."

She looked at Pritchard's eyes again. Something troubled him. "What charge do you think the prosecutor will file?" She hoped it would be manslaughter, feared it would be murder, maybe even aggravated first-degree.

"I don't know. Off the record, I'd say this case was blown back before this agency received it. Things might get messy now."

She nodded, agreeing but waiting.

"That comment's totally off the record. Pure conjecture."

She studied him a moment longer before deciding to trust him, then chose her words with care. "I'm residing with my uncle, Ragnar Hansen, near Poulsbo. The phone number is in the directory under his name. It's often difficult to reach me here." Impossible after today, but she wouldn't mention her decision to resign before discussing the matter with Keith.

Pritchard nodded. He pulled a card and pen from an inside pocket, wrote on the card's back. "I've added my home phone number."

"Thank you," she said, wondering why she'd need his home number. Keith appeared in the doorway.

"Just keep repeating, 'No comment,'" Keith said over his shoulder to Rachelle; then to her, "We need to reconvene. I have Jacob Carr on the speaker phone, and reporters closing in."

Jacob Carr, the agency's legal counsel. Kelda returned to the chair she'd occupied earlier. Keith fiddled with the phone and a tape recorder, and had each person speak for voice checks. Kelda's stomach rumbled. Too much coffee, too little food.

"Sounds like someone's hungry," Jake said. "You're coming through clearly. I'll interrupt only if there's a concern. Otherwise, carry on."

Keith's office closed in around them. The stench of cigarette breath and male ego threatened to turn Kelda's stomach growls into retches. Keith distributed copies of the Smith referral and intake notes like second-graders hand out valentines; grinning but uncomfortable, explaining more to the phone than to the detectives.

"In a nutshell, it came to us as a father-son domestic dispute that revolved around the girl. Cameo. Child Protective Services couldn't keep her in foster care, so we got her as part of the case. I gave it to Ms. Hansen because, quite frankly, she's had more experience with people from that demographic than have our other therapists."

While both detectives nodded, Kelda struggled to swallow bile rising in her throat. Demographic. A male word, objective and rational. Keep emotions out of it. Meehan had seen the Smith house and neighborhood, and rattled off a description: low income, mostly rentals, disrepair.

Alcohol and drug abuse, frequent domestic disputes. The description omitted a few things. The day-to-day despair of the occupants. The late stage moral decline of the chemically dependent. The fresh and fading bruises of physical abuse. The children with runny noses, and empty eyes, and brains not developing properly because they lacked intellectual stimulation. Their TV and neighborhood role-models taught them to problem solve with aggression and violence.

That demographic. Those kids from that demographic led Kelda deeper and deeper into counseling troubled families.

As Kelda answered questions, gradually painting a picture of each Smith, she thought she saw a change in Meehan. Even with Tory's confession, it might be difficult for the prosecutor's office to make a case for murder. Much would depend on the passion of the attorney assigned to Tory. With the current state of overwhelmed courts and public defenders, the case could possibly be plea-bargained to manslaughter. Prison, even with its horrors, might be a safe retreat for an adolescent old before his time. With encouragement and guidance, Tory could complete his academic education and enroll in vocational training. Of the two Smith children, he had the better chance of healing.

Cameo's chances were comparable to putting Humpty Dumpty together again. That could play a role in Tory's defense, as could the earlier death of their mother, ruled a suicide though at least one investigator labeled the circumstances suspicious. Hap had been questioned extensively, but no case had been made. But professionals who work with physically, emotionally and sexually abused women knew the continuum, knew it often ended in death if not stopped along the way. Whether the death is self or other-inflicted, the result is the same.

The men did their male-things at the interview's end: shot their cuffs, straightened their ties, shook hands. Their ability to practice linear thinking would direct them to their next task.

Kelda's thoughts circled back around to the children's lives, past and future. When did they veer onto this path? What chance did they have to leave it now?

The three men moved toward the door. Kelda sat, waiting for Keith to return. A hand on her shoulder made her jump.

"Sorry, I didn't mean to startle you," Detective Pritchard said. "I'll be in touch."

She nodded, confused by the message she saw in his eyes. It didn't fit the scene. At that moment, she couldn't say what it fit.

"Well," Keith said, rubbing his hands and grinning, "you certainly made an impression on Detective Pritchard. Too bad Meehan's such an ass-hole. Let's get some lunch. Your stomach's been growling forever."

"Keith, sit down for one more minute. Please."

"What now? Oh, shit, Kelda, don't even think such a thought." Keith sat heavily in his chair and tried his fixed stare.

"I'm resigning effective the end of this workday. I'll meet with Mandy and Shawndra Jenkins today, and the battered women's group tonight. After that, I won't be back. You might want to sit in with me. Or have another therapist sit in so someone will be prepared to carry on. I'll clean out my office during the time the Smiths would have taken. You could take the men's group through their last four sessions. The curriculum's all prepared. I'll write out my official resignation. You can send my final check and annual leave payoff to the Landing." She knew she was cramming too much in all at once, but she needed to get it said.

"Come on, Kel, you can't leave me high and dry."

"You shouldn't have dumped all the deferred criminal cases on me for the last two years. You didn't listen when I warned you that the cases were interfering with my coping mechanism."

"Okay, you're right, but you can't afford to quit. I know you need the income, and frankly quitting without a decent notice could ruin you professionally."

"You're threatening me? I've been handling these cases for you, and now you're threatening me? Cameo isn't likely to recover from her life circumstances. Tory is in jail, and you're turning against me when I'm devastated because I couldn't save them?"

"You'll need me as a reference when you apply for a new position."

She gave him her 'don't argue' look. "I permitted you to talk me into staying on a part-time basis when I asked for a leave. That's on me. I stayed, and got entangled in the Smith mess. It will follow me the rest of my life. But I'm through with this kind of work. I'll clean houses or cook, or whatever I have to do, but I will not work with disturbed families. It's making me sick, and I'm dragging Uncle Ragnar down."

Keith slumped, all bluff and bravado gone. "Burnout. I think I've seen it coming. I should have honored your request for leave. Encouraged it." He ran a hand over his face like he was checking whether he needed a shave. "Would it help if we backed up? You could start a legitimate leave today. Tomorrow, make it tomorrow."

"Keith," she started, her head shaking.

"How about a salary increase?"

"Any amount you could get by the board would be too little too late."

She saw sadness in his eyes. He'd been a decent boss because he was a decent man. Did he regret some of his business decisions? Expanding the agency's economic base by bidding on the state's social and health services cases looked good to the board of directors. Keith was a business man now, but he'd trained in psychology and social work. He mustered up a smile for her.

"Your stomach's still growling. You need lunch. I'll buy, and we'll talk about anything but the Smiths."

He opened his office door. Camera's clicked; lights flashed. Reporters asked questions. Over the babble she heard Rachelle's voice.

"I'm sorry. They pushed right past me."

*Truth always lags last, limping along on the arm of Time. - Baltasar Gracián, 1601-1658.*
*Spanish Jesuit, baroque prose writer & philosopher.*

# 21
## Arne

Arne felt like he'd been pedaling a stationary exercise bike; he was exhausted and sweating, sitting in the same spot. Not as bad as yesterday afternoon when he almost passed out in Kelda's office. He remembered his Beta-blocker pill this morning, but his stomach protested the doughnuts he'd inhaled for breakfast. Most mornings he grabbed an Egg McMuffin. Started doing that when Kelda started acting like a war was on, and bacon and eggs were rationed. She'd fix him oatmeal and toasted whole grain bread with a little heart-smart spread. Her old uncle could eat heaps of raspberry jam, wash it down with raspberry wine if he liked. But not Arne. She hid the jam from him. And served skim milk for the oatmeal. Geez, blue milk.

He went through the accountant's report one more time. Sure as hell wasn't the eighties with building booms and investors backing upscale developments, no questions asked. Now they wanted to see the Environmental Impact Statement before they released a dime. He had good money tied up in land on hold while some Greenie argued for the rights of insects.

Been bad enough when cutting a tree might upset a spotted owl living there. Seemed like everyone wanted to save trees these days, drive builders right out of business. How in hell did bankers think this economy got built in the first place? Shit, Weyerhaeuser and Boeing helped build this state, both relied on trees. Hadn't been for spruce trees used in airplane production, Boeing wouldn't exist.

And now this mess Kelda was in. Some frigging reporter takes her picture. Hers and Keith's. They've got starring roles in an incest-patricide case.

*Did agency ignore threats? Counselor resigns. Death Penalty for teen?*

Shit like that sells papers, gets TV viewers attention. Folks hear the 'no comments,' figure there's more to it. So, Kelda's all over the news, plus she's quit her job. Not that it amounted to much money, not much more than school teachers make, they've got to have master's degrees too.

Shit, he would have liked being a teacher himself. Vocational education. Only thing he really liked about his work anymore was getting on a job, handling wood, maybe swinging a hammer. One good thing about Kelda's job, they knew which day the check would come. Which helped, given the way Gerda and the girls went through cash.

But Kelda's quit, wants to go through Hedstrom Construction books, check the investments and annuities, see what can tide her over. Kelda, who never did more than scan reports and sign her name, wants to know investment details. Wait 'til she discovers her income about equals Gerda's expenses.

And this new wrinkle. Kelda wants him to move to the Landing, for crissakes.

He grabbed the ringing phone and barked, "Mac?"

"Yo, Arne, what's the emergency?"

Dan McClusky had been Hedstrom Construction's accountant from its incorporation. He'd been Arne's friend longer than that, and knew most of what there was to know about him and the company.

"This Seafirst annuity. How much money is Gerda going through every month, for crissakes? These figures can't be right, man. And Lauren's draws. Shit."

Mac's laughter came through the phone, and Arne's already hot, sweaty face heated even more.

"Your mother and your first-born both do their share to keep Nordstrom stock healthy. Gerda likes her TV shopping channel, too."

"Hey, Mac, glad to give you a good laugh buddy, but hear this. Kelda wants a meeting."

"No problem, Arne. Pick a time."

"She's quit her job. Wants to take out a chunk of money to put into growth stock to cover her expenses at the Landing."

"Well, there is money earmarked Hansen. Came originally from her trust. But, I think you've borrowed against it. Let me look at exactly what's where."

"She thinks we should sell the Shore Pine Point house, even at a loss. Cut expenses. She's suddenly getting concerned about the corporation's investments and property taxes. God knows what else she's thinking, she's a woman, you know how that goes, but she's not coming around on a gated community at the Landing."

Mac chuckled. "Hey man, cool your jets. I'm an accountant. Hit me with one thing at a time."

Arne could hear paper rustling. He ran his hand over his face and wiped the moisture on his pants. His chest felt tight again. Indigestion. Damn donuts. All that sugar, all the coffee he'd consumed to wash them down.

"It's going to be hard for you to lose on the Shore Pine Point house. Even if you don't get the mil it's appraised at you're bound to come out ahead. We've kept that mortgage clean. The boat moorage at the Point must be worth a hundred-thou alone, if you sell it outright."

"What about the boat? Just beach it? Christ."

"I don't know. Moor it at the Landing? The old dock's still there, isn't it? You know developing there's always been iffy. Long as I've known Kelda I never heard her budge on that one. Her brothers, I think, were considering it, but that's a moot point now."

"Yeah. Shit." Arne wiped at the sweat on his face. On the way home from the Hansen celebration he'd promised Gerda he'd bring in something cutting edge at the Landing within the next couple years. Far as he could see, it was the only way to get her off his case. Off Knut's case, God rest his soul.

Arne knew most of the Knut-Karli business was making a little homebrew, drinking it, melting lead to make fishing weights, reshaping other salmon fishing gear, tinkering with outboard engines, sanding and patching boats. Hell, keeping a boat seaworthy could take all a man's time. Especially that old wood-hull boat Karli and Knut owned together. That and their drawings to build more wood boats about the time that fiberglass came along. So, the old man told Gerda he and Karli were doing business. Kept her quiet in the short-term. All Arne wanted to do was protect his old man in Gerda's eyes. Then, finally, he could have his life back.

Knut used to refer to Gerda as the Commandant when he'd had a little nip or a few bottles of homebrew. "Just do what's expected, things will be okay," Knut would say. "Don't rock the boat, boys."

Trouble is, Knut damn near sunk the boat letting Gerda draw conclusions about business dealings, not to mention her take on that Wallace Taylor murder. Gerda thought Knut's investments paid her way, and that some truth about Taylor was additional insurance. Shit. He could hear Mac tapping keys on his computer; he could almost hear him thinking.

"Arne, you might want to sell off some options, pull something in, if Kelda's looking for a pay-out on the original Hansen investment at current interest rates, which is how it's obligated. You could do that without the business taking much of a hit. Your cash flow isn't the greatest, but your net worth's not hurting. I mean, it's all relative. You've been making good money, you've been spending good money. Unless you're thinking divorce. That's another matter." After a pause, Mac said, "You're not thinking divorce, are you?"

Arne didn't know what he was thinking, except that it was goddamn hot in his office. No air to breathe. Worse than Kelda's office yesterday when she'd dumped all the bad news in his lap. Well, not bad news exactly, just her sudden interest in Hedstrom Construction's investments. "Shit. I'm sure as hell not thinking about living in that old house at the Landing. Even with remodeled bedrooms."

Kelda suggested that. Take a wall out between two of the bedrooms, make another one into a den. He'd gone to her office yesterday afternoon, after she called about the press invasion. Figured it would be better to slip in there than have them hound her to his office. She'd sat there at her desk, calm as a windless sea, and run through options for their future. Ways to cut expenses, take care of old Ragnar, see to decent meals for Arne at the same time.

"Shit, Kel, you want me to start commuting across the Sound? My office is on this side for crissakes." He'd gotten a little dramatic, waved his arms, watched her. She just kept sitting, like she'd turned to stone. "Hey, you're not in shock or something?"

"It's an option, your living at the Landing." Then she'd looked right at him, her head tilted toward her left shoulder. "I want to be fair to you, but for now I'm going to live at the Landing. I don't think I'm in shock. Numb, maybe."

Answering like she was doing a boring weather report. He'd leaned across her desk, taken her hands, turned on his best smile that always melted her heart. "Now, hear me out on this, okay? Let's talk some more about something a little different at the Landing. Nice cedar cottages, each on an acre, keep all the trees we can, make trails, places for bonfires on the beach, nice lodge in the center, both wood-burning and gas-log fireplaces so folks could choose."

She'd let him talk, he'd give her that. Just sat there, looking from eyes that didn't seem to see. Then she'd asked the question. It always came to the same question.

"Why the Landing?" She'd tilted her head to the right, lifted that left eyebrow, given him the Kelda look. "You can build that rustic-modern development a hundred places. It would fit better on the Sol Duc river, or other spots on the Olympic Peninsula. Or in eastern Washington, where you could offer river rafting in the summer, snow sports in the winter."

Then she'd moved her head again, squared it on her shoulders. "It's Gerda, isn't it?"

He couldn't remember exactly what he'd said then, except, "No, of course not."

Sweat had erupted on his forehead, it was just so damn hot in her office, couldn't she open a window? His hands no longer held hers. She, for crissakes, had her fingers on his wrist like she was a goddamn nurse and told him his pulse seemed a little fast, had he taken his pills? Shit. Turns out he'd forgotten to take his meds, blood pressure got a little out of control. Next thing she's got him stretched out on a sofa in a therapy room, and Maria's on the way with his goddamn pills.

"You still there, Arne?" Mac asked.

"Yeah, I'm here. Talk to me about pulling in some of my options. And while you're at it, maybe you better talk to me about divorce. How that makes a difference to the big financial picture."

*A mother who is really a mother is never free.* - Honoré de Balzac, 1799-1850.
*French novelist & playwright, one of the founders of realism—sense of characters & place.*

# 22
# Kelda and Lydia

Kelda celebrated what she chose to call her early retirement by mixing up *Norsk Pannekaken*, using Lydia's stained, almost illegible, recipe card. Norwegian pancakes were a treat, a tradition learned early in her childhood, served to say 'I love you.' Her mother made them on Sunday mornings in this Landing kitchen. Kelda remembered the way her mother smiled when she folded the paper-thin pancake with a spatula and delivered it to a plate. Love shows on faces. This morning Kelda needed love. She poured batter into the cast-iron skillet, rolled it to cover the entire bottom, loosened the edges, then flipped to cook the other side. In seconds she placed it on a plate, buttered and sugared, and ate—a solo celebration at daybreak. The batter would improve with standing as the flour expanded, but Kelda wasn't waiting. It should be just right when Ragnar got up.

There would be left-overs cooked and waiting for Arne when he came to the Landing, if he showed up as he'd promised, to embark on the task of sorting out their lives. He shouldn't eat them, but he'd sniff the air in the kitchen, and then search in the refrigerator. He'd know, and this day it would serve her needs to let him indulge a little in food he loved.

The grief of failures and losses hovered about, a weight on her shoulders, a pressure behind her eyes. Not a migraine pressure, just sadness that collected over time. Yesterday she'd spaced out for a time, floated above herself and her life as a family therapist, watching events unfold in the offices that had occupied so much of her life for over twenty years. She couldn't save the Smiths from themselves or herself from grief of that failure.

She'd liked the view from aloft, remaining there when Arne arrived and started his pitch of cedar cottage housing at the Landing, paying little attention until she noticed his breathing, and the pulse in his neck. Then she'd snapped back to caregiver mode, while he'd gone right on being Arne. Scared but acting pissed, ratcheting up the impatience when Maria arrived. In the midst of the drama, Kelda suspected her life with Arne had reached a crossroad. She read more than concern in Maria's face and more than appreciation in Arne's.

Love shows on faces.

Maria tried to hide her feelings when she brought Arne's pills. She'd been hiding her feelings behind a commitment to Carlos for years. Strange as it seemed to her now, Maria's concern for Arne pleased Kelda because she cared about him herself. She just couldn't give him what he wanted most.

The Landing.

When she'd eaten one more pancake than she could comfortably hold and washed it down with one more cup of strong coffee, she went into the sewing room, the indoor place where she felt closest to her mother. She needed her mother, needed her guidance and wisdom, and sought it in Lydia's things; her bed and quilt, books and pictures, starched and ironed doilies, assorted items on the dresser that remained because they belonged to the room, to the comforting spirit that lingered in peach and white. Kelda sat at the old sewing machine used by Lydia and Magna before her, working the treadle, sewing air.

Then she gathered Lydia's journals and searched until she found the one she wanted, the one Lydia wrote after Olav died, before Kelda was born.

LYDIA'S JOURNAL
December 8, 1941

It is official. We are at war with Japan. Yesterday morning Japanese planes bombed the Pacific fleet in Pearl

Harbor. We have not yet received official word about Olav, but all of us at Hansen's Landing seem to be in deeper, more personal mourning than war news would bring at this juncture. We know he's dead. His ship was named as one now resting on the ocean floor. We are hearing ship names and casualty numbers on the radio, along with FDR's speech to congress. Now we wait for the telegram we all expect.

I am five months pregnant. Olav didn't know. I waited, keeping back the news of this pregnancy for the wrong reasons. It's true I don't feel quite right physically, but it is emotions that tied my tongue.

Blackout orders are being broadcast for the west coast and Puget Sound. I looked at the map and confirmed we are but a narrow ring or two off 'bull's-eye' on a target of strategic naval installations. We are preparing to cover the windows at night. The men will return to the Landing before dark, or drive without their headlights if they are delayed.

That's what Rolf will do, traveling between Brownsville and the Landing. I know he will come each evening for dinner, and for more. These Hansen men enjoy one another. They are sad and angry, and very close. And they are afraid, a new experience for them. They are fretting about the Indian family camped at the inlet, not for their safety as much as the possibility they might attract the enemy with their campfire.

To my shame, I'd forgotten about the family until my brothers-in-law reminded me. How long have I wallowed in self-pity because the man I married chose a life among men on the sea over a life with me at the Landing? I railed at Olav, called the Navy and the sea his mistresses, asked if I should build a Widow's Walk on the second floor.

I'm not alone; many women suffer the same torment. But there's no comfort for me in such a sisterhood. Instead, I find my comfort in nature, in the wild flowers, and with the Hansen men, especially Ragnar. I feel his love for me. It didn't stop because I chose Olav for my husband.

I went with Ragnar and Karli to the inlet in the late afternoon, to speak with the Indian family and offer them shelter in Karli's workshop. Seeing the woman's advanced pregnancy brought me back to the living. To my relief, Ragnar agreed immediately that we must enclose the workshop with a fourth wall.

The woman, Clara Morse, said the baby could be born in a month's time. The men will add the wall tomorrow. Rolf has some shiplap, they say. One or another of the Hansen men always manage to have whatever is needed. That was true even in the worst of the Depression. How fortunate I am to be with them, to be a Hansen, to lean on their quiet, steady strength, their no-nonsense approach to life. Even Karli, the most gregarious of the three Hansen men still here, is generous to a fault.

December 14, 1941

I am very taken with Clara Morse's son, Edward. He's seven and though he hasn't ever attended school, he is bright. He seems at one with his surroundings; he relates to nature in a way I suspect is innate. Still, a child needs formal training in these times. In any time, I believe.

Clara was reluctant to give permission for his enrollment in our schools. She fears education may carry him farther away from his people. She's already paved that path, choosing a Makah man as her mate. Finally, she agreed to Edward's schooling when I promised to take him and bring him home each day.

Clara was one of the Suquamish children sent to the Tulalip Indian boarding school. In her account, she served as an unpaid maid, learning little but distrust and defiance. Some of her friends died there, of what she called white-man diseases. Did that include sexual abuse?

I did not ask. She said only that she ran away often and left permanently during her eighth-grade year. I don't know her age; neither do I know for certain that Edward was born of a union long before Raymond Morse came into her life.

It is one of the sad truths of our times, and a shame-scar on our communities: Indian children in our districts were denied access to public schools because their parents didn't pay property taxes. Teachers should have fought that decision. Perhaps they did, and I am unaware. The law changed about the time I embraced this profession.

How quickly we newer Americans, born to European immigrants, forgot that the land taxed by our government was taken from the Indians. How thoroughly we ignore the bargains we struck. Not that they were much of a bargain for the tribes. Am I acting in Edward's interests or my own by taking him to school? I hold the belief that formal education is in his best interest.

January 25, 1942

We are having a quiet Sunday afternoon. Life does go on. Clara Morse gave birth to a baby daughter several days ago, with me serving as a midwife of sorts. The baby's name is Lucy. She is beautiful.

Clara accepted the flannel diapers I hemmed, but refuses to bring them here for washing in the machine. I must exercise caution not to impose my values. She did let Ragnar string clothesline both inside and out for her, and she accepted a wash tub and scrub board, and a collection of clothes pins. Edward made Lucy a blanket of woven cedar strips, and Clara lays it over the child when she's sleeping.

Edward already reads better than many of his classmates. He says little to me, but I see his eyes looking with hunger and wonder at each new stack of books I pass along to him. He and Erik have forged a friendship of sorts. They meet in the woods to play, if it's not raining too hard. For reasons I can't find the energy to explore, neither boy ventures into the other's home.

Oh, Olav, how could you leave me alone to handle all this, and to face what still lies ahead? I am so angry. That's not new. I was angry when you chose the Navy. Choices, always choices. Have any of us made the right ones? It matters not. They're made; now we must get on with managing what they bring.

That anger left me fast enough when I looked up from writing to see little Greg standing beside me in his pajamas, all pink from his bath, books tucked under his arm. Ragnar bathed him without a word to me. He is a wonderful man, a wonderful uncle to my sons. I know he desperately misses little Gunnar. We talk often of that wee one's death, and of Ruth. She remains my friend and Ragnar's wife, and is part of the strong bond between Ragnar and me. He predicts this child I'm carrying will be the daughter the Landing has long awaited, and that she will be strong and worthy of the name I've selected. I fear she will need the strength; I hope Ragnar will remain earthbound long enough to be here when she needs him, for he is the best of the Hansens.

There was more about Lucy and Clara, and about Edward's success in school. And then, dated April 5, 1942, Lydia's joy in Kelda's birth. Kelda had found what she needed for this morning. Lydia accepted her choices and the anger in sorrow, and went on with life. She grieved and celebrated, and did what needed doing. She sought and found solace in nature, especially in the most delicate wildflowers that grew and bloomed in the protection of the oldest trees. Only a few people ever saw dainty Ladyslippers and Fairyslippers, freckled Yellow Wood Violets (Lydia called them Johnny-jump-ups when she wasn't being scientific), ghostly Indian Pipe Stem. Lydia made seeing them part of her purpose, and from this day hence, Kelda would too.

"*Kär a?*" Ragnar called, an anxious note in his voice.
"I'm here, Uncle. In the sewing room, being maudlin."

But she wasn't, not really. She was just being a Hansen: proud, stoic, thankful for what she had, and ready to feel her grief and grow with it.

"There's *Norsk pannekaken* batter. I'll heat the pan again," she said when her uncle came into the room, his face all furrows and frowns.

"Oh, *kär a.*" Ragnar grinned at her. "It's a good day, this one. Lydia's helped you start it right, I'm thinking."

Kelda looked at her uncle, aware for perhaps the first time that he lived with Lydia in the present, that her mother and her uncle had a current relationship, at least in his mind. For a moment she thought she should say something, bring him back, make certain he wasn't slipping into Alzheimer's or some other form of dementia. Her head tilted to one side, like Arne said it did when she went into her counselor mode. And then she straightened it, and smiled. What had she just done but find Lydia in the present? Lydia's wisdom in words, and in things in a room painted peach and white.

"It *is* a good day. I think I ate seven pancakes." She laughed, delighted at the look on his face. "Well, five anyway. Come on, I'll cook for you."

Before Ragnar sat down to eat, he retrieved a stool from the laundry room and positioned it for her. "You'll need to be sitting, much batter as you've got there. Might be we should call Walkingstick and Joyce to come." He made it a question.

"No, let's keep it just us this morning. I think they've both gone to work, and Emma will pop in any time." Raymond, Joyce, and Emma had been there the night before when she'd driven in. They'd watched the news and worn down the worry so they could all help her unwind. She'd called so many times throughout the day that they knew she'd taken up a new worry: Arne's blood pressure.

Arne's spell, Emma named it. "You'd better not be counting on any help from that quarter." So saying, Emma put into words part of what Kelda felt—a lack of emotional support from Arne. Throughout their marriage, he'd always managed to have a crisis just a tad more pressing than hers. It had become one of the ruts in their relationship.

Later, after she and Ragnar had their morning together, and a little tea and cold salmon for lunch, Kelda went looking for Lydia's Fairyslippers along the trail to the inlet, the outdoor place she felt closest to her mother. When she found them, she ringed them with a wall one rock high, then leaned against a tree and looked them up in a wildflowers' book. The fir needles she'd brushed into a pile made a comfortable cushion. If she closed her eyes, she'd drift into sleep just like Ragnar had in his chair.

'*Fairyslippers, Calypso bulbosa, members of the orchid family, grow on bulb-like corms, usually in soil rich with leaf mould,*' she read. Lydia insisted the Landing maintain a few deciduous trees at the perimeter of the property so she could collect the decaying leaves. Lydia had known how to care for the environment before it became an issue.

The book said the delicate plant was rapidly being exterminated, largely due to trampling and picking. A picked or stepped-upon flower generally meant a destroyed corm. No wonder Lydia always placed more rotted leaves around them and ringed them as Kelda just had. She'd protected the plants because she found comfort in them, and because it was the right thing to do. It served a greater purpose.

She squinted to read the book's fine print in the tree-shaded light. The Haida Indians had called Fairyslipper corms 'black cod grease' because they had a rich buttery flavor. But even in the distant past, they ate only a few because of the plant's rarity. The Haida girls ate them raw to enhance their bustlines. It seemed women of all cultures and ages fretted over the same things. Had the Haida believed in the mythical Calypso, goddess daughter of Atlas? Did they accept the flower as a nymph hidden in the woods, and found by Ulysses when he was wrecked on an island? Or had myths transcended culture and written word to be carried by spiritual message to all people?

Kelda left her fir-needle cushion and stretched out face down to study the delicate flower. It did indeed resemble an orchid, and it had the bonus of a wonderful perfume. The dark rose, almost purple petals and sepals sat above a slipper-like lip of purple-speckled white. She closed her eyes and breathed in the scent. When her eyes opened again, she knew she'd slept because the fragments of a dream lingered. She wanted to let it register in her conscious mind; it seemed to have some symbolism. Something about the order of things, leaving them where they belong, or returning them to their natural habitat so they can heal and grow again.

Raymond Walkingstick sat on her needle cushion, engrossed in her book. She closed her eyes again, still too groggy to be irritated or embarrassed at being found. When she next looked up she saw his dark eyes watching her. He fit in here, in the trees, with sun ribbons and breeze music.

"How did you find me?"

"Ragnar told me where you'd be. He sent me."

"Hmm. That's odd. I didn't tell him. He'd already dozed off."

"Lydia told him."

"Oh. Of course." She sat up, brushed needles from her sweatshirt front, looked at Raymond's smile. In the days she'd known him, he'd now smiled at her twice. Had he ever smiled that summer when she knew him as Edward?

"Is Emma still with Ragnar"

"Emma's there. And Arne. They were having a verbal tug-of-war over something that looked like crepe suzettes." Raymond used his cane to get to his feet. "It's the first Fairyslipper I've ever seen. I'm glad you left the page marked."

"Did I?"

"With needles and a leaf-piece."

"Ah. Well, now I suppose you'll grow them for your nursery. Sell them to the public." For some reason the idea irked her.

"No." He was shaking his head and smiling still. "I can't imagine anyone that didn't find them growing as these could possibly appreciate them."

"Good."

"I've come with a message, not just to intrude. There's a reporter from the Poulsbo paper at the house. He's determined to see you."

"Damn. I gave him a statement this morning, over the phone."

"Right now, he's quizzing Ragnar about that old murder, sixty years ago this month. The one Arne's mother referenced at your celebration gathering. Ragnar's brother-in-law. I gather it's not the first time the reporter and your uncle have met. He'd come once before, for a history note. Now it seems to have taken on more importance."

Kelda frowned. "That old murder." Someone was digging. Or planting. A reporter would get little from Ragnar, but she wanted to be there, just in case.

Raymond stirred some needles with his cane. "There's another message. Ragnar said, 'Tell Kelda to listen to Lydia.'"

"Oh?" She studied the stirred needles, looking for an answer like a seer might look at tea leaves. "Raymond, do you find any of this strange?"

"Not at all. I had a little conversation with Lydia yesterday."

She laughed, nervous. "I meant the Poulsbo reporter connecting an Alderwood Manor murder and a north Seattle mental health agency to Hansen's Landing. I know my name got mentioned in the newspaper and on television, but not my place of residence. Which, officially is Edmonds." She'd told the detective, the nicer one, where she could be reached. But she'd almost bet he wouldn't give that information to the press. "There are dozens of Hansens."

"Arne asked the reporter the same thing."

So, Arne suspected someone. She could just hear Arne overloading the question with expletives. She could see him taking a stance that intimidated, squaring his shoulders and puffing his chest.

"Let's go. I need to get back to Ragnar." She looked at their surroundings, and at Raymond. She'd like to linger there with him, tell him what she'd read in Lydia's journal, but he needed to read it himself. She knew from reading that Lydia had loved the child she'd known as Edward, and wondered if Raymond knew that, and what he meant about having a conversation with her.

*Other sins only speak; murder shrieks out.* – 'The Duchess of Malfi' by John Webster, 1580-1634.

*English dramatist, playwright of the Jacobean era.*

# 23
# The Landing

Damn it all to hell, Ragnar was having enough trouble getting Lydia's messages straight in his head without all this other folderol. Arne and Emma arguing over pancakes like a couple kids arguing over the biggest half. This newspaper reporter back again, this time with a business card in his hand.

Travis Eklund, Reporter.

Still asking questions about that old murder, Wallace Taylor, sixty years ago, now adding questions about this new murder that had nothing whatsoever to do with the old. Why in Sam Hill the reporter put them in the same breath he couldn't figure. Lydia wasn't getting through his thick Norwegian skull.

Except 'Sam Hill.' Now that came right straight from Lydia. It had served as her bit of cussing. Well, he needed her help, so he guessed he'd use it. Anything to keep off the subject of Kelda and that new murder.

"Now why in Sam Hill would you be wanting to ask again about that old murder? Seems we settled all that, you and me, a week or two back."

The reporter held out his arms and lifted his shoulders. "It's an interesting piece of this area's history. You said yourself it seems tied in to bootlegging in Kitsap County. As for Ms. Hansen and her client, well, I'm quite lucky to be sent out on a current event."

Ragnar glanced at the card one more time, and then at the reporter. "Lucky, is it? An awful thing to be finding luck in someone's murder."

Darned if Travis Eklund's face didn't go red as his hair, blending in all the freckles in the process. Darned if he didn't have a charming grin.

"It's my job, at least it's a writing job. Someday I'd like to write a book about the people who settled Kitsap County."

"Seems there's already a book, done by the Historical Society folks."

Travis grinned again. "I'm interested in writing something that folks in other parts of the country might read. Something that explores the relationship between the early settlers and the Indian tribes. Some of what happened to the Japanese strawberry farmers during World War Two." He shrugged. "Why the federal government built so many facilities here. This peninsula's unique in many ways. I'm just lucky to have an assignment with a newspaper here.

But the book's somewhere down the road, and my editor thought there might be a local interest connection between that old murder and the recent one. Hansen family members investigated in the old Wallace Taylor murder—a younger Hansen with Poulsbo ties who knows the young man accused of this murder in this event. I talked to Ms. Hansen on the phone. She was very polite in saying she can't discuss the matter. My editor thought I should try to meet her personally. You know the drill: local interest in a high-profile case."

"Only drill I know much about's the drill I use to make holes in something needs a screw," Ragnar said. "Those connections I can understand. What you're talking goes beyond me. My understanding's prit-near worn out."

And darned if Travis Eklund didn't chuckle and say, "You old Norwegians have something in your genes. You don't say much, but you know plenty."

Over the years Kelda had heard more than one version of The Murder. The most interesting were those overheard in Karli's workshop when the men forgot she was there. She could tuck herself into a box of lumber scraps and read while Karli and Rolf turned out a baseball bat on the lathe or built a table for one of the cottages. Rolf conserved words even more than Ragnar, but he whistled when the work went well. Karli talked and laughed until Rolf said, *"Be tidde."*

A clam digger found Wallace Taylor's body all scrunched up, a little seaweed stuck to his clothes and hair, and figured he'd drowned. The clam digger spread the word until someone with a phone called the sheriff. Folks nearby kept their eyes peeled for a drifting boat. Then the clam digger scratched his head, or so Karli told it, and said, *"Hell, this ain't no fisherman. Dressed wrong. This here's a man slicked up for doing business."*

At that point in the story, Karli would shake his head. *"Poor old Wally, he'd be some upset about seaweed in his hair. Kept that wavy hair fixed just so, let the ladies pet it."* He'd shake his head again, then chuckle.

*"Let it be a lesson,"* Rolf would answer. *"Careful who you let get her hands in those curls on your head."* He'd give Karli his Rolf look, upper lip hitched up a tad on one side, eyes squinted just enough.

*"Yeah, I'm aware."*

Uncle Karli kept his hair longish, for the times. It had been white since Kelda's childhood, and she liked to touch the soft curls. No other Hansen in recent years had curly hair, but Magna had written that her own hair tangled some like Karli's. He'd been a beautiful baby, she wrote, and she named him Karli because it meant manly according to her early 1800s Norwegian name book. He'd need such a name, she noted.

She'd died before parents started using the name for girls. Karli had been called Karl away from the Landing and the Hansens, but he'd remained Uncle Karli to Kelda. She found delight in stories of his escapades, and his 'lady friends,' who brought treats for her and her brothers when they came to visit.

*"Whatever fool killed Wally should have held his head under water long enough for him to take a little in his lungs. Made it easier on the rest of us,"* Karli said. Then he'd be off and running about the FBI, missing money pouches, Wally always flashing a wad. *"Coulda been he just went to Seattle buying parts for the garage, some skid-roader seen all that money and done him in."*

*"Could be he'd invested up the creek,"* Rolf said.

Kelda had been ten before Erik explained that 'invested up the creek,' meant being involved in making bootleg whiskey along a stream somewhere deep in woods loggers hadn't gotten to. Or knew to stay out of.

Her aunt Ruth, Uncle Ragner's wife and Wallace Taylor's younger sister, told Kelda a different story.

*"We're all a little crazy, it gets us in trouble. Crazy comes with superior intelligence, you know. Wally knew things the government didn't want him to know. He owned that garage as a front for gathering information. The FBI investigated all of us to cover up the fact that they killed him themselves. How else could he wash up on a beach in the fetal position with no water in his lungs, no bullet or knife wounds, and no serious bruises? The FBI know how to kill without leaving a mark on a body, or traces of poison for the coroner to find."*

Ruth would lower her voice and gather herself up, shoulders drawn in, arms around her legs. *"They're after me, too, you know. That's why I can't stay long here at the Landing. I have to go back to the sanitarium before they come."*

Kelda learned to nod and pat Ruth's arms. Ruth suffered too much, Lydia said. Ill health, a brother murdered, a baby dying at her breast.

The most reasonable explanation came from Lydia.

*"Wallace Taylor carried two leather money pouches when he went to Seattle to buy for the garage and the store-front items. He tended toward flamboyance and braggadocio, and may have been careless. I suspect he was killed in Seattle, his body placed in the trunk of his car, his car driven onto the ferry. Then, somewhere between Seattle and Bremerton, his body was dropped into the Sound. His car remained on the ferry when it docked. That's when Ruth and the Taylors learned he was missing."*

*"Why two money pouches?"* Kelda had asked.

*"Because he likely did use the mercantile business as a front for buying ingredients for a bootleg operation. One pouch for the garage money, the second for the other business."*

Kelda preferred the more embellished stories she overheard in Karli's workshop. She wondered which version Ragnar had told the young man standing on the great-room porch. She wondered why Ragnar had never discussed it with her in all these years.

"Hello," she called, taking in the scene. Ragnar somewhat red-faced, which meant he was agitated. Arne, more red-faced and scowling. Emma, arms crossed, scowling too. The reporter, coming toward her, smiling. He looked like her brother Greg had looked about in his teens.

Her uncle said, "*Kär a.*"

Arne said, "Shit, Kel, this is a mess."

Emma said, "The newspaper seems to be knowin' a goodly amount about Hansen's."

"Ms. Hansen, I'm Travis Eklund. I know you said 'no further comments,' when we spoke on the phone, but my editor sent me. Mr. Walkingstick, hello again."

Travis stepped off the porch with the movements of one young and physically fit, and extended his hand. Kelda took it, noticed the freckles on it, on his face, even on his ears. The freckles of her worst summer couldn't compare. On him they looked attractive, endearing. He looked about the age of her daughters, and his grin charmed her into smiling back, though she wanted to be angry. She'd intended to use him as a receptacle for some of the frustration she felt. Instead she asked, "What color are your eyes?"

He shrugged. "Sometimes blue, sometimes green, I guess. At least, that's what I'm told. I don't pay too much attention, except that I have good vision."

"Shit, Kel, this isn't the social hour, for crissakes."

"Arne? Did you remember your meds today?" Kelda moved to sneak her fingers onto a pulse point, but he put up a chair barricade.

"I already asked," Emma said. "He is a test, eatin' all them pancakes like there's not a worry."

"Your uncle and I have talked twice now about the Wallace Taylor murder," Travis said. "I read the old news stories in *The Daily News Searchlight*. That's what the Bremerton paper was called then. Great name, huh?"

Kelda turned her attention back to the reporter. "Searchlight seems incongruent with daily. Nightly would be a better fit."

175

"That's what makes it great." He grinned, and the blue-green eyes almost threw off sparks. "Uh, Ms. Hansen, my editor told me to check for a human-interest connection between that murder and the case you're involved in. That is, not personally involved, but as a professional therapist."

Kelda looked at Raymond, hoping for some legal advice. He sat on the porch edge, his bad leg stretched. He nodded slightly, pulled a piece of wood from his shirt pocket, snapped open his knife, whittled. Carry on, he seemed to say.

"I've been wondering how your editor connected me with the Landing, and why the Wallace Taylor murder even came up. I mean, it happened in 1932."

Travis shrugged and shook his head. "I'm low man on the paper's staff. I just get assignments. Frankly, the old murder interests me more than the Smith case. I read the Seattle papers and talked to one of the TV station reporters. It's sad, but it's just another tragedy. Like I told your uncle, I'm glad to get an assignment on a current story."

Kelda agreed that the media's interest in Hap Smith's death would be brief. Other news, another family's tragedy, would replace it, and send reporters scurrying to find information before their competitors. The interest focused more on the agency involvement, whether they, and she as therapist of record, should have done more to prevent it. There would be a state investigation. She looked at the handsome young man and thought she'd welcome him as a date for one of her daughters, if he'd come for a different purpose.

"Did those sources mention Hansen's Landing, or that I'd be here visiting my uncle?"

"Naw, that came from my editor." Travis shrugged. "He said there could be a local-interest angle, if the info he got was accurate."

"Did your editor tell you the source of his information?"

"Hey, I'm low man on the reporter totem pole, I just scramble when he says go."

"Shit," Arne said, kicking a chair away from the table and plopping down alongside Emma. Ragnar paced. Raymond Walkingstick whittled.

"Interesting," Kelda said, watching the reporter's eyes. He looked so honest that she spoke honestly in turn. "As I told you on the phone, I'm a professional family therapist. There's nothing I can say about the Smith case without violating my clients' rights. But I'll tell you this, and you can create a quote . . . if you let me see it before it's printed. I requested an extended leave-of-absence from my job sometime back so that I could be more available to Uncle Ragnar, and to pursue other interests. My boss asked me to reconsider, to work part-time so I could continue with cases and classes in progress. I agreed. The case taking most of my time is now closed, so I've rescinded that agreement, and resigned."

Travis looked up from the small notebook. "That seems to be of interest to the press. Resigning in the wake of your client's murder."

Kelda tilted her head, lifted one eyebrow, studied Travis, who did his shrug and grin. "The press will make of it what it chooses. I can't control that. My main concern is my uncle. He needs help with this place, and I'm the helper."

"Just what are you doing with the place? Forty acres, am I correct?"

"Trying to save it, all forty acres of it, from the tax man." She squinted, looked at Arne, Emma, Ragnar. None returned a look that said they'd mentioned the acreage.

Travis smiled, a smile of innocence and unwitting charm. "Well, you've got quite a stand of trees, but I guess you're not interested in selling the timber to cover the taxes. Being an old timber family, you'd know the worth of the trees."

Kelda again raised her left eyebrow and gave Travis her look. "They have a worth far beyond the board feet value."

Raymond snapped his knife closed, positioned his cane, and stepped up onto the porch. "They're not just a stand of trees," he said, sweeping his arm to take in the whole. "It's a forest, albeit on a small scale. The understory includes flora, and quite likely fauna, that are threatened species. Both the Hansens are committed to maintaining the integrity of the forest. That might be a story worthy of a local newspaper."

Travis nodded. "I'd like to do that. Frankly, I'm impressed, considering how many places forests get trashed and shopping centers get built." He grinned, shrugged, held his palms up. "But, there's another thing my editor wanted me to check out. Are there babies buried here? Somewhere in this forest?"

Kelda saw Ragnar's face register what she felt. Anger not at the question as much as the source behind it. She moved to him, steadied him as he stood, his mouth in motion, Emma and Arne talking at the same instant.

"Damn it all to hell, I'm knowing where your editor's getting his news. First on, I was just wondering, but now I'm knowing. You go back and tell him that source is not so reliable."

Emma uncrossed her arms and slapped the table. "Gerda Hedstrom's been at it again."

"Damn." Arne stood and knocked over a chair.

"Let me tell you about those *liten babies*," Ragnar said "Buried proper, right out under those cedar trees along the lane. Births and deaths registered with the Lutheran Church, laid to rest the day they died, each of them. There's some who said Helgar and Magna Hansen just put them in the ground without proper funerals. There's few alive to dispute that, but you could be looking it up. They all went in *liten* cedar boxes built by Helgar, all lined with fine damask linen. Magna dressed them in hand-stitched christening dresses, every one, and made up a new dress the next time she had her confinement. It's in the church books who came to the Landing to share the grief, if you're wanting to know."

Kelda had one hand on Ragnar's arm, the other at his waist. She could see red scalp through his thin white hair, and feel him shaking with anger.

Red swept up Travis's face, and a frown darkened his eyes. "I didn't mean to upset you folks. I'm not certain why my editor's curious about the burials, but I'm interested in the history. There's almost no new-born-infant graves at the old cemetery. The children buried there had all lived for a few months, at least. Yet, stillborn babies, or those who died shortly after their birth, were common in those days. There must have been others buried on private land. At least you know where the little graves are located. How many little graves do you suppose might have been built over or bulldozed?"

Kelda's heart went out to the reporter. He looked stricken; his eyes clouded, and his face reddened so deeply the freckles disappeared.

"It's okay. We're a little over-reactionary right now. The Smith case is a tragedy. It's unfair to Uncle Ragnar that it's spilled over to the Landing." She heard the phone ring, watched Emma move into the house.

"I'd like to quote that, what you just said." Travis scribbled, then read. "Ms. Hansen said, 'The Smith case is a tragedy'" He read the entire quote back, then looked from Kelda to Ragnar, and back again. "And I'd like to write about the Wallace Taylor murder in a separate story, as history, with some information from the old Bremerton paper. I'll ask my editor to hold it for two weeks. The murder actually occurred on May 21, 1932, so it would fit. He turned to look at Emma waving the phone, its long cord snaking on the porch.

"Kelda, it's some detective, saying it's important."

Kelda took the phone, looked at those waiting, turned her back. "Hello?"

"Ms. Hansen, this is Dave Pritchard, how are you doing?"

"Well enough, detective." She felt heat, fear-conducted heat, in her own face.

"Please, call me Dave. This is a personal call, actually. I know this is a stressful time, and I'd like to help cheer you up. Buy you dinner, talk about pleasant things."

"Oh." Kelda glanced at the others and moved toward the door. "Do you have any news about how Cameo and Tory are faring?" She didn't want the news reporter to overhear.

"I'll have an update. We can make it lunch. I'll come to Poulsbo. I'd like to get to know you."

"Detective, may I call you back? There's a reporter here from our local weekly paper, and several family members."

"Tell the reporter, 'No comment.'"

"Thanks, I'm handling that, I'll talk to you later." She let Emma take the phone, let her say goodbye.

"What was that all about, for crissakes? Asshole detective hitting on you or what?"

Kelda waved her arms. "Arne, sit down for a minute. He's the detective who agreed to keep me informed about how the Smith girl is doing. Travis, I'm sorry. You were trying to get my approval for a quote." She looked at Raymond, caught his nod and something else she couldn't decipher. "I think what you suggested will be acceptable. Will you just read it back again?" Damn, she wished everyone would go away. She needed to think.

Travis read. She nodded. He shook her hand and grinned. "Now, I'm going to hold your uncle to a promise to show me some things in his basement."

"Good. Excuse me a minute." She didn't wait for anyone's response but dashed into the house and up the stairs to the bathroom. Even Arne probably wouldn't follow her there. She locked the door and sat on the edge of the tub. The dream symbol that she'd tried to hang onto in the woods had been dancing just out of reach, like an elusive Fairy slipper just peeking out of fir needles and waving slightly in the breeze. She was like that threatened plant; she needed special soil and conditions to thrive. That's why Uncle Ragnar started getting sick. He was bringing her back home for a reason. For her, not him. For something her mother wanted her to know. Some truth untold.

As she struggled for what that truth might be, another truth settled on her. Arne sensed that the detective might be calling for personal reasons, and now the others would wonder too.

*One must choose in life between boredom and suffering.* - Madame de Staël, 1766-1817.
*French woman of letters. Swiss origin. A Napoleon opponent.*

## 24
## Raymond

Raymond sat on the beach just beyond his cottage, whittling, watching the water lick the seaweed it left at its last high. The rocks on which he sat were unforgiving, but the discomfort to his posterior took away a bit from the pain in his leg. A small crab skittered, stopped, skittered again to disappear. Gulls caught the wind and drifted. Oh, to be so free.

But he didn't really want freedom, he wanted involvement. With the Hansens, both of them, of Hansen's Landing. "Damn it all to hell," he said, trying out Ragnar's words on the evening breeze, permitting a smile to relax his jaw a bit. He reviewed the day's most recent hours and decided he'd learned something about himself; he'd been more annoyed than jealous when his wife sought other men. Or if he'd been jealous it felt differently than the catch and twist in his midriff when he realized Kelda's phone call came from a man who was 'hitting on her,' as Arne called it. Arne was her husband; Raymond accepted that. But this faceless stranger, this detective that sent Kelda inside, away from all their watching eyes, brushed a coat of green over Raymond's heart.

He dragged the point of a knife blade over driftwood, etching fur onto an animal's body. He contemplated the animal from one angle and then another. Not bad. The jealous feeling wasn't bad either; it centered his world a bit more. Something important had happened thirty-five years ago, but he'd never admitted it, not consciously. He'd fallen in love with a young girl-woman, and it terrified him. He'd seen it only as lust, done the right thing; put her out of his thoughts, left her to grow up to have the life she was meant to have.

Meeting her again was part of his spiritual renewal. And part of his plan? Had he returned to this place to see what she'd become, to close that chapter in his life? Had Lydia's spirit sent him, as he often felt? Being here felt right, as though he was meant to help Ragnar and Kelda save the Landing from the development they feared. Kelda was married and attractive to other men. It didn't make his feelings other than they were, and he needed to feel them. He just needed to keep them to himself. He'd long ago mastered keeping things to himself.

He heard the crunch of footsteps on rocks and shells, and looked up to see Joyce Lindquist. She called to him. Soon she sat next to him, picked up rocks, studied them, dropped some into a plastic bag and others back onto the beach.

"What do you do with those you keep?"

"I polish some. I have a rock tumbler. Others go around plants. Shells go into dishes or small containers just as they are. See? Like this." She picked up a clam shell, scraped away larger rocks, searched, selected smaller shells, and dropped them into the clam shell scraper. "Here, you can add this to your decor. Set it and one of your carvings on a larger piece of driftwood."

"Thank you." He was moved by the gesture, and awakened to another of nature's healing wonders: touching and examining rocks and shells individually, not just as part of the beach.

"Have you seen Kelda today?" Joyce asked. "I wanted to check on her, but Arne's truck is here."

"I saw her." Raymond launched into an objective account of the afternoon and the reporter's visit.

Joyce looked at him. A smile started, spread, lighted her eyes. "Why Raymond, I believe you're in love with Kelda."

He looked at the little carving in his hand, turning it as though it might answer for him if he could hold it at the right angle. Then he let his eyes meet Joyce's. "I'm quite fond of her. And worried for her."

Joyce laughed a light, lilting laugh that floated on the air currents with the gulls. Her hands moved, arranging her thoughts, knitting them in a pattern he could understand. "The subtle change in your face, your eyes, even your posture, say you're more than fond. Most of the time you're a bit lawyerish, but now you're human, a bit vulnerable."

"I see." He nodded, looked out across the bay. "Well, I won't burden her with the depth of my fondness. Or with improper attention."

"You don't think she deserves to know?"

"She's a married woman, and she's got quite enough to cope with just now."

"Oh, Raymond," Joyce laughed again, "don't look so stricken. Kelda will cope. She has the Landing and her uncle. And us. We're part of the equation. She said that last night, remember?"

He did remember. Ragnar met Kelda at the great-room door. They came into the living room arm in arm, their love-bond making both glow. He, Emma, and Joyce all stood. Kelda hugged Emma first, and laughed at the woman's take on the situation. "Them folks will just have to sweep up their own messes without your help." She hugged Joyce next and said she might have to look for a job in old downtown Poulsbo herself.

Then she turned to him, smiled but blinked, like she'd been about to cry, and crawled into his arms. Or so it seemed. A heat had washed over him, and he'd wanted to kiss her. When she lifted her head from his chest and looked up, her eyes seemed to say she'd like that too. But didn't men always think women wanted the same thing they wanted? Hadn't he heard that bandied about the law offices more than once?

"I remember." He used his cane to push himself to his feet and get his balance, found a flat rock, and with a flick of his wrist sent it skipping along the bay's surface so it left crescent ripples where it touched.

"Wow, five skips. I'm impressed," Joyce said. "Have you eaten? I've got some lasagna thawing and things for a salad."

"If that's an invitation, I accept. I've got wine or beer. Which would you prefer?"

"Why not both? A beer while I toss the salad, wine with dinner."

*Marriage: a job. Happiness or unhappiness has nothing to do with it. - Kathleen Norris, 1947-*
...

*American poet & essayist/lecturer*

# 25
## Kelda and Arne

Kelda sat at the great-room table while Arne paced. She could hear Emma's voice, exasperated, drifting in from the living room where she played cribbage with Ragnar.

"Uncle Ragnar must be trying to sneak extra pegs."

"Yeah, well he can do it. Shit."

"Arne, please sit." They'd come to their moment of truth, she and Arne, and she needed him to settle, talk, respond with something other than expletives.

"All right, you're saying you're back at the Landing for good." Arne hooked a chair leg with one foot, bumped it away from the table, sat slumped. "The next move's mine. So, I either live here or I go it alone, is that it?"

"I think it's time for you to decide what you want to do about our situation." She looked at his blonde hair, and how well the stray grays blended in. She tried to read his eyes, but he kept turning his head. "Arne, why did you marry me? Do you remember? Did you ever know?"

"Shit, Kel, you were a hell of a good-looking woman. Still are. And you're a damn good cook. None better, far as I can tell, except when you get on your high horse about cholesterol."

Kelda sighed. She'd heard that answer before and let it go, but now it had to be faced. "You found me attractive, but I wasn't really the 'object of your affections.' Someone else was, but she didn't meet

Gerda's criteria. For whatever reason, you chose to follow Gerda's wishes rather than your own heart. I mean, looks-wise and cooking-wise, I'd do, but you didn't really love me."

He rubbed both hands over his face, which was redder than the warmth in the room would make it. "What's love? Really? If Gerda influenced me, well maybe it was for the best. We've had a good marriage, for crissakes. Haven't we? Two kids, nice home. I don't know what you want."

"I would like us both to be happy, and I don't think either of us is right now. Not as things stand. We don't need to stay married to continue being parents to our daughters. I want to live at Hansen's Landing with Uncle Ragnar. You've made it clear that you don't want to live here, but I think there's something more going on. I'd like to hear what you want."

"Okay, how about this. We stay married, you live here until Ragnar dies, or goes to a home, or whatever. Don't give me that look. Shit. Anyway, you stay here for now, I'll find a place on the other side, close to the office, we'll sell the house. Then, when the time comes, we'll figure it out."

"Stay married, but live apart?"

"Yeah." He grinned, relaxed, sat a little straighter. "Why not?"

"Because you don't love me, Arne. There's no passion in our marriage."

"We been married what? Twenty-four, twenty-five years? I think we do okay, considering." He grinned his lecherous little grin that she did find endearing. She slumped under the weight of what needed sorting. They didn't even speak the same language.

"I don't mean sexual coupling, I mean a passion for life. The things we value, the way we spend our energy for work and for fun."

"Shit, Kelda, I know you don't like sports, except when the girls played, you don't like golf, you don't go out on the boat, but that don't mean we don't have fun."

"That's exactly my point, Arne. Those are some of your passions, but they're not mine. Watching or participating in sports is not my idea of fun. I'd like a rowboat."

"Oh, for crissakes, a rowboat's just a way to get to a real boat."

Kelda laughed, though she felt like crying. She put a hand over her mouth, closed her eyes, shook her head. "You're right, for you that's what a rowboat's for. But for me it's a quiet way to be on the water. I don't like engine noise, or television noise, or the shouting that's part of sports. I like solitude."

Arne shook his head. "That's fun? Solitude?"

"For me."

The cribbage game ended, and Emma came into the great-room to say goodnight. "I'll be going, I've had enough of his cheating for one night."

Kelda saw Emma to her car, then went through her bedtime checklist with Ragnar. She gave him a hug, watched him climb the stairs, returned to the great-room, filled with the tension of her confrontation with Arne. At least he hadn't left, or turned on television. But his face color had darkened again, and a muscle in his neck twitched. She raised one eyebrow.

"So, Arne, what do we do next?"

He gave her his open-eyed stare that he used to intimidate lesser mortals. She could see that he'd been stewing in his own juices, as Lydia used to say, while she'd been out of the room. When he spoke, his words sounded like a hammer hitting nails.

"That's what's worrying me. Let's say we get divorced so you can have your solitude. All it costs me is everything. I give you half of everything, that leaves me without enough left to run my business, let alone keep the boat." Arne pushed away from the table, stood, lifted the chair and pounded it onto the floor. His biceps bulged, his jaw muscles twitched.

"Arne . . ." Kelda stood, reached out a hand. Arne slapped it away.

"Why don't you just cut off my balls with a dull knife, Kelda Ronalda Hansen? Cut 'em off and use 'em to fertilize one of your goddamn flower gardens."

"Arne, you have to calm down, damn it." She got hold of his arms. "Arne, I don't want half of everything. Whatever gave you that idea?"

He looked at her, and gradually relaxed. His jaw and eyes quieted, softened. He moved his head forward, squinted like he'd understand better if he could focus more clearly.

"What do you want, Kelda?"

"I want to save the Landing from development. That's my first passion. I want to stop feeling responsible for your happiness and health, and for the girls as well. I want to take care of myself, my needs. I want to be with people who appreciate me for who I am, not just for my cooking.

"You think that detective asshole's going to make you feel appreciated for crissakes?"

"Oh, Arne, that detective is just a guy who's trying to find someone to make his life more pleasant. I give off caregiver vibes. I have to do something to stop that."

And then tears burst forth and fell. She caught one with her tongue.

"Come on Kel, don't cry."

Arne put his arms around her, gathered her in, patted her back, then rubbed it up to her shoulders, down to her waist; up to her shoulders down below her waist; up a way, then down, his big hands cupping her bottom.

"Come on, Kel, you must be tired, crying like that. Let's go to bed." He pulled her toward the stairs.

She went with him, worrying that love making might not be good for his blood pressure, which she suspected had been soaring all day and evening. Then his moves, so practiced, so foreseen, so comforting, stopped her worrying. It was only afterward that she thought about the patterns in their relationship. Making love didn't resolve their issues, it only postponed them.

In time she went into her bathroom, showered and pulled on an old pair of flannel pajamas she'd left in a drawer for chilly winter nights. She crept down the stairs, collected a bottle of brandy from the kitchen liquor cupboard, pushed her feet into her garden clogs and went out into the night.

Seatlh found her on the dock, rubbed against her legs and nuzzled her neck before settling into her lap for some serious petting. Kelda sipped brandy and talked to Sea, who listened far better than Arne, and who answered with purrs. When she'd talked it all out, decided she would reassure Arne that though it was time to live their separate lives, she wouldn't ask for anything that wasn't fair and equitable. She carried Sea to Raymond's cottage and set him on the porch, returned to the main house, put the brandy away, and crawled into Lydia's bed.

Dan McClusky's private office reflected the man's conservative tastes; simple furniture, clean lines, Ansel Adams photos. Mac was on the phone, trying to pacify a client. Arne looked up from the papers Mac had spread out on the old hand-rubbed walnut work table. Maybe the calm surroundings would keep things on an even keel. His greatest worry these last few days was that Kelda would change her mind, decide she did want half of everything.

He'd tried to make her believe he'd be happy living separately while staying married, he'd just pop over to the Landing now and then. Problem was, he couldn't give up on trying to convince her she'd have to sell that property one of these days.

"Look at it this way, with me doing the developing, you get almost total say of what happens to every tree, every shrub, even the flower beds. We can dig up and move every rhodie and lilac, if that's what you want."

"I don't want anything dug up and moved, Arne. I want time to consider some options that aren't so invasive. If some of the land has to be sold, I want to plan the best way to manage that with the least disruption of Uncle Ragnar's life."

It always came down to her uncle. Maybe a bit to her own needs. Getting over that Hap Smith mess.

They'd agreed to discussing an amicable divorce. She'd gone through their Shore Pine Point house, packing clothes and books, some office stuff, a couple pictures off the walls some other art pieces. So far, she'd left the dishes, silver, glassware.

When she was going through books, he'd tried to distract her, get her to stay another day, then maybe another after that. "Hey, you like to read, why not curl up with one of those books, I'll make a cup of tea, heat a bowl of soup. Tomorrow we can start a reasonable plan for our lives."

"There's really nowhere in this house to read."

"House this size, this many rooms, no place to read?" He'd gotten a little dramatic, stomped around, slapped walls. "Look at the place. Over four-thousand square feet."

"Reading requires a certain ambience. This is a spacious, lovely, impersonal house. The architectural lines are pleasant, the construction is flawless, the amenities are superb. None of it reflects me or my needs."

Mac cradled the phone, pointed to the parking lot. Arne made it to the window in time to see Kelda climb out of the Bronco, dressed like she might be heading to her office. She kept her hair short and the color it had been during her teens. She looked good. Damn, why couldn't he love her like she wanted to be loved. "Shit, why didn't she just wear her gardening jeans."

"Maybe because she's not here to garden." Mac cradled the phone. "Hey, relax man, it's Kelda. She's a good woman, you're a good man. It's time to straighten out some financial matters. Stick to business, okay Arne?"

Mac hugged her when she came in, and Kelda hugged back. She smiled but Arne could see sadness in her eyes. Better sad than mad, he thought. "Hey, don't I get a hug."

"Sure, Arne." She hugged him, pulled away, patted his arm. "Well, let's get started."

Patted his goddamn arm for crissakes, what did that mean?

Mac took them through the papers, explained the financial picture, made certain Kelda understood. She nodded or asked for clarification if something confused her. They studied maps and aerial photos so she could see exactly where Hedstrom construction held land options. They reviewed proposals, even the one listing the Shore Pine Point house and marina moorage as a potential part of the deal. They went through the assets and depreciation schedules on all the equipment. She just kept nodding. How the hell can a man read a woman's nods?

When they'd gone through everything once, she said, "Do you have hot water and a tea bag, Mac? I have several questions."

Arne felt his insides wrench and then slacken, like he'd lost the muscles necessary to sit up straight. He studied his hands, listened while Mac asked his receptionist to bring tea, coffee, juice, and a snack tray. Then he snuck a look at Kelda. She still studied the papers in front of her.

When the tea came, she thanked Mac's receptionist, and complimented her on something. "Let's start with the company's equipment," she said. "The Bronco, which I've been driving, is depreciated out. Arne, I guess you can give it to Lauren. I've told her I expect my Honda back this weekend."

"Lauren called," Arne said. "She's really upset, Kel, she said she hates the Bronco."

Kelda shrugged. "Let her ride the bus then. I bought the Honda, and I'm still paying the insurance on it. I didn't want to loan it to her in the first place, but you talked me into it because it uses so much less gas than the Bronco. Which doesn't matter, since you've been paying her gas bill anyway." She flipped pages, found the one that showed Lauren's gas bills were being picked up by Arne's personal-expenses account, and gave him that Kelda look.

Arne let his head fall forward into his hands. He knew what would be coming next.

"Lauren's spending is out of control. So is Gerda's. I'd like to know why Gerda has such a huge allowance."

"She's my mother, Kel, for crissakes. What should I do? Throw her out on the street?"

"I'm not talking about the cost of the Kensington. I knew about that, and agreed to it, because it covers meals and all utilities except her phone. What I don't get is the additional two thousand or more a month for incidentals. How can she spend that much?"

Arne threw his arms up in the air. "I don't pretend to know what you women can find to buy." He tried to put on his charming smile, but Kelda had pushed away from the table and stood with her hands on her hips, giving him her look again. Shit.

"Oh no, Arne. I'm not buying that. Gerda's combined spending for housing and incidentals almost equals my annual salary. That pisses me off."

"Shit, Kelda, she's my mother."

"Oh, shove it, Arne. I've mothered you more than Gerda ever did, but that's my own fault. What really ticks me is Gerda never worked outside her home, and she didn't even work that hard at home as far as I can tell. She had a sweet, dear man as a husband, but he had to stay outside most of the time so the carpet and furniture didn't get soiled. Not dirty, soiled. Your father worked hard all his life, good honest work, blue-collar work, but Gerda spends like she'd been widowed by a bank president or a brain surgeon. I think that sullies Knut's memory."

"There were some investments . . . Knut got into some things . . ." Arne started, but couldn't find anywhere to go with the explanation, because it meant telling Kelda things he'd vowed were better left buried.

"What investments? What things? Hedstrom construction things? We paid off that land deal years ago. Hansen money helped with that. You, or Mac, I guess, rolled that into the initial Hansen investment."

Arne couldn't stand the look on Kelda's face, or the one on Mac's, for that matter. Kelda still looked more sad than mad, even though she said pissed. Kelda didn't cuss very often. And Mac looked complacent, for crissakes. He'd promised Arne to stay through the discussion, regardless of where it led, you'd think he could give an old friend some help.

It'd been nice having Mac take care of the accounts through the years, keep Gerda's and the girls' personal draws included with his. Mac kept everything straight and clean. Their income taxes reflected Gerda as a dependent. Kelda knew that.

"Just investment things, you know, some business crap with Karli." Arne hoped that would end it. "You know, Knut and Karli got thick there at the end, before Knut died."

"You mean their so-called boat business? Their K and K wooden hulls?"

"That, yeah, that." Arne was glad for something to grab onto.

"That wasn't a serious business. That was just a couple guys drinking beer, talking, dreaming a little."

"Well, but Knut cashed in his annuity."

Finally, Mac spoke up. "His pension annuity. He spent it before he died, which is why Gerda doesn't have much to draw on now. That's the trouble with taking a pay-out."

Kelda looked from one to the other, her head tilted, her eyes squinted, her mouth scrunched a little. Arne thought he could actually see the thoughts jumping around in her brain.

"Cashed it in for what? Uncle Karli and Knut didn't get that far into that boat thing. I know they didn't."

"Yeah, well there were some other things going on. It got spent, you can trust that."

"So, you're saying there was no money left for Gerda to live on?"

Arne shrugged, tried a smile. "That's about it."

"So, status-seeking Gerda used her husband's death and her son's construction business to climb a couple levels higher than she'd lived. And you just went along with it."

"Until now, until you started talking divorce, I figured we could afford it." He tried making his face look remorseful, hurt. If Kelda didn't get too greedy now, the company could still go on, things could get back to normal. Close to normal. Maybe he'd have to run over to the Landing now and then for a good meal. And he'd have Maria's concern. He almost let a grin slip at that thought.

"I don't buy it. I think it's a crock. You knew when that reporter came to the Landing with all those questions about Wallace Taylor's murder that Gerda had called the newspapers. You know something else, too, I just don't know what. Yet."

Arne rolled his eyes. He could feel sweat just about everywhere, even in his crotch, making it itch. "You know Gerda. She likes to upset you, Kel. It would have been easier for you if you'd gone along with the plan."

"What plan? Turning the Landing over to Hedstrom Construction? Apparently, that's the only thing I didn't go along with, since I seem to have spent years doing damn demanding work so Gerda could shop at Nordstrom and drip with diamonds and drive a Cadillac, though she hardly ever drives, she waits for someone to come get her. What else does she do? Bet the horses? Keep a gigolo? I know she's had face lifts and tummy tucks, there must be a reason.

Don't try to stop my mouth from running, Arne. I'm pissed, and I'm venting. I want to know what else you know. I want to know why you protect that nasty old woman. It's not because she's your mother. You don't like her any better than I do, but you're afraid of her."

"She's my mother, for crissakes. Can't we just take care of the rest of our business and leave my mother out of this? It's bad enough that she's not seeing the Landing developed like she'd hoped, she doesn't even get the land Karli promised Knut for the money Knut sank into their business. She's been waiting all her life for her piece of waterfront, now she's old and that's not happening. She'd have settled for my having part ownership, building something nice there, having it known the Hedstroms were involved in that goddamn Hansen's Landing. But no, Kelda, you and old Ragnar are so goddamn nearsighted you just want to hang onto the place, let it grow over." Damn, his heart was beating so hard his head pounded, and sweat was dripping into his eyes, blinding him.

"Arne, calm down old boy," Mac said.

"I don't want to calm down, I'm just as pissed as Kelda. I've invested a hell of a lot in this marriage, which it seems is now going down the toilet, and the hell of it is I've been protecting her, not my mother. I'm the one who's been caught in the middle of this whole mess."

"What mess, Arne?" Kelda asked.

He looked at her, miss cool-headed Kelda Ronalda Hansen. His chest ached, his vision blurred, he thought he might puke, he figured it wouldn't matter, he seemed to be having a heart attack, there'd be other messes for them to clean up, he might as well spit it out.

"Gerda's going to tell everything, unless you back off this idea of divorce."

"Tell what, Arne?"

"Your fucking uncles killed Wallace Taylor and tossed him off the ferry. She's got some kind of confession stashed somewhere."

*I believe that in the end the truth will conquer. - John Wycliffe, 1320-1384.*

*English philosopher, theologian; Biblical translator.*

## 26
## Kelda and Gerda

Arne went down with a thud not unlike a tree falling on hard ground. Mac, who'd made a step toward him before he fell, stepped back to the desk to grab the phone and punch in 9-1-1. Kelda was on her knees beside Arne, grappling with his flailing arms.

"Easy, Arne, let me loosen your belt and unbutton your shirt." She was prepared to do CPR, but Arne would have to be further gone before she'd be able to get past his beefy arms, which had become battering rams. His fear driven strength terrified her. Was it the power of the last gasp? For a fleeting moment, while her hands fought his, she considered knocking him out, but she could hear Ragnar's voice saying, "Too hard headed, half Swede, half German."

"Arne, try to relax, you need to relax, the pain will subside if you relax, Mac has called 911, help is on the way. Arne! Stop thinking about this mess. Everything will be fine, I can deal with Gerda, just relax. There, easy, think about Lauren and Reva. They need you to relax your breathing. Maria needs you to relax your breathing and stop gasping." She had found his pulse, erratic but strong enough for her to trust he'd be alive when the medics arrived.

He quit fighting her so suddenly she thought he'd died the moment her fingers left his pulse. His groans intensified. "Pains getting worse, face and head wet, "she said. She grabbed the napkins Mac's receptionist had brought with the tea and daubed his face and neck, all the while talking in a voice she'd used to soothe her children when they were young and trusting. Arne's eyes met hers for a moment, showing that same level of trust. He dropped the Gerda-bomb that had been controlling him for years. Now he trusted her to deal with it.

"Mac, take off his shoes and socks, the medics will want to look at his toes. Loosen his belt; he always buckles it too tight. Unbutton his pants. Arne," she said over his groans, "let me see your eyes." His face, now pale, had been crimson and ashen. His lips and fingernails were not blue.

He opened his eyes and looked at her.

"Listen to me. I am going to handle Gerda, and we will work out everything that needs to be done so we can both keep on living. I will always care about you, Arne." She watched his eyes accept that; she watched the relief in them. The medics came through the door, and she moved out of their way.

The inner shaking started, as she knew it would, but she paid it little heed. What if Gerda was right? What if the uncles had killed Wallace Taylor? If they had, there would have been a reason.

No, the gentle Hansen men she knew wouldn't do such a thing. They just wouldn't, though they would withhold information if they deemed it necessary. They were known for being conservative with words, for not discussing subjects they deemed private. They might obstruct an investigation to protect someone.

Why did it matter now, sixty years later? Who, other than Gerda, really cared? The young reporter, Travis Eklund? He seemed interested only because it was history.

She heard a voice that sounded like her mother's say, *"Let Ragnar handle it."* Her eyes darted about the room. "What?"

"We're ready to transport him to the hospital now," the younger medic said. "Edmonds General. You can meet us there at Emergency."

She watched Arne as the medics rolled and then carried the gurney out of Mac's office. His eyes were closed, his color near normal. "Yes, I'll head there now," she said long after they were out of hearing range.

Calming Lauren, who sat sniffing in the waiting room, had consumed the last of Kelda's adrenalin-rush energy. Reva, who met fear more head-on, stood behind Lauren massaging out knots in her sister's neck. Maria Sanchez paced, her lower lip clamped between her teeth, her eyes blank. The click of heels along the hospital's ICU corridor signaled Gerda's arrival. Kelda drew in a deep breath.

"Kelda," Gerda said, her voice sharp, "now what have you done to my dear Arne?"

Gerda had dressed for this emergency in a periwinkle linen dress and matching coat. The dress-pumps that had clicked along the hall had a low heel, but a heel none-the-less. Gerda's perfect white hair reflected a touch of the linen's color. The crossbody Louis Vuitton, clutched by diamond-ringed fingers, was one of many expensive bags Gerda owned.

"Sit down, Gerda, and I'll tell you."

"Mother." Lauren came to her feet, a warning in her tone, and moved to her grandmother's side. Kelda had told the girls only that she and Arne were having an argument about Gerda's spending habits when the heart attack started.

"Lauren, dear." Gerda clasped her favorite granddaughter's shoulders and gave her an air kiss. "Why don't you go wash your face and fix your make-up while I talk with your mother?"

"Yeah, that's like really important," Reva said.

Gerda ignored Reva to look at Maria and scowl. "What's that woman doing here?"

"What the rest of us are doing; worrying and waiting."

"Surely this is a family matter."

"Arne considers Maria family. I'm sure he will want to see her when he's stable."

Gerda lifted her shoulders, stretched her neck and peered at Kelda from half-closed eyes. "I'd think he'd want to see his mother and his children. And you of course, dear, but then he's seen you, hasn't he? You were there, weren't you, dear?"

Kelda nodded "I was there, Gerda. We were going over the Hedstrom books looking for places to cut spending. Including yours."

"You know Arne doesn't like discussing money issues. You should leave such matters to his accountant."

Kelda narrowed her eyes, and spoke just above a whisper. Migraine warnings stabbed her left eye, and her chest ached. "Tell me what Arne does like to discuss, outside of sports and food. He doesn't like dealing with any real issues."

"Kelda, you need to calm down."

"Saying this will calm me. Just before he collapsed, Arne told me what you've been saying about the Hansens and that Wallace Taylor murder, and how you used that to control him all these years."

Kelda had been at the hospital well over an hour, made the necessary phone calls, comforted her daughters and Maria. She'd calmed Mac and sent him back to his office, spoken with Emma and Ragnar, and heard the worry in her uncle's voice. Worry for her as much as for Arne. Her clothes were rumpled and sweat-stained, her hair mussed from running her fingers through it, and there sat Gerda dressed and coifed like she was going to tea at the governor's mansion.

Gerda fanned her fingers over her chest. Diamonds caught the light. "Surely you're not suggesting that I'm responsible for my dear son's heart attack."

"Your *dear son* has let your dislike for my family eat at him until it ate a hole in his heart."

"Why Kelda, dear, I don't dislike all the Hansens. Just Karli. He manipulated my dear Knut into all sorts of sordid behaviors. Brew-making . . ."

"Mrs. Hedstrom?" The ICU nurse materialized in front of them

"Yes?" Gerda stood, her fanned fingers now spread over her throat. "I'm Mrs. Hedstrom."

"I mean Mr. Hedstrom's wife."

"I'm Kelda Hansen, Arne's wife. How is he?"

"He's stable. You can say hello. No more than two at a time. Stay for a minute or less each." The nurse looked the group over. "You are all family?"

"Yes," Kelda said, over Gerda's, 'all but one' remark. "Our daughters, his mother, and his business partner, Maria Sanchez."

"Family only, this time. I'm sorry, Ms. Sanchez. Perhaps next hour."

"I'll go in first," Gerda said, already on her way.

"One moment." The nurse's authoritative voice stopped Gerda. "Just say hello. No heavy conversation."

Gerda nodded once and continued toward Arne's room.

"Reva, you go with your grandmother." Kelda watched her younger daughter lift one eyebrow as she picked up the unspoken message. They never referred to Gerda as grandmother in her presence. Reva took her grandmother's arm.

"I should have been the one to go with Gerda." Lauren's lower lip quivered, her eyes brimmed with tears.

"You go with me. I'll stay in the background and let you have a full minute. But try to contain the tears."

"Oh." Lauren saw the advantage had shifted back her way. She sniffed, dabbed her eyes, smiled. But the tears came again when she saw her dad in the hospital bed with monitors and tubes, his eyes closed.

"Shh, Lauren," Kelda whispered. "Look, this is a standard IV. That screen shows his heart-rate. Let's not send it racing."

Lauren nodded and took Arne's hand. "Daddy? Does it still hurt?"

Arne opened his eyes, smiled and shook his head. ". . . fine . . ." he said. His eyes closed again. "Lauren?"

"Yes, Daddy, it's Lauren."

He gave a slight nod. "Help your mother with Gerda."

"Okay, daddy." She turned to Kelda. "Can I give him a little kiss?"

"Of course. And you can squeeze his hand. You don't have to hold it so loosely."

Lauren squeezed, planted a kiss. "I love you, Daddy."

"Arne," Kelda whispered, "you're looking much better. Maria is here, but the nurse said she'll have to wait to visit."

She sensed him relax as she kissed his cheek, squeezed his hand and led Lauren out.

"He squeezed my hand back, mother." Tears streamed down Lauren's face. Out in the corridor, Kelda took her first born in her arms and let her sob.

"What do you want us to do now?" Reva's eyes were damp, but she maintained her composure. "We can't go back in for an hour."

Gerda grasped Kelda's wrist. "Well, I can't just sit around here. Kelda, you'll need to drive me home. I was so distraught that I came by cab."

"I can take you, Gerda," Lauren said.

Gerda smiled at Lauren, then glared at Kelda. "No. Your mother and I need to talk."

Kelda tilted her head, raised her left eyebrow. "Yes, we do. Lauren, give me the keys to the Honda, and tell me where you parked. You girls and Maria might get something to eat. Reva, will you call the Landing again and tell Uncle Ragnar that your dad is stable. Lauren, you can use the time to wash your face if you like." She caught Maria's eye, said her name, then shook her head. This wasn't the time to discuss anything with Maria.

The heavy traffic demanded Kelda's attention. She put her anger back in check, let Gerda talk. The Smith case, the end of her career, the decision to discuss divorce, Arne's life threatened. She was trying to handle it. At times, her head felt detached from her body.

Gerda rambled, words without a theme, glancing at Kelda, then out the side window. She opened her handbag, fished around, came out with a compact and lipstick, checked her face.

"You Hansens have always acted so superior. What were your uncles, really? Nothing but a bunch of dumb Norwegian loggers. All they knew to do with wood was cut it down. Not like my Knut and my dear Arne. They're skilled artisans."

Kelda clasped the steering wheel so hard her knuckles went white. "Arne is certainly an artisan, I'll give him that, and I believe Knut was too. But I've never seen any workmanship better than Uncle Ragnar's or Uncle Karli's, or even Uncle Rolf's, though he worked more with metal. Sorry, I can't agree with that one, Gerda. The Hansens all built both utilitarian and aesthetic things, and you know it."

"Your uncle Karli was the worst of the lot." Gerda continued as though Kelda hadn't spoken. "Bootlegger, womanizer, siwash lover."

"*Hold kæft!*" Kelda's open hand landed a bit hard on Gerda's left leg. "If you want to make it home, do not say another word. I will not permit slander or racial slurs in my presence."

"You needn't get violent, Kelda dear."

"When I get violent, it won't be with a hand on your leg. We're going to talk, Gerda, but not in the car. Not while I'm driving. I plan to take notes."

Gerda snapped her compact shut, dropped it into her bag, snapped the bag's clasp, opened it and snapped it again. And again. "Drop me under the porte-cochere."

"You can walk from the parking lot with me."

Gerda huffed when Kelda drove past two open slots in the Kensington lot.

"Here, this gives you room to get out without having to brush that lovely garment up against another car." She grabbed the tote with her notebook and handbag, and went around to help Gerda out, locked the doors and grasped Gerda's arm.

The Kensington's lobby projected the building's understated elegance with soft lighting and music, expensive hard-wood floors and plush carpeting, good furnishings and accessories. The fresh floral arrangements alone must cost hundreds a week. A woman rose from one of the sofas, adjusted the belt on her silk dress, touched her hair with both hands and came to greet them.

"Gerda, my dear, dear girl, how are you? How is your sweet, sweet son?" The woman had one hand on Gerda's arm, the other on Kelda's.

Gerda put on her 'worried but enduring' face. "It's touch and go, I'm afraid. But he's being very brave. Have you met his wife? Kelda, dear, this is my friend and neighbor, Rose."

"Rose Taglia, it's so nice to meet you, your husband is such a sweetheart, and so handsome." Rose sucked back drool that was trying to find its way over her lips.

"Taglia?" Kelda moved her body into a blocking position to bar Gerda's interruptions. "Would you be related to the Taglia Brothers business?"

"They're my dear, sweet sons." Rose fished in her dress front for a hankie.

"I see." Kelda watched Rose Taglia catch drool on a lacy wad of cloth. "Rose, will you excuse us? Gerda and I are going up to her apartment for a nice cup of tea before I return to the hospital."

Gerda's kitchen had marble counters and top-of-the-line appliances; cupboards held expensive pottery for everyday service. The dining room's glass-front cabinets contained fine china and crystal, including special wine glasses for reds, whites and champagne. The entire apartment, done in creams and beiges, accented with oriental rugs and good antiques, boasted good taste. Expensive taste.

"The kettle's on, Gerda. Now, tell me about the Taglia brothers and why they showed up at the Landing with a plan to build a golf-course."

"Why, I'm sure I don't know. We'll have English Breakfast tea. Rose and I talk, perhaps she got some notion or other."

Kelda squinted and stared at her mother-in-law until knife-point pain stabbed behind her eyes. Hatred would blind her.

"How dare you look at me like I've committed a sin when it's clearly your family who are the transgressors." Gerda's hands, splayed and crossed, covered her heart. "Well, I'll tell you a thing or two. Your uncles and your own father conspired to kill Wallace Taylor because he was paying romantic attention to your mother, to Lydia Berg before she married Olav. Four Hansens against one poor man. They murdered him and dumped his body in the Sound. Lydia, being the flirt she was, owns much of the blame for the poor man's death."

Kelda set her tea cup back on its saucer, which rested on a gilt-edge tea tray on her lap, and willed her legs to remain steady. She stared at Gerda; stared, without speaking. Whatever she'd expected to hear hadn't included such a far-fetched notion as that. Lydia's journals, from the moment of her meeting the Hansens at a Lemola dance, were filled with her delight in them and her hope that one of the brothers might find Ruth attractive so the two young women could continue to share their lives after marriage. And though Lydia hadn't written much about Wallace Taylor, she'd noted sorrow that her friend had to *endure such an embarrassment as Wally"*

Gerda railed on, ending with, "Your mother had all four of the Hansen's under her spell. And crazy Ruth, too."

If Arne had based his life choices on appeasing Gerda in exchange for her sealed lips, he'd struck a pitiful bargain. Gerda Hedstrom vented her spleen in less time than it took one fragile bone-china cup of tea to cool. Veins bulged in her neck and red spots dotted her scalp under her blue-white hair.

"I expect I'll never forgive you for this, Gerda. Now you've gone this far, you may as well tell me where my uncles allegedly committed the murder."

Gerda's nostrils flared, and her thin lips almost disappeared as she pursed them and stared at Kelda. "In Seattle somewhere, I don't know exactly. They may have sent some Indians from the tribe over there to do the dirty work."

Kelda released her held breath and tilted her head. "The written confession in your possession doesn't provide those details? The actual who or where?"

"Your Uncle Karli wrote it all down, like a confession, and told it to my Knut, and then locked it some old box. My Knut knew all about it."

"Arne thinks you have a written confession in your possession, Gerda. You've been controlling your son with that for all these years, and all you have is one alcoholic's story told by another alcoholic? Really?" Kelda stared back at her mother-in-law and wondered what it would have been like to have a loving woman fulfill that role.

"Knut Hedstrom and my Uncle Karli Hansen were bonded by alcoholism. I've tried to discuss this with you before, more than once. And with Arne. Neither of you want to deal with the reality of what alcoholism does to families and to truth."

"Are you suggesting that my Knut drank like Karli? Are you saying my Knut was a drunkard?"

"I used the word alcoholic. Drunkard is your word. I worked through the impact of Karli's alcoholism as part of my therapist training." Twice, but Kelda didn't say that. First in her formal chemical dependency training, then when Uncle Karli died. They were tearing down the old woodshed. Ragnar had gone to the house basement for a tool while she and Karli tugged on a stubborn board. He grunted, a sound he liked to make. It turned into a noise she'd never forget. The same noise Arne made in Mac's office a few hours ago.

Later, the doctor said Karli was dead by the time he hit the ground. She knew that; she was there when his body relaxed, released its fluids. She'd watched her Uncle Karli die. She loved him, but she'd learned to avoid him when he drank.

"Knut Hedstrom was a dear man, but also an alcoholic, Gerda. Admit it or not, that's up to you."

"You dare to sully my Knut's name? You? A conniving Hansen? Knut invested good money in the Landing, and never got his name on the deed. That inlet land belongs to Hedstroms. Karli and Knut owned that together, for their business, and then Knut died, and Karli kept the land and building, and all the proceeds from selling their boat designs." Gerda's eyes, pupils dilated, darted left and right, though her head didn't turn. Her face and neck were purple; her chest heaved.

For a moment, Kelda feared Gerda would have a stroke and felt a frisson of sorrow for her mother-in-law. Gerda tossed down her tea like Knut and Karli tossed down whisky. "You grew up with all those conniving Hansen men, you must have known what they were up to. How do you think they came by so much land? They poured liquor down more than one man's throat, and then stole his land."

Kelda closed her eyes, drew in a deep breath and concentrated on ignoring the perspiration trapped under her breasts, and the sadness trapped in her heart. "Gerda, what did you tell Arne to convince him to court me and marry me? You coerced him, I know that. What leverage did you use?"

"I couldn't let him marry that horrible Daphne. That New York Jew. Her family made even the Hansens look reputable."

"Daphne?"

"Or maybe it was Delila."

"Do you mean Deborah? He was dating a woman named Deborah before he started dating me."

"I should never have let Knut get involved with those Norwegians," Gerda said, her head turned, her eyes wide and staring at a wall. "Filthy Norwegian loggers, and that dirty old Indian." Gerda's tea cup rattled on its saucer. "Never trust an Indian. That one you've got at the Landing now? Do you know what he's really after?

He wants that inlet land. Watch out Kelda, he's an attorney, he might well have filed to take that land away from you. It's in his eyes, that Walkingstick's."

Kelda blinked twice, aware that Gerda was awash in old issues and fantasies. Talking with her wouldn't solve anything. She stood and picked up her tote and handbag. "I'm going back to the hospital now. When next we meet, do not demean Hansens, or Raymond Walkingstick, or any Norwegians or Indians in my presence. Spend your energy on helping Arne heal. He needs to hear you say that you want him to concentrate on getting well."

Kelda carried the burden of Gerda's anger with her on her return trip to the hospital. She tried deep breathing and pep talks to throw it off, but it stuck. *Sticks and stones may break your bones, but words will never hurt you.* Gerda's words hurt. At the same time, they increased Kelda's understanding of Hansen history and gave her something to investigate. As she navigated through traffic, she heard a voice say, *"Let Ragnar handle it."* Her mother's voice again. Those words again. The steering wheel jerked. Kelda righted it and looked at the empty passenger's seat. "Yes, Mom," she said.

*Night is the mother of counsels. - George Herbert, 1593-1633.*
*Welsh born metaphysical poet, devotional lyricist & Anglican Priest.*

## 27
## Ragnar and Raymond

Ragnar figured time had come for him to speak up for all the Hansens past and present, present being Kelda and himself. Lydia had been trying to get some messages into his brain clean on back to the time before she died. Some Hansen history things to help Kelda. Some of them truths untold.

How in tarnation it got so wrapped up with that old Wallace Taylor murder didn't quite make sense. Why was Gerda Hedstrom resurrecting Wallace Taylor and dressing him out in angels' wings and halos? After sixty years, it seemed Wally should be left in peace. He'd paid a price for his pastimes.

Wally had an eye for women and cars, and didn't pay much attention to relationships or ownerships. He liked his whiskey and didn't let Prohibition interfere with his imbibing. Truth be known, he made it work for himself, buying whiskey from them who distilled, getting into the hands of them who bottled it up for selling.

Gerda Hedstrom raked the past like a man might rake dug-out beach gravel for little-neck clams. Far as Ragnar could tell, Gerda had been threatening Arne with what that rake might bring up for umpteen dozen years already. Gerda told as fact a thing or two the FBI might have suspected. In the end, the FBI men maybe learned some things they'd as soon forget, and left well-enough alone. Left it to Indian Affairs, that government bunch that looked out for tribes. That's how Ragnar always figured it, based on rumors flying about back then.

When Karli died, Ragnar did just what his next older brother had told him to. He took the old steamer trunk out of Karli's workshop, soldered the lock, and moved that danged heavy piece of Hansen history into a spot deep in the darkest corner of the basement. He'd never opened it, though he knew it held Lydia's last journal. They'd decided together, he and Lydia, to place it in the trunk along with other papers Karli kept for one reason or another.

There had been a time when he considered rowing it out of Liberty Bay, past Keyport, into the deeper waters of Puget Sound. One problem, the thing was too heavy for a Hansen rowboat. Then he'd forgotten it for a good many years, too busy worrying over property taxes. Now he s'posed he'd better open it, give Karli a chance to speak, compare notes with what lingered in Ragnar's head and what Lydia was sending him. Least that's what Lydia's voice seemed to be saying, and he trusted that woman's voice in his head more than he trusted most folks still alive and breathing.

Damn it all to hell, he liked Arne Hedstrom, stubbornness and all. He just didn't much like him for Kelda. Arne had deserved a better mother than Gerda, and Kelda deserved a man who looked a little deeper into life than the sports pages. Looked now like saving Kelda for the Landing meant saving Arne Hedstrom for something or other, too. Could be Karli locked the answer in the old trunk.

Ragnar was tugging the trunk past an old grinding wheel he'd parked in front of it when he heard someone on the stairs. Next thing, Walkingstick called his name.

"Here, back in the depths, in Karli's corner wrestling with his ghost. Weighs more than the man himself ever did." He pulled a handkerchief from his back pocket and mopped sweat from his face. Damn it all to hell, he hated to use 'em, but Emma fussed that a man needed one, 'specially a working man. Said they washed up just fine in the machine, and took just a swipe of the iron, not even enough to call it work.

"Let me give you a hand." Raymond lifted the grinding wheel, grunted and chuckled. "Not much danger in this being packed off."

"Karli liked things solid, same as him. Built things in his own image. His head sat down in his shoulders same as this wheel sits in its box." His brother had built the heavy, round stone into a frame of two by eights, and then attached that to four by twelve support beams. He'd rigged a belt-drive with a motor from a wringer washer Lydia wanted off the place soon as she got an automatic. Some days Ragnar would find Karli at the wheel sharpening axes, knives, even shovel blades, making tunes and fireworks as metal touched stone.

"There's something rather remarkable about the resourcefulness of your family. I've noticed several things on the property that I can tell are crafted from flotsam and jetsam. The ram you used in the creek to pump water to the gardens; many of the hand-tools you loaned me; the electric lawn mower in the cottage garage."

Ragnar chuckled now, remembering. Emma's old washer motor, that one, attached to an old push mower. "That one I built. Still like it, too, but I kept cutting the cord when I made a turn. Careful with your bad leg, I don't want to be the cause of more troubles."

Raymond had both hands on the trunk, ready to lift. "The leg works when there's something this sturdy to hold onto. Where're we taking it?"

"Just out of the corner. Out of darkness into light. Might be I'll need to load a gun and blast my way in. This lock's been sealed tighter than a tomb for prit-near twenty years."

"There's likely an easier solution, unless you're seeking the dramatic, in which case I'll stand . . . uh . . . stand out of the way."

Ragnar looked up. Walkingstick's attention had leapt from the trunk lock to a highly polished stick with a rounded point on one end hanging crosswise on the wall. He took the stick down from its perch, held it in one hand, caressed it with the other.

"Aah." Ragnar nodded. Another wondering-about was getting answered.

"What is this?

"What do you make of it?"

"A clam digging stick. I remember watching one in use."

Ragnar waited, but Walkingstick kept remembering, and that made the wondering come clearer. "A digging stick it is. Indian Joe's clam digging stick. He left it with Karli. They done a lot of clam digging together. Used to fire up that old wood stove in Karli's workshop and steam little-necks. Course that was before we put up the fourth wall. You could smell clam nectar clean over to Poulsbo."

"Indian Joe. You've spoken of him before. Did he use a last name?"

Damn it all to hell, Lydia was lighting fires in too many parts of his brain at once, he couldn't grab hold of her thoughts. "Hansens mostly called him Diggingstick. Indian Joe Diggingstick." Miller? Was that it? No, that was the bay cut in west of Indianola. Something like Miller. He could see it in his mind's eye. Seemed he'd heard it said not so long back, but Lydia hadn't been helping him pay attention that day.

"Diggingstick," Raymond said.

Ragnar could hear the musing in the man's pronouncement and tucked that away to ponder on later. "Stick's yours, now, I can see that. It needs an Indian man's hands on it, I'm thinking. Not that Norwegian hands can't keep it polished up good, but it's taken to you."

Though Raymond watched him with those dark eyes, Ragnar knew he was looking backward in time, seeing some of what had been and how it led to what is now. Might be Karli's trunk would help clear that path. He let his fingers get reacquainted with the trunk's tin-work casing, wood bumpers, leather handles, iron corners and lock. It took him back, it surely did, but Emma brought him to the present again, calling down the stairs.

"There's dinner want's eating. Kelda called, fussing and worrying over you starving with only me here to cook, but Joyce come carrying a casserole that's perfumed up this kitchen."

"Damn it all to hell, Kelda shouldn't ought to be thinking about me, she's got enough worries." He worked to make his voice properly annoyed. He heard Raymond Walkingstick chuckle, second time he'd heard that since the man had come into this corner of the basement.

There had been a time but a few weeks back that he'd thought the man's face muscles had been ruined right along with those in his leg. Walkingstick barely spoke then, and never once so much as smiled.

"Come on, then," he said, turning his back so Walkingstick wouldn't look too closely, see sentiment in his eyes. He led the way up the stairs, stopped in the laundry room to wash up, pulled the handkerchief out of his hip pocket to dry.

"Ha. When you finally figure out how to reach around for your hankie, you think it's a towel." Emma grabbed it from his hand and tossed it into the laundry hamper. "Here's a proper towel, now be moving aside, let Raymond have some room."

He moved aside as Emma disappeared. When he reached the dining room, she handed him a snow-white handkerchief, pressed and folded into a square.

"Here, put this in your pocket. You're never knowing these days when you might be needing one."

Raymond Walkingstick made his way through the trees to Karli's workshop, and then beyond to the rocky beach where he'd lived for a time in a driftwood and mat shelter. Generally a patient man, pleased with the seasons and the order of the universe, he'd grown restless waiting for the shield of darkness on this mid-May night. The digging stick he carried felt alive, as anxious as he to seek a connection with its owner.

He would have postponed this quest for another night, or several, if he could have gone to Kelda's side to offer his friendship and support while she waited outside Arne's hospital room for her next one-minute visit. He'd made the offer, wondering all the while what use he'd be. She'd faced one crisis after another, and handled them with aplomb.

In truth it was his need, not hers, that generated the offer. He wanted to find logical answers to questions bombarding his conscious thought. Why had she and he both returned to Hansen's Landing at this time? She'd come to care for her uncle, her acknowledged reason; he'd come for spiritual renewal, his acknowledged reason. Still, something unspoken hovered in the air, something he didn't feel once he'd gone beyond the Landing's boundaries.

"Thank you, Raymond," she'd said over a somewhat static phone connection. He could hear hospital bells signaling in the background. "That's generous of you, but I have the girls and Maria with me. We'll snooze in the waiting room."

He hung up, repeated the conversation to Ragnar, who'd nodded to him, three nods. "Let Kelda have it her way. This is a time for some healing, maybe some growing up for her girls. We might have a game of cribbage before you settle for the night. You and your digging stick."

His digging stick. He hadn't noticed it, resting horizontally on galvanized nails in the basement's far corner, until he and Ragnar had the trunk out in the light. Then he'd felt a breeze, smelled the sea, heard a voice, and his eyes moved to the sorrel hued stick. It seemed ready to leap off the wall into his hands. How had he missed its presence when he'd tugged at the grinding wheel? It seemed to take on substance when they moved the trunk.

Now it caught the light of stars that dressed the night sky and accented his loneliness. Lights shown from windows here and there across the bay.

His eyes adjusted to the darkness, the phosphorescence of the beach, the subtle uniqueness of each ripple on the bay, each rock on the shore.

Raymond scratched rocks just above the water's edge, and felt the stick come to life, like a divining rod he'd once held over an underground stream. An ethereal image formed and floated over the water. His own image? Similar, but not quite the same. His own face lacked the deep creases, his chin the tuft of beard, his eyes the wisdom.

"Grandfather?"

The image dissolved, the stick turned rigid.

Clams squirted, flirted, waited for the rising tide. The stick would not disturb them this night.

He stood, anchored by thoughts not his own trying to tunnel their way out of his cerebellum so he could process them.

In time, the boy he'd been found the cedar tree he'd loved, and he sat, leaning against it. He closed his eyes and let his fingers explore the digging stick. They felt knots, swirls in the grain his eyes had missed. The stick told him it had danced in flames to harden its core. The stick told him its surface had been polished with deer horn and seasoned with fish guts. The stick told him it should be used only for digging little neck clams. A longer, heavier stick was needed for geoducks and horse clams.

The stick suggested he'd chosen his last name not only for the cane he used, but also from wisdom he denied.

His fingers moved to the stick's rounded point, and back to its slightly thicker upper end. The stick told him he'd once been loved.

His fingers stopped moving. A tear snuck out from under his closed lid; another followed; then several. He opened his eyes and saw his teardrops standing on the digging stick. The wood drank them in one swallow. His fingers moved again, over the place where they'd been.

The stick told him he'd be loved again.

When Sea wakened him at four to be let outside, the first birds were calling to the sun and bidding farewell to the stars. Raymond filled Sea's food and water dishes and set them on the porch. The black Bronco Kelda drove was parked on the drive near the great-room porch. Was that good news then? Or bad?

He crawled back into bed, closed his eyes and willed sleep to return. What had actually happened at the inlet last night, and what had he dreamed? Had he cried? He believed tears helped cleanse the soul and restore the spirit, though he had no experience to support that notion. Wanting spiritual renewal didn't make it happen. He knew only that yesterday's first glimpse of the digging stick summoned strong emotions and he wasn't ready, at four in the morning, to face any of them.

Training in the law, and earlier in debate, permitted him to immerse himself in linear thinking, logical reasoning, objectivity. If the training masked his nature, as he sometimes suspected, the mask was multi-layered.

His long-standing interest in ethnobotany, and his recently-opened native-plants nursery, reconnected him with his people's origins, but not with the people themselves. Though they'd welcomed his help with legal matters through the years, they'd remained reserved, distant.

He'd experienced life outside their tribal womb, and they saw him as tainted by the white culture. He longed for a bridge to his past, and therein lay the danger. Such longing, such emotion, might fool the mind, especially the mind of one so briefly acquainted with feelings.

As he drifted, neither awake nor asleep, he saw the digging stick in repose, waiting for him. He sensed it would soon uncover information, and some of it would bring a new degree of concern. But concern for whom? Or what? He let himself drift on the edge of sleep, waiting for the answer.

*Fate rules the affairs of mankind with no recognizable order. – Lucius Annaeus Seneca, 5 BC – 65 AD.*

*Roman Stoic, philosopher, statesman & dramatist.*

# 28
# Kelda

Kelda sat on the Landing dock waiting to greet the sun, or be greeted by it, but low clouds kept it hidden. The first rays of light turned shadows into trees and buildings, boats and water. Liberty Bay looked like dishwater left standing overnight; dingy grey and cold.

She'd arrived at the Landing the night before to find her uncle sleeping in his chair. He looked as haggard as she felt. She got him up the stairs and settled into his bed before closing herself into the sanctuary of her room, the room filled with her own ghosts, the room where she'd admitted to herself that she and Arne should consider divorce. He wasn't happy with her decision to return to the Landing, but his discontent went back further.

Seeing Maria at the hospital, talking with her, answered a long-lingering question. Maria and Arne shared a love they'd never acknowledged aloud. In Arne's case, he may never have acknowledged it to himself.

Reading had always been part of her night routine, but she'd felt too tired to hold up a book and focus on the print. The moment her head touched the pillow, her brain kicked into overdrive and dragged her back through a day that had been one of the most trying of her life. Finally, after noting each hour and the half-hour following, she'd gotten up at five, started a pot of coffee, and ventured out into clean Hansen's Landing air where she could think.

Shortly after four o'clock the afternoon before, the waiting room nearest the ICU unit had filled with Hedstrom Construction workers. They'd come straight from the job, still in denim or khaki work-pants and sweaty shirts. They sat on their haunches to save the hospital's furniture, and sipped sodas and bottled water. Their eyes met Kelda's, then looked away.

"Guys." Maria waited for quiet. "Word is Arne's stable. When he's back on the job I want all the junk food out of sight. No donuts, no chips, no candy bars, and absolutely no McDonald's meals. If you want to clog your arteries, that's your business, but you keep it away from the boss. Most of you know Kelda and her reputation as a cook. You also know she's been trying to keep him on a 'heart-smart' diet. She knows Arne cheats, forgets to take his blood-pressure meds, and generally bitches about being starved, and she knows we fall for it. Well, no more. Right?"

The guys nodded, grunted, joked, punched one-another's arms. Guy gestures. All of them wanted to know where it happened, just what Arne was doing at the time, who was with him.

Kelda said, "We were with our accountant, going over the books."

Stan Percy, foreman and friend nodded to Kelda. "That'd do it all right. How close a call was it?"

"I didn't even get to practice my CPR skills. Arne might have been in pain, but I couldn't get past those big arms."

"Yeah, man, that's Arne, baby! He'd go down fighting."

Stan scowled at the others. "What did the doctor say?"

"He won't know the extent of the damage until tomorrow. They used medications to open the blockage, and then did a balloon angioplasty."

"They talking by-pass surgery?"

"Not yet. But the cardiologist wants him out of the hospital as soon as possible."

"Yeah, hospital's where the germs are," Stan said. "We just went through that with my wife. They did surgery on a Tuesday afternoon, sent her home Thursday, less than forty-eight hours."

After Stan and the other men left, the waiting room seemed too quiet, too antiseptic. The young nurse who'd taken over at shift change said Arne was progressing as expected. Dr. Drury, Arne's cardiologist, would be by for evening rounds soon. He'd had another emergency. Lauren and Reva were restless; Maria looked exhausted. Kelda needed to start giving directions.

"Girls, I'm going back to the Landing once I've talked with the doctor. Reva, go get whatever you need for your photo-journal report and meet me back here. There's no sense in driving two cars across the ferry; we'll leave one at the park and ride. Lauren, keep your date, it really helps to stay busy, but check your answering machine regularly.

Lauren came to hug her, clung heavily and cried again. Kelda patted and reassured, and sighed when the elevator door closed between them.

"I don't need to stay, either," Maria said.

"I thought you wanted to hear what the doctor had to say."

Neither spoke for a full minute. Kelda sought a topic other than Arne, settled on asking, "How's your gran?"

"She's well. I called her. She's saying her prayers."

"Good. How's Carlos?"

"He's doing fine, considering."

"How often do you go to the prison? I know it's not easy visiting there."

"Oh, Kelda, it's horrible. I try to make it at least once a month. Carlos wants me to come every week, but I just can't stand it. He understands. Well, he says he understands."

"Do you love him?"

Maria turned her brown eyes on Kelda. "I care about him. I didn't ever really love him. He knows that."

"Do you love Arne?"

Maria's face went pale, then red. "How can you . . . I mean . . ." She looked away, at a far wall, then at her hands, one rubbing the other as if they were cold.

"Did Arne tell you why we were meeting with Mac?"

Maria looked down at her lap. "Not really."

"Do you know what Gerda has been using as her whip all these years?"

"I know it's always an ordeal when he goes to visit her." Maria picked at her nail polish.

"Do you love him? Because I'm certain he's in love with you. Knowing you love him could make the difference in how he heals."

Tears streaked down Maria's face.

"I'm sorry, Maria." Kelda leaned her head against the chair back, closed her eyes. The voice in her head said Arne could start to take care of himself.

"Kelda?"

She startled, stood, looked at Dr. Drury, who needed a shave and a good night's sleep. It was after ten. Twelve hours since Arne's attack. Reva was slumped in a chair, one leg over its arm. Maria stood, waited to be introduced.

"Doctor, you look . . ." Kelda left it unfinished. He needed a shave, sleep.

"It's been a long day. Arne's stable. I'd like him left undisturbed through the night. No more one-minute visits. We can talk more tomorrow." He glanced at Maria, at Reva who rubbed her eyes.

Kelda introduced them. "Maria is Arne's business partner."

"I see." He drew a hand over his face, and pinched the bridge of his nose. "Go home and get some rest, Kelda. All of you, get some rest."

Rest had alluded her, so she would rely on the Landing, the sea and trees, the order of things unexplained to see her through this crisis. It would absorb her fears and offer up the comfort of changing tides and salt air, cedar scent and fir needles. It would give her trilliums and fairyslippers each spring, Indian pipe stem and red vine maple each fall. It would endure, and so would she.

She stretched out on the dock and dangled one hand in the water. Cold; maybe forty-five degrees. Had Wallace Taylor been dead when the Sound embraced his body sixty years ago? Or had he died of shock from falling in? Could it have been a heart attack that forensics of the time couldn't detect? Or was Gerda's story a variation of the truth?

Lydia thought someone had killed him and then tossed him into the Sound. Someone who didn't know an autopsy would reveal lack of water in the lungs. The Hansen men certainly understood drowning. They'd talked of that in Karli's workshop, perhaps forgetting her presence in the wood-scrap box, or assuming the book that held her attention prevented her from hearing. They'd even remarked on drowning's peacefulness, at least for the barn cats they'd rowed out into the bay.

"The lungs fill so fast, makes dying easy." That was Uncle Karli explaining to her when she'd still been a child. Had she actually been a child? Why hadn't she protested? Even as a child she'd understood that Hansen's Landing hadn't needed more cats.

Morning chill and moisture permeated her cotton robe, and reminded her that good coffee was brewing in the Landing kitchen. On the way back along the dock, she paid close attention to the planks. Not all of them would need replacing.

She would need to find work Arne could do during his recovery, for she'd made the decision that he would have to spend time at the Landing. Without projects to keep him busy, he'd make life miserable for the rest of them.

Kelda eased the entry door open and closed, and breathed the scent of good coffee. Norwegian coffee fit for Norwegian loggers. For one Norwegian logger, long since retired, and his niece, recently unemployed. One-hundred percent dumb Norwegians. So dumb they owned forty acres of land on Puget Sound, water on three sides, lush timber with a rich understory, nice old house, four cottages sturdier than many houses currently being built, and the determination to do what it took to hang onto the land, the trees, the buildings, and the love that started it all.

"*Kär a*, you've had no sleep? Your eyes have the purple-under."

Kelda started, splashed coffee down her robe and onto the floor, set the cup down and moved into her uncle's arms for a morning hug. "You'll get stains from the coffee I spilled down my front, Uncle." As she hugged back, she realized her head rested right alongside his. He'd shrunk down as he aged. None of the Hansens had been tall; maybe five-ten at the most. Still they had logged the land, wrestled trees and heavy-equipment, and returned home at the end of their workday to rest up for the next.

The three who'd remained at the Landing hadn't hung out in bars, gotten drunk and disorderly in public or abused their families. They'd stuck together, one helping the other through bad times, all working and doing what needed doing to rear her and her brothers, and to pay for Ruth Taylor Hansen's care until her death. True, they'd made a little beer, and enjoyed it. That didn't make them tied to an unsolved murder.

Ragnar was grinning at her when she stepped back from their hug. "Ah, now, I'd not be minding a few coffee stains. Give Emma something to fuss over. Spilled coffee, spilled milk, keep her from worrying about other things."

His smile, his blue eyes, made the room seem sunny even on this cloudy morning. "What things are worrying Emma?" Kelda watched her uncle shake his head. One shake, pause, another, pause, a third. "Oh dear, she's worrying backward?"

"*Ja*, that she is, and ready to take on the world to make things go right for you. She thinks you've been visited by too much worry of late."

Kelda tilted her head and studied Ragnar. His w's were coming out v's which meant he was worrying backward himself. "I love you, Uncle." She squeezed his hand. "Now, let's have some breakfast and get things organized for Reva to start her journal project. Then I'll go visit Arne. The hospital said they'd be doing another test this morning and moving him out of ICU if he remains stable. They expect the doctor between eleven and one, so I'd better be there if I want true facts, not Arne's version."

"*Ja*, Arne can rearrange the truth. Might be we all do, a bit. It would be my turn to fix breakfast. Give you time to be reading this." He handed Kelda a thick envelope.

"What?" She tried to read his eyes, but he'd started searching the refrigerator.

"Just read it, *kär a*."

She pulled the papers from the envelope, unfolded the pages, looked at Ragnar again, and then at the document in her hand.

## Last Will and Testament of Emma Mildred Stern

*I Emma Mildred Stern, being of sound mind . . .*

Kelda sank back into the chair. Tears welled in her eyes before she got to the content. Emma's will named Kelda Ronalda Hansen as her sole heir after specific small bequests to each of her living relatives. Kelda would inherit Emma's land and house, and any monies left after meeting her final debts. The date on the will was ten years back, so this wasn't something Emma had decided in the light of current worries. Kelda dug in her robe pocket for a tissue, blew her nose, read the attached note written in Emma's hand.

*You one time said I could move into one of them cottages, or even into the house at the Landing. Well, maybe we should have a talk. We can sell my house and land any time so there's money for the Landing taxes. I know its worth would only cover three years or so, but you seem to be learning a bit about investing to make money grow. I don't need this place, and none of my family need it neither. It's mine, free and clear, and I'm ready to do whatever it takes to help you manage. You've been like a daughter to me in many ways, and like a sister and even a mother to me in other ways, and I'm needing to say my thanks while I'm still alive. – Emma*

Kelda set the papers down, jerked tissues from the box on the kitchen counter, wiped her eyes, blew her nose, sniffed. "Uncle? Did you know?"

"No, I'd not been knowing before yesterday. Emma handed it to me and ordered me to read it, just like she orders me to lift my feet when she's vacuuming. 'Look here, at the date,' she said, talking at me like an army sergeant, stabbing her finger up and down, like I might miss it. 'Nineteen hundred and eighty-two,' she said. 'When I turned sixty-two and started my social security draw.' She made certain I understood she'd decided and done it back then."

"I saw the date."

Ragnar chuckled, slapped his thigh. "She's seventy-two this year. More than ten years younger than me, and she's all the time trying to boss me around."

That made Kelda laugh while she still needed to sniff or blow her nose. "Okay, what's for breakfast. I need some sustenance to think this one through. I'm not sure I can accept the terms of her will."

"You'd not be thinking you can refuse." He drilled Kelda with squinted eyes gone steel blue. "A last will and testament's a serious decision. She made her decision in sound mind, just like it says, and with good advice. Abe Tosenrud's a good, honest man, and he wrote the papers, but Emma's the one made the decision."

"Yes, all right, I'll mind my manners and say thanks. But, Uncle, are you ready for Emma to move in?"

He shrugged. "When want comes to need. Damn it all to hell, she prit-near lives here as it is." He shook his head, but just once. "In one of the cottages, I'm thinking, not in the house. You'd not be wanting her underfoot just now, what with things going on. There's some cleaning out needs doing first."

Now Kelda squinted her eyes, trying to copy the look Ragnar had given her. "What things? What cleaning out?"

"Things would be Arne's heart attack, and Gerda's mouth running, and all that what-not from your job. Cleaning out would be Karli's trunk, that would be all."

"Karli's trunk?" She frowned. "What trunk? I don't remember there being anything we didn't go through when he died."

"In the basement, in the corner. Under the old canvas tarp. Me and Walkingstick dragged it out yesterday, after you called about Arne." Ragnar busied himself while he talked, pulling raspberry jam out of the refrigerator, bread out of a drawer, cereal out of a cupboard.

"Stop being so busy and look at me, Uncle. Let me see your eyes. What's in Karli's trunk?"

He stopped and looked at her, his blue eyes clear, a grin increasing the depth of his face wrinkles. "Now how would I be knowing that? It's soldered shut. I figure we'll open it together, you and me, when you're ready."

"Is it going to tell us who killed Wallace Taylor?"

"Might be. I'm not for certain about that."

"Was Karli involved? Gerda says he was." She pushed those words past what felt like a cotton ball in her throat.

"Gerda talks, but she's not for knowing much. Karli talked some too, and I 'spect he knew some things, but he'd not be telling Gerda Hedstrom."

"But did he tell Knut? About the murder? Did he know if it was a murder?"

"Might be. But it wasn't Karli done it, or no other Hansen neither, that's prit-near for certain."

"How certain is 'prit-near for certain'?"

"Certain enough for opening that soldered trunk, I'm thinking."

"Why was it soldered? Damn, I'm on the verge of having a heart attack myself, worrying about what Gerda's going to say next, who she's talking to and what it all means for Arne. Damn it all to hell, Uncle, what am I going to do about Arne? We were talking about the possibility of divorce and division of property when he had his heart attack."

She hadn't meant to tell Ragnar that, not yet. Her hands were on his shoulders, shaking him just a little while she looked into those blue eyes. God, they looked just like the ones she saw in the mirror when she leaned in to put on lipstick. He was nodding; one, two, three.

"About Arne, you're going to do what you started. It's time he quit using you to hide behind where Gerda's concerned. I'm knowing a good bit about that woman. Arne deserved better for a mother, but there's no more you can do about that. You said no development at Hansen's Landing, no more tree cutting. I planted them firs to make up a bit, and I'll plant another thousand if need be, to get the message through."

"And Karli's trunk? Why was it soldered?"

"To seal away the truths untold. Likely there's more'n one truth buried in that trunk. Times were such I thought some things weren't meant to be talked about. I cogitated on dumping it in the bay, back when."

"You were going to dump Karli's trunk in the bay? Something of Karli's? With some Hansen history in it?" My god, where had she been?

"*Ja*, back before I was concentrating on dying. But then you come home and made me that beef-barley soup."

"You were concentrating on dying?" Her hand flew to her chest where a pain had been building.

"Now, *kär a*, I changed my mind some days back. Damn it all to hell, you make some good soup, and I've got Walkingstick here for the cribbage. He's going to help with what needs doing."

"Help how? With what?" Kelda knew her heart was beating too fast, but probably no faster than if she'd run in from the dock. "Maybe we should all just take to our beds."

"You get Arne settled here, and get Gerda's mouth closed up for a minute. Walkingstick and me, we'll work on the rest."

*There is no love sincerer than the love of food. - George Bernard Shaw, 1856-1950.*
*Irish playwright with extensive influence on western theater.*

# 29
# Arne

The twenty-four hours or so Arne had been confined to bed was the longest he'd ever spent in a hospital, and he'd had enough. So, he'd had a little heart attack. Well, Kelda was here, she could drive him home, but being Kelda, she was stuck on dragging him to the Landing.

Maria had been here earlier, before they wheeled him off somewhere for tests. Shit, man can't even tell where he's going. She'd watched the time, said she'd leave before Kelda arrived, let them discuss going home without her interference, be back later to see what they'd decided. Shit, he'd already decided.

"Home means home, not the goddamn Landing, for crissakes, Kel." He tried giving her his stare, but she just stood there with her superior Kelda look.

"Arne, please try to avoid getting upset. Please. You leave here when Dr. Drury releases you. If you refuse to go to the Landing, you'll have to get Gerda to stay with you."

"Shit, Kel," he started, then turned his head toward the sound of footfalls. "Hey, doc, got your pen handy? Sign me out of here. People die in these places." Arne watched the doctor, hoping for a sign the man agreed, but saw only a serious look on the man's face and a loosened tie at his neck. He figured the doctor for his mid-forties, give or take, and respected him because he'd seen the degrees hanging in the man's office.

"Lucky for you these places exist, Arne. Good morning, Kelda." Dr. Drury flipped pages on a chart. "Blood pressure's not too bad today. Temperature's okay."

"Yeah, I'm good to go. Just get me my pants."

"Sure, Arne, in another forty-eight hours. We've got a few more tests to run."

"More tests? Shit."

Kelda sighed. Arne watched her edge her way past the bed, look out the window. She looked tired around her eyes, more tired than he'd ever seen her in twenty-five years of marriage. She probably needed to be in bed more than he did.

Dr. Drury stuck a hand under the blanket and felt one ankle. "Arne, I hope you realize a heart attack isn't just a bad pain that goes away. It's death of part of the heart muscle. Its permanent. We got the artery open with the PTCA yesterday, but the EKG shows some damage. We won't know how much until we run a CPK on your blood."

"Hey, doc, I'm just a blue-collar kind of guy. You know, a dumb-shit."

"I know, I live down the street in one of the houses your blue-collar talent built, remember? There's no reason you should understand the terminology." He held up his hands and ticked off explanations of the terms.

Arne noticed the doctor's hands looked soft, nothing like a construction worker's hands. Well, he supposed doctors scrubbed so often and did so little other than doctoring that their hands would be that way. Odd. He'd never really thought about that before.

"The PTCA was the balloon we used to push the blockage out of the spot where it had lodged in your artery. A clot built up on some of that plaque I've been warning you about. That's the cholesterol taking its toll. PTCA is percutaneous transluminal coronary angioplasty, more commonly called balloon angioplasty."

"You pushed it out of the way, so I must be good to go. I'll take my meds . . ."

"Kelda? Does Arne have a good insurance policy and an up-to-date will?"

Arne watched Kelda turn, lift an eyebrow, shake her head. "It gets worse," she said, and turned back to focus on the window.

"Arne, I'm not releasing you until I've determined you're ready to go. That's my job. The CPK test–that's creatinine phosphokinase–will tell us how much muscle protein enzyme was released into your blood. That indicates the amount of heart muscle that died. Your EKG, electrocardiogram, showed some areas where the heart muscle had been deprived of oxygen. Now we need to know how much and for how long." The doctor narrowed his eyes and watched Arne. "Now, you want to cooperate with me?"

"Another forty-eight hours, you say?" Damn, he'd be in danger of dying of starvation and boredom.

"In the hospital, yes. Once you're released I want you in for cardiac rehab once a day, and regular checkups twice a week for a couple weeks. Cardiac rehab's in the same complex as my office. It's a gym similar to those in athletic clubs, but with trained exercise scientists. Once I'm convinced you're doing proper exercise, you can choose a different workout site."

Arne grinned. "Looks like I won't be able to stay at the Landing, Kel. Got to do my rehab at the doc's complex."

It took Kelda some time to give up looking at whatever the hell she could see through the goddamn window. Then she looked right over him, directly at the doctor. "I'm living near Poulsbo, with my uncle. I'd intended to take Arne there for whatever length of time he needed to just rest. That way I can try to monitor his diet. I think you know he cheats."

"Cheats. Shit."

The doctor looked right past him too. "Is there something more I need to know? Some additional stress besides leaving your job at the mental health agency?"

"Yeah, she's abandoning me, probably permanently. Like in divorce. Shit, she's probably going to be like every wife, clean me out, take everything I've worked for all these years."

The doctor raised one eyebrow but stayed focused on Kelda, who just kept talking to the doctor, telling him stuff he didn't need to know.

"Divorce is an option we've discussed. We were in the midst of going through Hedstrom Construction books with our accountant when Arne had his heart attack. Nothing's settled, but you should know a few things. First, I'm not interested in creating financial havoc for Arne or the business. Second, his mother is, and has been, a major problem in our lives, for Arne especially, though he won't admit it or do anything about it. I've promised him I'll deal with her for now. Third, I'm not returning to our Edmonds home. That's why I need Arne to do his R and R in Poulsbo. I promised my uncle I'd be at the Landing for him, and there's a room on the main floor for Arne. No need to climb stairs."

"No. Nope. No way. It's NBA playoffs, Landing's TV's about the size of a thong bikini's front patch."

Dr. Drury laughed. "That's a new analogy. I've heard postage stamp. So, Arne, you going to prepare decent meals for yourself?"

"You mean like Egg-beaters for breakfast? Taste like the chicken squirted 'em out the wrong hole? She's tried feeding me that crap."

The doctor stared at him, and Kelda started to cry, for crissakes. Just stood there, tears falling, arms hanging down at her sides. Then she wiped her eyes with her fingers, like a kid would. And that was that.

"Sorry, doctor, I didn't really sleep last night. Our younger daughter, Reva, said she'd move back home. She's got about three more weeks before the college term ends. I'll make regular trips over from the Landing. Gerda, that's his mother, can stay with him to help out." She shrugged. "But if Arne doesn't cooperate, there's not much either of them can do."

"Arne?" the doctor said, standing there, looking like a school principal waiting for a kid to confess to smoking in the john.

"Hey, I like good food. What can I say?" He held his arms out, put on his charming smile. The doctor ignored him to look at Kelda.

"It's up to Arne to watch his diet and do an exercise program. It would be best to have someone living in the same house. Heart disease, like any serious disease, is a family matter." Doctor Drury paused, squinted. "I respect your decision to remain with your uncle.

I suspect you need to start taking care of yourself, too. I'm guessing that move is part of your needed therapy."

Arne looked from Kelda to the doctor, to Kelda again. She didn't look good. Looked like she might cry again. He'd caused some of that. Well, most, he supposed, dumping that shit he'd been hearing from Gerda.

"Hey, Kelda, don't cry. I'll eat right, okay? I just won't go to the Landing. Hey, doc, talk to her, will you?"

Dr. Drury checked the fluid level in the IV, took Arne's wrist and timed his pulse, patted his shoulder once. "I'll tell the nurses to take you off the liquid diet, but you'll be on a cardiac diet here. I suggest you start developing a taste for low and no-cholesterol foods."

"Yeah, okay. Hey, can you get them to take the block off the TV?"

"Sure, but if your blood pressure escalates, the block goes back on." The doctor's eyes bored right into Arne's brain.

"Yeah, whatever."

"Kelda, can I have a minute with you?"

Arne waited until they'd reached the door, then called, "Hey, Kel, Maria said she and her gran would stay with me, see to my diet, no need to have Reva there."

Kelda spun around. Now her eyes bored into his brain. "You might have interjected that fact into the conversation a little earlier."

"Interjected? Shit, Kel, lighten up with the language."

"Already lightened, Arne. I trust Maria to keep you on your diet. Just to make it clear, I'm still pissed."

"About what?" he said, but she was leaving him

*It is a long lane that has no turning. –*

*American idiom.*

## 30
## Raymond

The great-room vibrated with the tension of long-unspoken messages, or so it seemed to Raymond Walkingstick. He watched Reva and again saw Kelda in her, though the daughter lacked the powerful presence of the mother, a presence and allure Kelda didn't know she exuded. It drew others to her and drained strength from her. Though this day would remain a wonder in his life, he would always find sorrow mixed with joy because Kelda wasn't with him for the discovery.

He'd returned to the Landing in the late afternoon after busying his body and mind with plants at his nursery, and was easing his damaged left leg out of the pickup when he heard Reva call across the distance. "Mr. Walkingstick, you need to come see what I found." She waved something, but didn't step off the great-room porch. "Come on, hurry." She seemed to bounce, an excited child, then returned to serious adult. "As soon as you can. I'm sure you want to freshen up first."

Reva, Ragnar, Emma, Joyce, Travis Eklund and half-a-dozen spirits waited for him to learn what they knew. The young newspaper reporter's presence baffled him. Reva handed him the object she'd been waving, an old sepia photo of three unsmiling adults squeezed together at the photographer's command, a voice he heard in his memory, and over it, Reva's.

"It's you, it looks just like you."

He looked at the photo, at the Old-ones he recognized from the large portrait in this room. He'd grown accustomed to their knowing eyes that followed him, and to the comfort their love imbued in this house.

The figure between them took longer to absorb, perhaps because the mind can't process emotions as fast as the eye can see. The figure was taller than both Helgar and Magna, a slender man whose face resembled Raymond's own—indeed seemed to be his own. The man's hair was white, much like Magna's, and long enough to fall below his shoulders. He was clean shaven, though the other night at the inlet, or in the dream, he'd had a tuft of beard.

Raymond sat on the nearest chair, his cane not offering adequate support. The man in the photo was an earlier version of him, clearly his genetic pattern.

"Grandfather." He spoke to the photo, then looked up at the smiling, waiting faces. "This is my grandfather."

"*Ja,*" Ragnar said. "It's what I've been knowing and not finding in my old man's mind. Look on the back."

He turned the photo over and read, *Helgar and Magna Hansen with their friend, Joe Williams, 'Indian Joe Diggingstick,' May, 1928.*

"My mother's name was Clara Williams."

"*Ja,* Williams was Indian Joe. I kept getting Miller for his name. I could see it in my mind, the first part of the name, but I made it upside down, the W. I didn't know Clara was his daughter."

Raymond squinted, trying to remember the truth in what he seemed to know. Did his mother ever say her birth names was Williams? Where had memories of his grandfather and the Williams' name been hiding?

Ragnar was nodding his one-two-three nod, as if reading Raymond's memories. "The Old-ones died within the year. Neither was here for the arrival celebration in 1929."

Joyce's eyes were wet, happy wet. Her arms went out in an embracing sweep, a gesture Raymond had come to recognize. "Let's go make some coffee or smell some flowers while Raymond absorbs this."

"*Ja*, I'm thinking some raspberry wine on the kitchen patio. Walkingstick, you join us when you like. Reva can explain about the picture finding."

Raymond watched them go, and realized whatever had brought Travis Eklund to the Landing this time, it was Reva Hedstrom who kept him here. Raymond understood. Eklund's face said he experienced the same feeling when he saw Reva that Raymond experienced thirty-five years ago when he first saw Kelda.

The room vibrated like it might in a mild earthquake, no longer than a second or two. Raymond Walkingstick accepted it as his world settling into place. He'd found his connection to this earth, to his past.

He held the old photo to his chest, closed his eyes, and watched memories of his childhood, of visits from his grandfather, who hadn't lived on the reservation, like they were movie clips playing on a screen. Where had he lived? Why had there been such tension between his grandfather and his mother? He saw a bottle being knocked from her grasp by weathered brown hands; heard a deep voice say, "*Let me take the boy . . .*"

Raymond sank deeper into the chair, hearing the rest, and the reply.

*Let me take the boy back to the Landing, to the Hansens.*

*So that he will be white, like you've become? A reader of books?*

*He can be Indian and read books, too. Give him a chance, Clara.*

*He stays. I've lost too much. You left me, his father left me, Lucy's father left me. The boy is mine. He stays.*

*He will grow to hate you, Clara, for the drink. Give up the boy or give up the bottle.*

*Go away, Father. Go away and leave me to my comforts. My boy and my bottle.*

Her boy. Had he ever been her boy? Before Raymond Morse entered Clara Williams' life, he'd been a child of the tribe. She took him from the tribe, and he became a child of his surroundings, of nature. Lydia Hansen found him, and he became a child of books, and of a world not ready for Natives to succeed.

He tried to return to the Indian world through his marriage. Maybe he had managed, in a sense, for the Indian world of those years was lost in drink and despair, and his wife found that to her liking. Perhaps it was her destiny. She'd needed to be an Indian of her time; he'd needed to return to the Landing and the Hansens to find his grandfather.

*Light tomorrow with today. - Elizabeth Barrett Browning, 1806-1861.*
*Prominent English poet of the Victorian era, popular in both Britain & the U.S.*
*Wife of poet Robert Browning.*

# 31
# The Landing

Kelda sat in the Bronco, deep in a line of cars waiting for the ferry to Kingston. She'd missed one, and might miss another on this May weekend, with the great exodus from the Seattle metropolis to the Kitsap and Olympic Peninsulas in full swing. She'd called Maria, who met her at the Shore Pine Point house. Together they went through food that needed to be tossed from the refrigerator and removed from cupboards before Arne returned home. Their meeting was awkward at first, but then it was just Maria helping her get a chore done.

Kelda was ready to drive away when Maria whispered, "I do love him." Tears erupted. Maria gulped air and continued, almost stuttering a declaration that said she'd never deliberately hurt Kelda.

"I know, Maria. I'll thank you some day. Right now, I just want to go to the Landing. I want to go home."

She called the Landing, left a message about the ferry line, said she'd pick up something for dinner, and then leaned back. A honking horn jolted her awake. The Bronco resisted starting, her cell phone rang, the car engine caught, she lurched forward while Reva was leaving a message that she and Joyce were cooking, no need to stop. Kelda picked up in time to hear Reva ask about her dad.

"Complaining about the food and being stuck in the hospital."

Reva giggled. "That's good, right?"

"Well, there's probably some damaged heart tissue."

"But he'll be okay, if he just watches his diet and follows an exercise program, right?"

"Right, he'll be fine if he does those things. Reva, I need to hang up, I'm boarding the ferry and getting dagger looks from the attendant." When she had the Bronco positioned to the attendant's liking, she headed upstairs for coffee and the fresh air of the passenger's deck.

In her sleep-deprived state, the Edmonds ferry slip and shoreline seemed to rush away from where she stood—a land mass shrinking while she watched. She grasped the rail with her free hand and gulped the coffee.

Seatlh crouched in the middle of the lane leading to the Landing, his eyes alert, his tawny fur rich in the evening light. Kelda gave the horn a little toot. Seatlh raised his head, stood, stretched one leg out behind him, brought it back, stretched the other, lifted his tail straight into the air and walked toward the Bronco.

Kelda pushed the button to lower the window. "Hey, Sea, get out of the road." Sea's ears went back, he darted out of her vision. "Sea!" She dared not move until she saw him again. In that instant he leaped through the window and settled, purring, onto her lap.

"Well, thank you for the welcome home." She scratched his head with one hand and turned the wheel to pull up by the great-room porch. A car she'd seen before but couldn't place had parked far enough over so she could have her usual spot.

She sat for a moment, too weary to move. Sea purred against her chest. Raymond was standing on the porch, an unusual look on his face. Reva bounced through the door like a child playing hopscotch, one foot down, then both.

"Mother, wait 'till you see what I found. Where is it, Raymond?"

Ragnar appeared while Reva and Raymond chattered.

"*Kär a*, now even the cat beats me to my hug."

Kelda handed Sea to Raymond, who'd just handed something to Reva. She hugged Ragnar before Reva pulled her into the great-room. The moment she crossed the threshold, tension lifted from her

233

shoulders like someone had removed a yoke. Funny. She often felt that someone wrapped her in a sweater in this room. In the ensuing confusion of voices and explanations, she felt that comfortable old sweater settle in place.

Emma came in, arms crossed. "Reva, give your mother a minute to be collecting her wits. Can't you see she's worn to a frazzle?"

"Emma, I haven't even had a chance to thank you," Kelda said.

"Now you just be never minding 'bout that right now, you need to be sitting down." Emma steered her to the sofa, where she fell more than sat. Had it been this morning she'd read Emma's will and accompanying note?

"Mother." Reva's voice dragged out the word. "Look what fell out from behind one of the pictures in the Old-one's album. We were doing a layout for a shoot, taking photos out of their folders, you know what I mean, and this just fell out."

Kelda took the photo that seemed to be the center of everyone's interest, looked at it and up at them. "I know, I saw it the day of the celebration."

Stunned and frowning faces looked back at her. She looked at the photo again. "Not the photo, the pose. Raymond, you were standing with the Old-one's right out there on the patio." Kelda pushed herself off the sofa, grabbed Raymond's hand, and headed down the hallway, past the kitchen and dining room, outside. "Right here." She tapped her foot for any who followed to see.

"I saw that very picture in my mind. The Old-ones sent it into my head. I was worried they were coming to take Raymond away."

Five pairs of eyes watched her. Ragnar nodded, one, two, three. His blue eyes comforted her, letting her know that he'd had the same vision.

Travis Eklund took Reva's hand in his, and she let him hold it.

Raymond's hand was still in Kelda's. She looked at it, at its shape, the length of his fingers. Something moved through those fingers into hers, and suddenly the Old-ones, Indian Joe, Lydia, Karli, and Rolf drifted around them like clouds drift through trees.

She was hallucinating. She drew in a breath so deep it hurt her chest. "Oh, dear God, I need some sleep."

She retreated to the sewing room, the peach and white room that held so many reminders of her mother. It served as Lydia's bedroom from the onset of rheumatic fever, a disease she'd caught from a student who hadn't seemed that ill. For a time, Kelda thought of it as a sickroom. Now she thought it would be an ideal library-reading room. She'd recreate it once she'd had some rest.

She peeled off her clothes, dropped them in a semi-neat pile alongside the bed, and crawled between clean sheets. In twilight sleep she listened to kitchen music, one of her favorite symphonies. It took her back to a time when Lydia had been alive and well, and busy in the kitchen preparing food for her children and her brothers-in-law.

Over the kitchen music, she heard comments about Raymond Walkingstick and his renewed connection to his family. That Raymond had grown to so exactly resemble his grandfather surely meant a completion of something left unfinished in the grandfather's life. Both faces looked carved, not molded, a distinction Kelda saw as significant in the owners' purpose in life, their place in the scheme of things.

Raymond belonged to the Landing because Indian Joe, about whom Kelda knew so little, was part of the Landing's soul.

Reva, then Ragnar, then Emma came separately to Lydia's room to see if Kelda was ready to eat, and she almost wakened each time, but her mind wasn't ready to descend from the gloaming. Her resting body let her mind work on the message about Indian Joe and Raymond. That's what the Old-ones had been trying to convey when she'd been caressing Helgar's old wood plane. *Take off another layer. Go a little deeper.*

Now, at the edge of consciousness, it made perfect sense, as did the fact that six apparitions gathered together on the patio to get the message through. She felt deeper sleep coming up to take her. Deeper? Another layer? The trunk, of course. Karli's trunk. Tomorrow, she thought, letting sleep take her where it would.

She wakened in full darkness, aware of the sound of the house. Conversation and laughter. "Reva?" she called. In a moment her daughter stood beside Lydia's bed where Kelda lay.

"Mother, are you okay now?"

235

"Yes. Why? Wasn't I okay before?"

"Well, you seemed sort of weird."

"Yes, well I am sort of weird. It's to be expected when crisis piles atop crisis, and there's too little sleep. The subconscious takes over. Who's still here?"

"Everybody. Uncle Ragnar and Raymond are playing cribbage. I guess Raymond has won a couple games, so that could go on all night now. They're sipping a little raspberry wine. Emma and Joyce and Travis and I are playing Scrabble. Joyce *hates* Trivial Pursuit, and Emma doesn't get it, but she's great at Scrabble. She wrote 'fart' on a triple word score, can you imagine?"

Kelda, chuckled, took her daughter's hand. "Emma *is* great, isn't she? Reva, I need a robe, but first, why is Travis here?"

"He brought some copy for you to approve, for a news story."

"But why is he still here? It's what? Ten o'clock at night?"

"Almost eleven, Mom. You really slept."

"Mom? I'm Mom tonight?"

"Oh, mother, you're always Mom, but you're, you know, a little *imperious* at times."

"I am? Imperious?"

"Well, intense and efficient, and *serious*."

Kelda sighed. "That bad, huh?"

"It's not bad, it's just hard sometimes to try to measure up. I mean, I understand why you're that way. Daddy is pretty much useless when it comes to anything that has to do with family responsibility, and Lauren is so much like Gerda I could just puke, and I always wanted to be like you, but I always seem to fall a little short of the mark, but Uncle Ragnar said today he thought maybe I was getting more like you by the minute, and Mr. Walkingstick likes me. I think he likes me, he said I could call him Raymond."

"Oh dear."

"Oh, Mother, I don't mean likes me in a *romantic* way. I mean he likes me as a person like he likes you and Uncle Ragnar, and Emma, and Joyce."

"Good. I'm glad for that. Now, tell me why Travis Eklund is still here at almost eleven o'clock at night."

Reva giggled, a delightful young girl's giggle. "He's smitten, according to Emma."

"I see. How do you feel about him? Beyond enjoying the power of having someone smitten."

"Well," Reva turned serious, "he's almost too good to be true. He's a good writer. He helped me with wording my layout. He admires my photography, which he should. I'm really quite good, you know."

"Yes, I do know."

"He's either beyond the disgusting early-twenty-male stage, or never went through it. He's quite nice looking, don't you think?"

"Very. He reminds me of your Uncle Greg about thirty years ago."

"And, Mother, he thinks I'm pretty. He didn't say beautiful, which is such a dorky word, at least the way most guys use it. He said 'pretty.'"

"Oh dear, this *is* serious."

"Please don't say 'it's too fast' or 'you've only just met' or any of those cliché things. You know I'm smart enough to exercise caution."

Exercise caution? "I won't say any of those things if you'll do one thing for me."

"Sure, Mom. What?"

"Get me a bathrobe so I can sneak upstairs to my bathroom. I really need to pee."

"Pee? My mom said 'pee.' I can't believe it." The girlish laugh lingered in the room, making Kelda's eyes sting.

Raymond heard Reva laugh and tell the others in the kitchen something about her mom. Emma and Joyce laughed, too. Dishes and utensils clattered. Raymond pictured the refrigerator and cupboards being opened.

Travis wandered into the living room, said the women were getting some food ready for Kelda and wandered back out the minute Reva returned to his side. That made sense to Raymond, who was watching Ragnar to gauge his reaction. At that moment he learned another lesson about love. The older man's face changed, though Raymond couldn't describe how, because Kelda was awake and others were tending to her needs.

In time Kelda came into the living room, wrapped in a blue bathrobe the color of her eyes, her hair wet and a darker golden than when dry. She went straight to her uncle and planted a kiss on his forehead, leaving a fresh-fruit fragrance in her wake. Raymond had smelled that same scent on Seatlh's fur one night when the cat came in from his prowls. Kelda turned, smiled at Raymond, and gave him the same greeting. Heat of youth washed his body.

"Okay, guys." She turned on her serious look. "Before anyone comes in from the kitchen and interrupts us, I need to know which one of you is transmitting mind-pictures into my head."

So, she did see what he saw: spirits, apparitions, messages from the past in human form rather than just brain memories.

Ragnar smiled, and his eyes took on a light that Raymond could identify only as pure wisdom. He nodded his head; nodded it three times.

"Ah now, *kär a*, I'm thinking Walkingstick here is the ground wire our circuit's been needing."

She tilted her head, lifted one eyebrow, studied her uncle, then turned that intense gaze on him. After a moment that in fact seemed electric, she smiled.

"Well I hope we don't short everything out when we open Karli's trunk."

Ragnar chuckled. "*Nei, kär a*, we'll make a new connection."

While Raymond pondered that, Kelda hugged her uncle again, and told him she loved him. Raymond looked for his cane; he needed to stand, to move, to remove himself from the intimacy. Just as his hand found the cane, Kelda hugged him, and the warmth of her breasts burned his chest. He clutched the cane handle with one hand, the chair arm with the other, or both hands would have moved to her.

"Raymond, thank you for coming here, to the Landing, to Ragnar and me."

Her blue eyes looked just like Ragnar's; as much alike as his own resemblance to Indian Joe. Before he could grasp that, Emma's presence broke the spell.

"Kelda, we heated you some food, you need to be eatin' it before is goes cold again."

While Walkingstick's attention was diverted, Ragnar stole a peg or two on the cribbage board, then watched to see if the man would notice, or if he was too lost in the wonder of human emotion. Ragnar knew the man loved his niece, and that suited him just fine. It was meant to be, just as Ragnar and Lydia were meant to be, but paths meet on their own schedule and in their own way.

Ragnar had wanted off the earth-bound path, wanted to rejoin Lydia, ever since he bought back her sons' share of the Landing. Then came Walkingstick, down the lane like he knew the place, parked his truck, eased that bum leg out and leaned hard on his cane as he came up onto the great-room porch.

Raymond introduced himself and said something Ragnar didn't hear because Lydia was talking at the same time. He hadn't heard what Lydia said either, or heard but not understood until now.

*Here's Indian Joe. He'll give you a hand.*

It was the first time he'd actually heard Lydia's voice in his head, though he'd been talking to her plenty during the time just before, telling her about the worrying backward and getting ready to be with her.

Ragnar kept an eye on Walkingstick getting reacquainted with his cards, then the cribbage board. He saw the face-change that was almost a grin and nodded once. "You ready to let me finish the winning?"

"A hug from Kelda's worth a couple pegs."

"Your admitting that's worth taking 'em back." Ragnar pegged back where he belonged. "Your play."

Walkingstick lay down a card. "Seven."

Ragnar slapped down his eight. "Fifteen-two. There, got those pegs anyway."

"I played right into that one."

"*Ja*, your mind might be on something else." Ragnar watched Walkingstick's eyes. Sure as shooting, the man blushed. Man looking for it could see it even in those black eyes. "It'd be fine with me, you thinking my *kär a's* special."

Walkingstick looked up. "It would?"

By golly, if the man didn't grin prit-near ear-to-ear.

Kelda looked at the two women sitting with her at the table. "Emma, Joyce, thank you. I can't remember when food ever tasted so good."

"Seems like food always tastes better if someone else cooks it," Joyce said.

"Depends on who's doing the cooking," Emma said. "Now you had some rest and some food, might be a good time to talk about how we're handling Arne when you bring him home. Guess we'll be fixing up Lydia's room for him, moving in a TV set."

"Arne refuses to come here. He's going home to our Edmonds home."

"That man is a test. Now what's he expecting you to do? Leave Ragnar? Or run between the two of them, see if you can do yourself in, end up in the hospital too?"

"No, what he seems to expect is that Maria and her gran will move in with him."

"Well, I'll be," Emma said, slumping back into her chair and pushing her pin curled hair back from her face. "If that don't beat all. Why would Maria be willing to take on that man? You'd think she'd know better, working with him and all."

Kelda took one of Emma's hands in hers. "She loves him, Emma. And he's in love with her."

Emma's head started moving from side to side. "No! That's just not right. Right's right and that's wrong. You been doing for that man for all these years, and he goes and falls in love with someone else? Now, when it's time he learns a little lesson, maybe a little appreciation, he gets to go and fall in love?"

"Shh, I haven't said anything to Reva yet. She's going over to see him tomorrow morning, so I suppose I'll have to tell her before she leaves."

"No, let that scoundrel do the telling."

"I think she'd rather hear it from me." Kelda smiled at Emma's look, one that showed how much the older woman cared for her. "It's okay, Emma. It's a relief in some ways, though it's sad, too. We were discussing division of properties with Mac when Arne had his heart attack. There's still Hansen money invested in the Hedstrom firm, and I'm going to take regular draws to pay back the Hansen account."

"Your uncle knowing this?"

"Yes, I told him. Just this morning, I guess it was."

"Get a good attorney," Joyce said. Then she laughed. "Raymond will love this."

"I don't think Raymond did much with domestic law. I doubt he'll want to get involved in advising me in a divorce."

"No, he didn't, he wouldn't. Never mind, that's not what I meant. It's just something I was talking to Raymond about." Her head was shaking, but she kept grinning. "Sorry, it's only funny to me because I'm up about three hours past my bedtime." Still laughing, she pushed away from the table and headed for the bathroom.

"You know she gets up about five in the morning," Emma said. "Says she can't sleep any later, then falls asleep about nine at night. You know, Kelda, I like her. Even your uncle says she's got a good head on her shoulders."

"She does. And a good heart and soul."

Emma nodded, leaned closer to Kelda, lowered her voice. "Now, 'fore she comes back, I'll say my piece. You can sell my place anytime, invest the money. You and Arne getting divorced, that could make it harder still for you to meet them taxes on this place."

"Unless you're in a hurry to move, I think we should leave things as they are for now. Give me some time to get through other things. I think we're going to manage the next half taxes, because I'm taking a draw from Hedstrom Construction's investment fund, even if it means Gerda Hedstrom has to go one month without a new Nordstrom suit and accessories."

Emma's head shook, nodded, and nodded some more. "No, not no hurry, just ready. Only real problem I see is those old dogs." She squinted her eyes. "So, you're going to call a halt to Gerda's spending?"

"It's time. It's out of control, but Arne just keeps saying, 'She's my mother, for crissakes.'"

"I'm knowing a thing or two about Gerda's spending habits from back when. She near put Knut into bankruptcy, near lost him that piece of land he bought from Lydia."

"When? How do you know that, Emma?"

241

"I been doing for all the Hansens and other folks out this way so long, I know near most everything there is to know, including a little about Gerda thinking she'd become a Hansen after Knut died, but Karli wasn't much interested."

Gerda? Become a Hansen? She wanted to ask Emma about that, but Joyce was returning to the table.

Emma said, "That's something that'll keep for another day. Might be we should talk about that daughter of yours, entertaining that reporter like she's known him all her life. He's smitten, but that don't mean she needs to go falling for him."

Keep for another day? Kelda blinked, aware she had much to ponder, and said, "Reva told me she's 'exercising caution.' She does seem a bit smitten herself, though."

"Reva said that? 'Exercising caution?' I swear, that girl's getting more like you, Kelda. She's a caution herself at times, just like you."

"Just what does that mean, Emma? I've always wondered, when you've said that."

"Why, it means you're just about too special for words."

*Never cut what you can untie. - Joseph Joubert, 1754-1824.*
*French man of letters who wrote on philosophical, moral & literary topics.*

# 32

## THE LANDING

The Hansen basement, where Karli's trunk awaited opening, felt chilly to Kelda, especially after a walk out onto the dock in the warm May morning sun. She'd consumed too much coffee and spent too much time worrying about the trunk's contents. Overhead, Emma vacuumed with a fury, cleaning up after the houseful they'd had the night before. Ragnar fiddled with the trunk lock. Raymond stood off to the side, statue-stiff, a reluctant participant in what he said should be a private family moment. They'd argued about family, its complex definitions. Raymond spouted law and Kelda countered with sociological family theory, until they looped around to the Old-ones and Indian Joe.

"Your grandfather, who I now know as Joe Williams, and my grandparents were family because they grew to rely on one another. They held dear and close the same values for land and spirit. They traded food, labored together, shared joys and griefs, and they remained close for a long period of time."

"We don't know that. That's pure conjecture."

"Oh, Raymond, stick that back in your law book. *I* know that because I helped my mother rewrite all the Old-one's journals. Indian Joe is all over in them. He brought fish and clams and oysters. He taught them how Indians rake smelt and smoke salmon. He helped them bury their three daughters. He brought Magna bundles of dried vanilla-leaf to scent the house and keep flies and mosquitoes away."

"Vanilla leaf?"

"You know, that fan-shaped plant that smells like vanilla . . . three leaves . . . white spiky flower that's blooming right now. There's some over by the fairyslippers."

"Oh, deer foot. I've always called it deer foot."

"Deer foot, vanilla leaf, whatever. I wonder why we stopped using it. Most people couldn't gather enough, but we could here, at the Landing."

"I'll bring you some."

"See? That's just what your grandfather did for my grandmother. That's family."

A tool clanked on the cement floor. Kelda gasped, and Raymond's cane jumped. Ragnar grinned at them.

"There, it's open, figure lock's good as new."

They gathered by the trunk, inspected the lock, a distraction from what really mattered. Kelda's heart pounded she took a good look at the lock. Her uncle had chiseled and chipped to salvage it and the trunk for future use. Pure Ragnar. She took his left hand, laced fingers with him, grabbed Raymond's right hand and squeezed.

"Open it, Uncle Ragnar."

A mothball-must odor wafted into the air. An army uniform of heavy, drab brown wool covered the trunk's contents. Dust motes danced in the slice of light from a small window

Ragnar ran his hand over the uniform jacket. "Gunnar's. World War I. I was but ten years old when word came that Gunnar died in Europe, in France fighting Germans. I didn't understand war. Still don't. Used to be I hated Germans, but time went on and 'fore long there were too many others to hate, so I gave that up. Takes too much energy, hate."

Ragnar swiped at his face, like one does if an insect lights there. Kelda took her hands back from both men, and helped Ragnar lift the uniform out of the trunk, stirring up more mustiness. Under it the huge empty eyes and misshapen snout of a gas mask stared up at them. It rested in a hard hat turned upside down, so it looked like a corpse stretched out.

Kelda gasped, let go her hold on the uniform, and stepped back onto Raymond's foot.

"Easy," Raymond said, a hand on her arm. Like the night before, his hand transmitted a current. Ragnar was arranging the uniform over Karli's grinding wheel, draping dog tags atop it.

"I'd 'most forgotten Karli made up this collection. Magna wanted only the tags."

A canvas army bag came next. Ragnar lifted up the bag, soiled, cracking along its folds.

"Mess kit, canteen, Sterno." He swiped at his face again. "Damn it all to hell, there's memories flying around down here, acting like mosquitos." He set the bag aside, lifted out the first of several brown cardboard boxes stacked in one corner of the trunk.

Kelda pulled up the flaps. "Our old blocks. Uncle Karli made them from scraps and sanded them smooth." She caressed the wood pieces stained from children's hands and Karli's workshop floor where grease and oil from assorted machines mixed with sawdust. Her eyes moved to the next box in the trunk. It had its top flaps tucked one under the other to make a stable lid.

PROPERTY OF JOE WILLIAMS was printed with grease pencil across the flaps.

Ragnar pursed his lips and nodded. "Next one would belong to you, Walkingstick. Go on, lift it out."

Raymond draped the cane over his arm, picked up the box, looked for a place to set it down. His hands shook.

"Here." Kelda pulled up a heavy oak stool Karli had sat on when he filed saws. Raymond looked like a child waiting for an adult to say it's okay to open a Christmas package. "Would you like to open it now? Or would you rather save it for when you're alone?"

"No. No, I want you here, both of you." He looked at them, snapped open the flaps, lifted out a sheet of paper, scanned it, closed his eyes. "Kelda, will you read it?"

She took the paper, a typical Uncle Karli piece of paper from the tablet he kept on his workbench, stained and yellowed with age. A faint cedar scent rose from it. The first notation, in Karli's open, loopy hand, had been written with a fountain pen and ink. ome of the letters had run a bit.

>*August 1943: My friend Joe asked me to hold these things in a safe, dry place for his grandson, Raymond Williams, until the boy's grown a bit, not so dependent on his mother's wishes. Seems Joe and his daughter Clara don't see eye-to-eye on things. Joe says his time is near, he's expecting to hear the owl call his name.*

Kelda looked up. "The next part's written with a different pen, did you notice? With a ballpoint, not a fountain pen, so it must be a lot later, but there's no date."

"Just read it, *kär a.*"

>*I went to the tribe to look up Raymond, asking for Edward Morse like Lydia told me. Found Clara, the boy's mother. She's not doing so well. Far as I could learn, the boy's in Korea, like Lydia thought. No one at the tribe claims to know any Joe Williams, not even Clara, but that's tribal. They learned a long time ago to know nothing about anything when white men come around.*

Karli had drawn a line under that paragraph and written another with yet another pen.

>*Indian Joe's gone and so's Lydia, and nobody seems to know what came of Raymond Williams (or Edward Morse). If he's not found, after I'm gone, these should go to the Suquamish tribe. They're museum quality, far as I can tell. Indian Joe made them himself. Made the hand adze in my workshop, and sharpened the other blades on my grinding wheel. He left his digging stick for me, and two canoe paddles for Raymond. I use the digging stick, only way I get clams nowadays. The canoe paddles are too big for the trunk. They're wrapped and stored with the maple burls and some good redwood underneath the main workbench, unless another Hansen has moved them. I'm not pretending to know my time is coming the same as Indian Joe knew, not being a true Indian, but he taught me things, and I'm getting messages, so I'm*

*packing up. I'd like whoever gets these things to know Indian Joe was*
*as close to me as my closest brothers, Ragnar and Rolf.*

Kelda read the last through tears for Karli. He'd been a good man who sometimes drank too much. She sniffed, swiped her face with a tissue and looked at Raymond. He seemed bathed in light, more luminous than the old overhead fluorescents could generate.

Raymond lifted an item from the box, caressed it, spoke softly to the item more than to Ragnar and Kelda. "I remember using this. It's a canoe bailer. I remember being in the canoe with . . . him, my grandfather. He let me bail. Canoes took on water, especially in storms." He turned the bailer over, rubbed it's under surface, turned it back, inspected the cedar bark strips that lashed its handle to its base. "I tried to make one once, when we lived at the inlet. I couldn't get it right."

He took the bailer and his cane, and walked away.

"He'll be needing some time," Ragnar said. "We found the digging stick, here on the wall. I knew soon's he touched it that it belonged in his hands. I'm thinking I know where to look for them canoe paddles."

Kelda stood frozen, fingers pinching an earlobe where she'd forgotten to put in an earring, stuck somewhere in processing and sorting information her brain had been gathering of late. Like a canoe taking on water, her brain had gotten swamped.

"Uncle, when you said something about the inlet going back to the Indians, did you mean to the tribe?"

"Now I'm knowing for certain Walkingstick comes from Diggingstick, I'm meaning just one Indian."

"Why didn't you know all this information that Karli recorded?"

"Now Kelda, you'd be remembering Karli. He stayed close to home lots of days, making furniture, tinkering in that workshop, sharpening saws for other folks. He and Indian Joe dug clams for selling. Fished some. Sold smelt, and oysters too, back when folks could trust other folks to handle things right. Karli's legs and back got stove up when that rebel log got him, and him still young, you'd be knowing that."

"Yes, I remember." She remembered other things about Karli. He liked to read and write, and he told wonderful stories.

"Now me, I was the one kept taking down trees, taking down trees, must be why I'm the one who lived to put a few back." He turned, took another box out of the trunk, this one a gift box like sweaters or shirts come in, with *Bremers* in raised letters on the lid. "Might just as well keep digging. Here, you open this one, I'll look in the other looks just like it."

"Bremers." Bremerton's fine department store, long since closed, once connected with Frederick and Nelson in Seattle, also closed. She removed the lid to see an assortment of letters, loose photos, a pocket-size notebook and a hand-tooled leather wallet. She set the box on the stool, opened the notebook, flipped through the pages. "Notes about homebrew making." She laughed, a light sound similar to what she'd heard from Reva the night before.

The twin box Ragnar opened had similar contents plus a beaded handbag with a long silver chain. Kelda pictured Lydia in a twenties hairdo and fringed dress with such a bag bouncing from her shoulder while she danced. Ragnar opened it, removed a piece of paper and handed it to Kelda.

"Karli's writing again. *Found in cottages after some Seattle folks had a party. Never claimed.*" Kelda sneezed, and said, "The only thing I ever found in the cottages was moldy bread and dirty socks."

"*Ja*, and heaps of other's left behinds not worth the effort burning took. We'd better take these up to the great-room, and these last things, too."

Kelda looked in the trunk. A huge, leather-clad dictionary and a rectangular wood box covered the bottom. She touched the dictionary, then lifted it out. Lydia had salvaged it from the old school and given it to Karli for his crosswords. She remembered it sitting in his workshop on a table alongside an old overstuffed chair.

"Over two-thousand pages, I remember." She held it while Ragnar removed the last item, a box made of walnut, about fourteen inches by twenty-four inches, and four or five inches deep. It had brass hinges and clasps.

"Are you remembering this from Karli's workshop, *kär a*?

"Yes," she said, her voice just a whisper, her heart pounding so hard her jaw ached. "He kept it on a high shelf. He said it held some truths."

"Truth's best left untold," Ragnar said. "*Ja*, I'm just remembering that too, just now, holding onto it."

"He always laughed, and even danced about a bit . . ."

"Like Indian war-dances in the movies."

"Sometimes with an old blanket draped over his shoulders."

"And his eyes twinkling. Must be full of love letters from all them lady-friends he had."

"Yes, I'm sure that's what it is."

"We go upstairs now, *kär a*."

"To the great-room. We'll open it in the great-room, Uncle Ragnar."

# 33

# Raymond

Raymond Walkingstick hadn't intended to head for the inlet, but that's where he found himself. He leaned against a cedar tree, breathed perfume the sun drew from its branches and stared out at the horizon just as he'd leaned and stared hours on end as a child.

Now, canoe bailer in his hands, he knew he'd been watching for a canoe with a white-haired man, hoping the man brought two paddles so the boy could use one. Those times the man came, he spoke words the boy didn't understand. The man said it did not matter, for his words were directed not to the boy's ears but to his spirit.

After his mother took Lucy and him back to the Suquamish tribe, Raymond went every day to the tribe's beach and stared out at the water. One day, a low-tide day, he walked along the beach, left reservation land, crossed privately owned land, climbed up banks and down again along Agate Passage and beyond to a spot called Point Bolin, a distance of three miles. Quite a distance for a boy, it seemed at the time.

There he sat on the beach of another piece of reservation land, and remembered a time he passed the point in a canoe with his grandfather. As he sat there, a boy much confused by the world, he saw a vision of his grandfather, and heard him speak the words he hadn't understood then, words imprinted in his brain.

*There is a place few of our people know or care to use. I will show you, my grandson, so you will find your way when it is time. Go first to the grave of our chief, now called Chief Seattle, and look to where the sun rises. Put a canoe in the water there. Paddle south and west along the shore until it turns to west and north. Enter that passage at its middle, and paddle west and north past the place called Keyport, where white men make torpedoes to rip through ships of their enemy. Go on beyond the place called Keyport, and the next point, still dark with trees. Enter the small water, and you will find a welcome place where the salmon go to leave their spirit. Step out onto the shore facing toward the rising sun. That place you may call home as long as Hansens own it. They are my white brothers.*

His grandfather had called him to that point that day to say goodbye. To transfer his spirit. But the boy had been known as Edward Morse, already confused by a world more white than Indian, more complex than fishing and digging clams. The grandfather's spirit had to wait while the boy found his way to the place where body and spirit could join.

Raymond Walkingstick looked out at the water and let the emotions he'd long buried emerge. He expected tears, but heard keening, singing, words that meant nothing to his ears but everything to his soul.

All through his reawakening, and for some time after, his eyes stayed on the water, the place where he'd known his grandfather. Raymond Walkingstick watched a canoe paddled by a rusty faced, white haired man and an almond skinned, black haired boy. As he watched, the boy grew and the man shrank, the boy's hair softened from black to silver, the man's hair lengthened and twisted down his back, until two figures were one, and the canoe brought the one to shore.

## 34
## Hansens of the Landing

Karli's box held an assortment of notebooks, most pocket size, one school paper size, a couple in between. Kelda wanted to study each, weigh its worth, its reason for being locked away in the trunk for all these years. Wanting to know fought fear of learning something better left unknown; her teeth clamped tight, as if that barred portal protected her brain and heart. For a moment she closed her eyes, then opened them and stood as close as possible to Ragnar.

He opened one of the smallest notebooks, read the first page, fanned through it, shook his head, just one shake. He looked at her again and grinned.

"Poetry. Karli liked poetry. Used to get Lydia to read to him. We all liked that, Lydia reading to us. Gathered around in the great-room like a kinder class. Karli borrowed her books, saying he liked to read while he sipped his homebrew. Read some before he turned out the lights at night." He shook his head again. "Look to be copied."

He set the notebook on the table, outside the walnut box, outside the fortress walls. Its secrets revealed, it no longer needed protection.

Kelda reached into the box and selected another small notebook bound at the top like the first. She lifted the cover for a quick peek and felt rigidity melt from her jaw. "Robert Frost."

"Ah, yes, much our favorite for Lydia to read."

The stack of small notebooks outside the box grew. How quickly they'd learned the pattern—how quickly they'd come to trust it. Small top-bound notebooks equaled secrets long known, poets' souls, not Hansens', bared.

Their removal uncovered a larger, cloth-bound tome. Folio, it proclaimed in Old-English gold. With the weight of other notebooks removed its cover eased up a millimeter or so, papers crammed between its pages begging to be read. Kelda startled, as if a jack-in-the-box leapt out. One hand flew to cover her heart that beat too fast, or perhaps beat not at all.

"There would be some order, this being Karli's." Ragnar lifted the Folio, from the box; light glinted from its gilt-edge pages. He opened the cover.

*Words of Truth and Soberness, and No Bad Intent*
*We Are the Sons of Hansen's Landing*
*It is Our Land to Protect for*
*Future Generations*

Ragnar, as the last Hansen son at the Landing, hadn't meant to abandon responsibility when he'd decided to take to his bed. He'd been worrying about the dwindling bank accounts and increasing taxes, and no way in sight to save the land. He'd figured once he'd bought out Erik and Greg's shares Kelda would have to give in to Arne, let him develop the Landing, better Arne doing it than someone not at all connected to Hansens.

Better Ragnar didn't live to witness that. But then Lydia moved into his head. She'd found Walkingstick, sent him to the Landing, sure as sunrise. She was here now, reading him a poem that comforted him. He couldn't get the words, he was that tied up inside, but he got the comfort sure enough. Something of Frost's about a tree, just the part about never letting the curtain be drawn, but special to him and Lydia in another way.

Kelda's presence calmed the turmoil stirred up by Karli's words. *In truth and soberness*, a Karli saying borrowed from the Old-ones.

"Work hard and tell the truth," their father often said when they were boys. Or so it translated from the Norwegian. They'd studied Norwegian at the church school in the early grades, but then Poulsbo schools and the church dropped the requirement and the Old-ones practiced English at home, wanting to be part of their new country. Ragnar had forgotten most of the old language now, just as he'd forgotten some of the truths.

Lies, now they were another matter. They stuck around, got twisted, mostly carried bad intent, and came back to worry. Or maybe never went away in the first place.

He turned a page, prepared to read what truths required soberness for Karli to fill so many pages. First, a postscript written in the shakier hand of Karli's later years.

*I fear we joked about Wally's death once too often in Gerda Hedstrom's presence. About all of us having a hand in his murder. This story is the truth. Karli Hansen ~*

## The Death of Wallace Taylor

The death of Wallace Taylor marked a bad time for the Landing and for Hansens. Most of us didn't much care for Wally or his doings, and maybe even said some things like, 'Served him right,' when we got the news. Might be that's how we all had a hand in it, his murder by person or persons unknown. Might be we could have stopped it from happening if we'd done some things differently.

I tried to get Lydia to do this writing for me, but she said some things come more honest between a man and a piece of paper if they're direct, like the pen knows what the man is feeling, not just what he's thinking. Lydia spoke some words to me, a quote from John Donne: . . . *every man's death diminishes me, because I am involved in mankind; and therefore never send to know for whom the bell tolls; it tolls for thee.*

She got me to read Hemingway's novel, too. It sets a man to thinking on how events come to be, who lives and who dies. Wally died, and here's the best sense I can make of it.

I believe Wally's death was related to alcohol and money. He died in 1932, the thirteenth year of prohibition in a country where alcohol need and want met up with money need and want. Those of us who knew Wally watched his misbehavior, his 'continuing moral decline' Lydia called it, but did little or naught to stop it. And then one day much like any other, Wally's body, dressed out in a suit, washed up on a beach on Bainbridge Island.

The next day the FBI had a list of suspects that included all of us at the Landing, and near half the population of Kitsap County. In the end, when the FBI gave up, most of us went on suspecting some others, and doing little to prove our own innocence for fear it might prove a friend's guilt. In that sense, we all had a hand in his death, or so I'm thinking.

Olive Taylor, Wally's wife, was the first questioned by the FBI. Olive was a mere slip of a woman, and that ruled her out, unless she hired it done. Which is what they poked at. Still, one of the G-men kept saying, "She bore four children. That takes some uncommon strength." Turned out that man's wife died in childbirth.

They were right when they said Olive had reason to be miffed at Wally. He'd leave her tending both the garage and the children while he went off drinking and dancing. Now, Olive was a smart woman, she knew what went on with Wally slipping in and out of beds where he didn't belong, and she didn't much like it. She'd have liked leaving him and moving home, but her widowed mother had sold off most of the old homestead by that time. Only a small house remained, and it poorly heated, what with reliance on neighbors to provide firewood and cut and stack it in the bargain.

Thus, Olive did what needed doing to keep those children fed and clothed, and gave up fighting with Wally over his comings and goings. She likely paid even less mind when he slipped out in a rowboat in the dark of a cloudy night. She knew he bought bootleg whiskey and sold it too. Could be she showed him how to burn sugar to a caramel color to make the stuff look more like whiskey, less like moonshine.

It's for certain Wally's death cut into the money Olive had for those children, but more folks picked up bread and milk at the little store they kept alongside the garage after his death than before. Once Olive took over, she turned that wee store into what's now called a minimart, and she got all four through high school, each of them helping out with clerking and pumping gas.

Olive swore she'd no idea who would want to kill Wally, or why for that matter, but she knew right enough that the man packed around money in those leather pouches. She knew, and she took out what she needed when Wally fell asleep after his nights out. Looking back now, I'd say Olive thrived after Wally's death, but not enough so folks would think she'd killed him for the money he'd been carrying that day. But she didn't do much mourning. Some folks found that suspicious.

Right away, the agents got just as interested in the bootleg as in the murder. They sure wanted to find the men who made the whiskey Wally passed along to them who bottled and sold but, far as I know, no one ever gave up a name. There was more than one good still in the woods here and about. More than one good family connected to them.

Lots of folks went cold-stone sober real fast after Wally's death, and stayed that way a good long time. No sense risking a drive, or even a hike, into deep woods. No telling who watched and who'd tell what they saw. There's some prominent Poulsbo families likely don't know they come from bootleg backgrounds, or that bootleg paid for their Sunday shoes and barrettes for their hair. Or, maybe they do know now but just don't bother talking. Some truths are best left untold.

If you go by Lydia's measure, all those folks had a hand in Wally's death. They needed customers, their families liked the money, and Wally was about the best customer any of them ever had. Still, some of them grumbled about that part, too, his being a good customer, because he took their product for a price deemed fair in those times. But then Wally watered the drink, so the story goes, and if he got a complaint from a customer, he blamed the manufacturer, not himself.

Bootleggers got wind of that, but they kept their peace. What else could they do? Kill the man? Well, maybe they did, though that doesn't make good sense. Wally got the product from distillers who didn't want their names or sites known. The FBI gnawed on that idea a good long time, but they couldn't prove it without finding the bootleggers themselves. Oh, they rousted out a few suspects here and there, but nobody who made enough to meet Wally's needs.

Wally's sister, Ruthie, got questioned about ten different times, new questions on each occasion. The G-men, agents they called themselves, really liked going after her. She was a pretty woman, though not so pretty as Lydia Berg, and she didn't have much of what you'd call feminine wiles, so they figured out right off that she didn't much like her brother.

I've wondered since what Wally did to Ruth when they were younger, besides make fun of her health problems, but I'll have to keep wondering. Ruth's mind couldn't find the truth of that now if she wanted it to. But the thing was, she didn't go about mourning his death like a sister might be expected to mourn. In fact, she seemed glad to be shed of him, so the FBI agents saw guilt written all over her. Even some years later, when time changed the view, Ruth still had little good to say about Wallace, and some folks find that doesn't add up to innocent.

Wally's parents are another story. They moaned and cried and carried on enough for themselves and Ruth. Most of us, Ruthie included, figured Wally passed along some of the money he made on that watered-down, burned-sugar-colored whiskey, and the older Taylors missed that after his death. They quit caring about the man for himself or as their son, they just cared for the money he brought by. That might clear them to the FBI's way of looking at things, but it makes them guilty in the moral column. Or so I figure from what Lydia taught me.

We Hansens were next on the list, all four of us, because Ruthie spent so much time here, and Wally came and went by car and boat. They figured he could be using the Landing dock. They even questioned Lydia, still a Berg then. One true fact I learned from that, men don't quite know what to think when they run up against a woman smart as Lydia. She could talk circles right around them, and poke holes in most of their theories. She and Ruthie both spent a good amount of time at the Landing.

There were four of us Hansens living here then, more or less. Rolf had his cabin down in Brownsville, but he stayed close by to see the rest of us through that ordeal, him being the oldest of those of us left here. He put up more smoke screens than a mess of slash burns on a rainy day, but the G-men (agents, I'm meaning) caught on to the beer making out here in the shed. I called it a workshop even then, before we put up that fourth wall, but they figured a three-sided building's nothing more than a lean-to.

But before they found the beer they picked at Lydia's life-long friendship with Ruthie, and then on the ins and outs of the Hansens' fondness for Lydia. They figured out before we did that we were all in love with her, and they tried to make something of that, get us riled, get us to say something against one another. All they ever got was a wall four Hansens wide, and little to nothing about Wallace Taylor.

"Your brother Olav's been heard to threaten Mr. Taylor at a dance," agent Clayborne, the lead man, said over and over. "Said Taylor would have him and his brothers to answer to unless he stayed away from Lydia Berg. I'm guessing that means Olav didn't want Mr. Taylor dancing with Lydia." Then he'd grin and poke a kitchen match in his mouth.

"You got it wrong," I told Clayborne. "The threat came from Wally hanging around where Lydia taught school, trying to talk her out of the car she drove. It was a Hansen car, and Wally wanted to borrow it. She'd have it now and then to carry some things between her place and the Landing. Wally'd given up on getting the car from us, figured he could get it from Lydia easier. But she took good care of property, hers or others, and wouldn't go loaning away something wasn't hers in the first place."

"Why you figure he'd want to borrow your car, he had a car of his own? Plus a garage with others easy enough to use anytime he chose.?"

"You're the agent, you'd know better than me, but the way I figure, Wally used his car for his garage business but other folks' cars for his side business. Wasn't unusual to see Wally behind someone else's wheel."

Next, they got after me about my lady friends. I'm not one to deny I liked the ladies, but I put myself in a different class from Wallace Taylor. First off, if I took one as my wife, that would be it, I wouldn't be courting others. Second, any woman another man took as his wife wasn't available for courting. Now, having a turn around the dance floor with a married woman's an okay thing, far as I can see, long as it ends at dancing.

There was a time Wally took an interest in a widow woman I'd taken to, and that led to some gossip. Clayborne kept peeking under that rug looking for more dirt, but he didn't find much. That's when they come after all of us here at the Landing pretty heavy for our brew making, but home-made beer didn't violate the law quite the same as bootleg whiskey, not if you didn't sell it. One of the G-men, not Clayborne, even sipped a glass of brew with me, after they'd more or less given up their investigation. Clayborne smashed a few bottles when he found out they themselves had a worth. Bottles were hard to come by in those times.

No Hansen man was dumb enough to keep much beer, or empty bottles for that matter, stored in one place. The smaller crocks was stored neat and clean beside the dills and bread-and butters. By the time the snooping got to us, one of the crocks held our sauerkraut. We'd put it into jars and sealed it up once, but it didn't take much imagination to dump it back into the crock. Ragnar's the one did that, and he's the one sealed it up in jars all over again once the FBI pulled out of here.

One true fact, no Hansen ever sold any brew. Now trading, that's another matter, but all you need to do is read history of the times. Folks helped folks make it through the bad times, and those were some bad times. No one was buying timber, no one was building houses. Most of the brew we traded went to our closest neighbors. Old missus Carlson liked a little glass along with her dinner. We'd tuck a bottle or two in a sack of spuds or a box of apples. She'd send back a cake or a quilt, or mend the sheets for the cottages. That woman could make a mend you'd never spot. That's neighborliness, plain and simple.

That trading never found light of day, but trading with Indian Joe did, and was neither him nor Hansens gave up that news. That's where I'd have to say those G-men earned their money doing some detecting. Those were Blacklist times. Indians couldn't legally buy alcohol, not even beer, before or after Prohibition. The agents kept poking at that one. Guess they figured if they couldn't find a murderer or a bootlegger at the Landing, they could get us for alcohol sales to Indians.

That didn't pan out for them either, but they tripped over another piece of information. There'd been an Indian boy turned up dead in a ravine out toward Hansville. There was some talk at the time that the boy, Frank was his name, was related to Indian Joe. I never found out. Indian Joe said all the tribe were related, all people were related somehow, which fits with Lydia's ideas. He called us his white brothers. He'd been around the Landing longer than any of us, he remembered us being born, but we didn't know much about his family, except for the bit he told me. I knew he had a daughter name of Clara. I knew it was her who came to live for a time at the inlet and then in this workshop.

Anyway, as for Frank, not last name known, some kids found him. He'd bled to death in the car, which he'd stolen from a dance hall. Then somehow that led to more sad news. Frank had a sister named Sarah, and she had a young girl-child that turned up drowned in a creek out by Indianola. Indian Joe said there was some talk of the child being half-white, and Wally's name came up as the father.

No one accused the Suquamish, or any particular Indian, of killing Wally, but some said it made more sense than the other theories. Some, the same ones for the most part, say Indians were seen on the ferry that night that Wally went overboard and left behind his car. They like to think the tribe's that close, a wrong done to one's the same as a wrong done to all, and could be they're right. I'll be long dead and cold before any at the tribe talk to the FBI.

There's some who say the G-men found out Wally provided whiskey to the reservation, so they turned their investigation on looking for alcohol at the tribe and run up against silence. There's others say Wally did the country a favor, just give it time. Alcohol will destroy the Indians. Blacklist laws have changed now, and alcohol's done its share of harm to the Indians just like it's done to Norwegians, truth be told.

There's one more story deserves telling. Clayborne, the G-man who poked around here the most, went to Rolf's place in Brownsville to snoop, ask some questions about Rolf's reputation as an avid hunter, insinuating Rolf was a killer. "Wouldn't waste a bullet on Wallace Taylor," Rolf said.

"Man was strangled, not shot," Clayborne answered.

"Only thing I ever wrestled to death's a bear," Rolf said, and invited the man in to see his bear skin. Rolf says Clayborne went over that hide looking for a bullet hole.

"Proves you've got the strength," Clayborne said.

"*Nei*, only proves I was that hungry. Hansens only kill in season, and only what they can eat."

Then Clayborne asked him what he'd take for the skin.

"It's yours no charge when you leave the county, long as you're gone tomorrow and don't try taking any Hansens or any Indians with you."

I still don't know who killed Wallace Taylor, but I admit to not missing him. Lydia thinks that Wally just got a little oiled-up (my words, not Lydia's) that day in Seattle, and started throwing money around a private saloon that no one admitted existed. She thinks Wally's murder was done by a person or persons who saw the opportunity and acted on it.

Some of us wondered why the killers didn't steal the car, but Lydia explained that they mightn't have known how to drive, or more likely, just wanted to stay on the ferry for the return trip to Seattle where they could get some more of the whiskey they were likely drinking with Wally.

At any rate, Wally's widow and the oldest boy both learned to drive and used Wally's car to make small deliveries for the store. The boy had been tinkering with cars all his life, and took up garage work, not that many could afford to pay for what most of us knew how to do ourselves.

About a year later, Rolf got a letter from Clayborne asking if he'd part with the bear skin since they never made an arrest. Rolf wrote back, polite as could be, that he'd since given it to a widow-lady friend for her parlor, though I know it was old missus Carlson, and she kept it alongside her bed. Said it felt good on her feet, and if anyone came prowling in the night she figured she'd just drape it around herself and growl.

Karli Hansen (Karl to them outside the family)

*The apparent serenity of the past is an oil spread by time. - Lloyd Frankenberg, 1907-1975.*
*American poet & poetry critic; author & editor of literary biographies and anthologies.*

# 35
# Kelda

Kelda remembered the bear skin rug, remembered, too, the younger Mrs. Carlson demanding it be removed right after the old lady's funeral. Rolf took it back, put it on the floor in the small extra bedroom where he kept a mounted deer head, a stuffed beaver, assorted horns and racks, a heap of tanned deer hides ready for making slippers or gloves, and other memorabilia of a bachelor's life.

Kelda hated that room as a child, hated being watched over by the deer's glassy eyes, hated the coldness and smells she associated with death.

The day she found Rolf dead his entire house had that cold feel and death smell. Her arms went goose-bumpy as she shivered with the memories.

"Too bad we can't just tuck Rolf in here with his things, out beside the girls under Magna's cedar trees," Ragnar had said, but they'd buried him in the old cemetery, close to the Old-ones. There'd been some talk of moving the infant girls' graves at that time, but that remained worrisome. What would be left to move now, eighty or more years later? Even cedar coffins would likely be rotted away.

She, Ragnar and Karli had packed up all Rolf's things, closed his house and sold the land, after a time, to help pay the Landing's taxes. "Are Rolf's things still around?" Kelda asked. "The rug, and the deer head and hides?"

"*Ja*, in the basement, one place or another, musty smelling by now."

The basement. Filled with Hansen history, the foundation of a family also getting a little musty. Kelda lifted one eyebrow and looked at her uncle. "Who do you think killed Wallace Taylor? Now that you've read Karli's account again?"

Ragnar held the Folio, and glanced at the portrait of the Old-ones. "I'm not one to say a man deserves murder, but I think one that goes so long unsolved tells its own tale."

Kelda smiled. Those Hansens could still form a wall. She could cajole and wheedle, but she'd gotten all she'd ever get from her uncle on that topic. She opened one of the loose papers tucked into Karli's Folio. An accounting of a loan to Knut Hedstrom, signed by both men, *Paid* and the date written across the figures and signatures. At the bottom, a more recently dated note, just months before Karli's death:

> *This one for past-due property taxes Gerda hadn't paid. Knut figures he's to blame, he didn't keep up with the bills. Him and me both sunk money into that boat building company in Tacoma, long since gone bankrupt. Sunk money, sunk the whole business, it seems.*

"This one? Are there more?" She pulled out other loose sheets, opened and read them. All loans to Knut, some marked *Paid*, some marked *Forgiven on Death*. All with notes added after Knut's death, some with an explanation of the loan, others just Karli's thoughts, several about that boat-building business in Tacoma.

> *Gerda's got some notion Hansens owe her a piece of the Landing. Ragnar and me returned all Knut's tools he'd left from time to time. Gerda thinks there's more should be his. He never mentioned the boat-builder business, so I'm keeping quiet.*
>
> *Gerda's a determined woman, bent on becoming a Hansen, but I'm not getting caught in that game. Now she's pulling strings to get our Kelda to marry Arne, that's clear to me. Arne's decent enough, takes after his dad.*

*Reason I kept these papers, I figure they're Norwegian insurance.*

Ragnar patted her hand as they read, patted and patted.

Kelda said, "I know that, about Gerda pulling the strings to get Arne to marry me. I've just finally taken those strings out of her hands and given them back to Arne."

"*Ja*, you're a Hansen, you do what needs doing."

"But I didn't know about their hope to get a boat built."

"They paid good money to have their designs drawn up professional, more good money to get that Tacoma outfit to do the building. Karli never said how much money. Boat builder went bankrupt, I'm remembering that, now. Remembering how Gerda set her sights on Karli, but he never took to her that way."

"A woman scorned. Did Gerda pursue Karli out of desire, do you think? Or just as a means to own a share of the Landing?"

"Karli had a way with women, truth be known, but Gerda wasn't one who cared much for men. Her desire was more for the land."

"The other . . . Norwegian insurance? Karli meant . . ." She hesitated, watched Ragnar nod.

"To help you against Gerda, I'm thinking, if need should come. Legal need, like. Karli said some things back when he sealed up the trunk. My mind's not so good, I'm not remembering all I should."

"I remember something he said to me. I was disgusted with Gerda, I can't even remember why, and he warned me that sons can be like their mothers."

She looked at Ragnar, and then at the room, the great-room, a sanctuary, where other memories lingered. "And then another time he said something about me being drawn to men who can work with their hands. That's true, it comes from growing up with men who can do anything, and Uncle Karli said, 'Arne's good with his hands, true enough, but Gerda's got other plans for Arne.' I remember that, things like that."

"*Ja*, we all worried, you with no mother, Olav dead before you were born. We all knew sorrow can come with love. Karli said his worries out-loud more. The beer helped him say what maybe we all thought."

Karli's wisdom, spoken over a glass of homebrew. She'd focused on the beer, heard it as 'beer talk,' and discounted the wisdom. "I spent twenty-five years in a marriage that shouldn't have happened."

"*Nei, kär a,* that's not the truth. The marriage brought us your daughters."

"Lauren's so much like Arne. No, like Gerda." Her uncle had his arms around her now, comforting her like she was a child. In a sense, in that moment, she was a child. She relaxed into the comfort.

"Lauren has a piece of growing to do. Might be she'll take a lesson from Reva."

"I doubt it. Lauren's older." She separated from her uncle, found a tissue in her pocket, wiped her tears, planted a kiss where Ragnar missed a couple gray whiskers when he shaved.

"And Reva's wiser. In the end, wisdom will out." He nodded, one good nod.

"Whatever happened to the rowboats? There used to be rowboats here. Magna's and Karli's and yours. Rowboats and rowing them are good for sorting thoughts."

Her mind had been doing that of late, moving from one thing to another without a bridge, leaving others to find their way between one spoken thought and the next. She wanted a rowboat, wanted the peace and solitude of floating on the bay, rowing from the dock to the inlet like she'd done as a child, first sitting on Ragnar or Karli's lap, finally being trusted to take the boat around the point herself. One of the uncles always waited at the inlet. She frowned, wondering if they crept along in the woods, watching her row, but made it look like they'd just gone across to the inlet to wait.

"I s'pect I can find a rowboat. Parts of rowboats. There's things yet uncovered in that basement and out in Karli's workshop. Need to clean that shop out, deed that land to Walkingstick, don't you think?"

"Yes. Do you think he can afford the taxes?" Just like that. She said 'Yes' just like that to giving away part of the Landing. It's what had been on Ragnar's mind since she'd first come back home. Before, even, she guessed. It felt right. Raymond would be a good neighbor, a good steward for the land.

"Ah, now comes Emma, kicking up dust." Ragnar had narrowed his eyes to focus, looking over the reading glasses perched on his nose

She picked up Karli's Folio. "There's more to read."

"*Ja*, we keep reading, Emma can start somewhere else."

They watched Emma come into the great-room, watched her eyes take in the two of them with Karli's notebooks.

"Well, you two keep at what you're doing, I'll stick with the kitchen and cleaning."

Ragnar shook his head, one shake, and grinned. They read an emotion-packed letter to a child Karli believed he'd fathered, but who grew to manhood in another man's family. "Who?" she asked, but Ragnar shook his head, an I-don't-know head shake. After that, several pages held sketches of boats Karli wanted to build.

"Good drawings," Kelda said.

"*Ja*, good boats. But too expensive for the times. Fiberglass came along, you know, and wood boats went, just like that, right along with the builders."

"They're coming back." Kelda turned the page, read a goodbye letter to a woman Karli had loved and watched die after an accident. She'd been hit by a drunk driver in a time when such acts were forgiven by reason of drunkenness. He'd sat in the hospital in Bremerton for two days, hoping.

*Not one drop of brew for two days, plus, and then too many drops, but sorrow doesn't drown so easy.*

Kelda massaged her temples. "I can't read any more just now." She knew more about the Old-ones than about the generation just ahead of her, the one that reared her and released her into the world. She needed to give this new reading time.

Raymond returned, knocked on the great-room door, came in still carrying the canoe bailer. His eyes had softened. His cane dangled from his arm when he walked in, and though he limped his walk looked steady enough. His eyes fixed on Kelda, and she felt little pins sticking her flesh.

"Raymond, you're giving off static electricity. I think I'll fix something to eat." She pushed away from the table and whatever she read, almost read, in Raymond's eyes.

The vacuum cleaner hummed from the living room. The old kitchen clock ticked. She dug in the freezer, found the ham bone she'd frozen after Easter dinner, put it in a soup pot, poured in dried lima beans and a chunk of onion, covered it with cold water, set it to cook. Found some celery tops, and tossed them in. Good course ground pepper. Started dough for oatmeal-honey bread for rolls, she thought, using quick rising yeast. The dough smelled good, alive. Growing, not dying.

Emma came into the kitchen, fussed, washed up things. The men talked in the great-room. Kelda heard snatches of conversation, some of it about Wallace Taylor, some arguing over land.

"Not without paying for it I won't." Raymond's voice.

Kelda grabbed the mixing bowl and beater before Emma got them dried, mixed a batch of cookies, coconut-oatmeal. She started yearning for them when she'd dug into the oatmeal box to mix the bread.

While the first pan baked, she dug in the freezer again, came out with a package of stewing beef, put it in the microwave on defrost.

"Now what mess are you planning on making?" Emma's hot-water reddened hands rested on her hips.

"I don't like ham and limas." She pried still frozen stew meat pieces apart, floured and browned them for Kelda's Deviled Beef, a recipe she made up as she went along. Today's would be different than every other time. The bread dough was ready. She punched it down, said, "Ah, yes," with the whoosh that released more yeasty freshness into the air, and lost herself in the tediousness of shaping uniform rolls.

"What time you going to the hospital?" Emma asked, spooning ham pieces and limas into a bowl, blowing on a spoonful, setting bowl and spoon down to grab up a wet cloth, wipe off a counter on its way to getting messy again.

"Tomorrow morning. Dr. Drury wants me there about ten."

Ragnar and Raymond stopped in the kitchen doorway, still in conversation.

"Bear skin's still in the basement, 'long with a stack of tanned deer hides. You up to another trip down them steps?"

They were already on their way, and Kelda knew Ragnar meant her to overhear, to know what they were doing without making a point of telling.

"Tanned hides?" Raymond's voice, excited, drifted back.

They returned to the kitchen with bottles of beer in their hands and the basement's smell of dust and cement walls on their clothes. Both seemed taller, stronger, carrying thoughts of animal skins and hides and glassy, dead eyes right out in front of them. They'd liked looking at those things. Liked talking about the old murder, and whether Indians did it as a revenge.

Ragnar brought the cribbage board to the kitchen. Cards slapped, men chuckled or frowned. Rolls came out of the oven. Kelda turned them out onto a linen dish towel; an ironed linen dish towel. Emma tucked a few rolls into a napkin-lined basket. Cards and cribbage board got shoved aside while men slathered butter on hot rolls. Butter dripped from fingers and mouth corners. Fat grams to break the scale. Food to fuel the discussion about the inlet land.

Ragnar used a napkin Emma shoved into his hand to wipe butter from his lips. "Only right you should have that land piece along the inlet, given how much time Joe Williams spent there with Karli, not forgetting you lived there yourself. Figure you should have the land, Karli's workshop, some decent trees."

"Not without a fair purchase price, documentation of land-use agreements, any restrictions you want, to protect it for another hundred years, and a hundred after that."

Emma dished up some more ham and limas. "I'm just tasting', not eating. Kelda's gone and made two dinners. I'm calling Joyce."

Later they moved to the dining room for the deviled beef, rice pilaf, more rolls, fresh asparagus, salad. The men and Emma had sampled all afternoon, then ate again like they'd just come into logging camp from a day in the woods. Kelda took a bite of the deviled beef.

"Not bad. I should write this one down."

But the men didn't hear. "They're still worrying that same old bone," Emma said. "Raymond's right, if you and Ragnar are thinking of letting him have a piece of that inlet, he needs to pay for it, and you all need to agree on what's going to be done with it."

"Hmm," Joyce said, and her hands went to work drawing pictures in the air. "Why don't you form a partnership and create a healing retreat here at the Landing? For small numbers of people at a time. I went to one once, in Utah. Rustic comfort. Only four to six people permitted, adults only; herbal soaks, walks in the woods, a rain shelter, quiet places to read and think. A get-away for those who have been working too hard."

The room went silent. No one talked or scraped up food onto a fork or moved a chair.

Joyce looked right at Kelda. "Businesses and industries love them for their top management. They're great for over-worked professionals like you, Kelda. You could be your own first customer, no charge. Others you'd charge about three, four, five hundred dollars a day, depending on what you served for meals."

"A healing retreat?" That's exactly the idea Kelda had sought, without knowing what it was, still with no idea how it worked, her thoughts now moving down two tracks at once. "Exactly. I've been meaning to plant a few potatoes and tomatoes. And cucumbers and corn. Some Swiss chard, if it's not too late."

Her words floated in on the echo of Joyce's laugh, the same echo that drifted through the house and neutralized all the negative energy building the last few days. Outside, sun rays turned green leaves brighter. Though she couldn't see them, she knew the dahlias were coming up.

The others looked at her like she'd dropped from the sky. Joyce's face had gone all frowns and furrows? "What?" Kelda asked.

"A retreat for growing potatoes and tomatoes?" Raymond asked, his voice flat now, not like when he talked about the tanned deer hides.

"No, for healing." Kelda's exasperation rang across the table. Were they all that slow? "Joyce just reminded me of that. Planting potatoes and tomatoes is what I planned to do to start healing from that awful Hap Smith mess." So, maybe she'd left out the bridge between thoughts again, but it couldn't be that difficult to follow.

Raymond almost smiled, turned his attention back to Joyce. "The place in Utah had herbal soaks?"

"People pay money like that for a walk in the woods?" Ragnar shook his head, one, two, three.

"You might consider planting some lettuce, way this bunch goes through salads," Emma said.

Joyce started to laugh, laughed until tears ran down her cheeks and she needed to excuse herself to get a Kleenex.

*Don't be afraid to take a big step if one is indicated. You can't cross a chasm in two small jumps.*
*- David Lloyd George, 1863-1945.*
        *British Liberal Politician, Chancellor of the Exchequer, Prime Minister 1916-1922.*

# 36
# Kelda

They talked long into the dark hours, the five of them, discussing the idea of The Retreat and Rest Spa at Hansen's Landing. Kelda's brain still sorted mental images of Hap Smith shot dead, Tory Smith holding the gun, Cameo Smith spattered with human remains.

Of detectives probing, her boss Keith Burgess and the agency, and the boxes of things she'd taken from her office, stacked somewhere.

Of Norwegian pancakes and a fairyslipper search meant to heal.

Of Arne talking about Maria and, later about him calling her uncles murderers.

Of Wallace Taylor, whose body washed up on the beach sixty years earlier, whose ghost came back and hovered like a dark cloud over the Landing.

Kelda heard scratching on glass. Seatlh. She opened the patio door to let him in. He circled her legs, rubbed against them, led her into the kitchen like he'd been there before, meowed, kept meowing at each offering, gurgling when she pulled a can of tuna from a cupboard. After he ate he found her seated with the others at the dining room table, jumped onto her lap, circled, curled up.

"I could think better in the great-room." Kelda scratched around Seatlh's ears. The discussion continued. The others were comfortable, focused. They talked, negotiated, drew maps and layouts, made notes.

She concentrated on the cat's purrs. Her head lifted from her body, floated over the scene.

Raymond, who it seemed could draw quite well, sketched the house and cottages, the lane leading to them. He added the creek, ponds, Magna's cedar grove, the skid-road, flower and shrub gardens, lawns, beaches, dock, forested areas, trails, Karli's workshop, an Indian driftwood encampment.

He looked up, let his eyes rest on Kelda's, trying to tell her something. It felt like another electric shock.

Taxes. Money. That's all that came to her mind. "There's enough money for the October half of the taxes, but that's about it until I work out something with Arne and the business. There's no start-up money. I know it needs start-up money. I can't focus on this until I sort out what's going on with Hedstrom Construction." She went on, repeated herself, heard 'taxes' coming from her mouth again and again while the others watched.

"You already have four cottages," Joyce said. "You could actually start a rest retreat right now, let your guests prepare their own meals or have them delivered. Then, as money comes in, start building a small dining lodge with a hot tub, fireplace reading room. What's Karli's workshop like? Could it be converted?"

"I'll transfer the deed on my place, it's yours anyway," Emma said. "Use it for borrowing against."

Kelda and Ragnar both shook their heads and spoke as one. "No. Not yet."

"There's money," Raymond said. "Rather a good sum. Money I saved in the hope you'd sell me a small piece of the Landing."

"For growing native plants." Kelda remembered that conversation, knew it went back only two or three weeks, though it seemed more like two or three years.

"Actually, I think I'm buying the old orchard across from the Kerry's for plantings. This is a special sum."

Kelda felt Raymond lift the hand that scratched Seatlh and hold it. Her head floated farther from her body so his words had to drift up to reach her ears.

"When I came to the Landing, after Korea, you gave me an envelope from Lydia. It contained savings bonds to use toward a college education. I used that money, then repaid it, with the interest it would have earned, once I started practicing law. I invested it, and dreamed of the day I could return it to the Hansens for the Landing.

Then my life took a detour when my wife and son were killed. More money came of that. Insurance money. That's been invested, too. There's money. Lydia's money will be spent only here. The other money will go to the nursery business and to learn more about medicinal herbs and their uses. I believe that's the way of the future."

For a time, no one spoke. Seatlh's purrs were the only sound Kelda heard. Then Raymond said, "Kelda?" and squeezed her hand.

Lydia materialized, or a sense of her, with her arms around the Landing. Kelda's unsorted thoughts flew off into boxes and their flaps closed.

"I want to see literature on such retreats—how they're set up, how they manage, what kind of profit they turn. Joyce, you're the MBA, you'll be responsible for that, and for all the myriad details. You'll have to develop a proposal, too. Somewhere along the line, we'll need a bank's involvement, but I will not permit the Landing to be mortgaged. We'll use Emma's offer, if we need to. Determine what you need for a salary. Can you do that and keep your other jobs?"

Without waiting for Joyce to answer, she said, "Raymond, you'll get all the legal duties, and you and Ragnar need to come to agreement about the transfer of land to your name so if this all comes to naught you have your own place and your own taxes to pay. You two can work on what needs to be constructed where, and how electricity, plumbing and septic systems will be managed. Ragnar knows every inch of this land. Whatever happens, I don't want any major trees cut.

"Emma, I want you to continue managing this old house. I'm going to live here, and so is Ragnar. Whatever comes of this, I don't want our home to be its center."

Seatlh stood on Kelda's legs, arched his back. "Sorry, old boy."

"He felt your energy shift."

"Yes. Well, so did I. Here's one more shift. I'd like to take some time to write, to see if I have the creativity it takes to be a writer." She watched Ragnar, concerned only about his reaction. He grinned. Chuckled. Nodded one, two, three.

The next morning Kelda carried a mental picture of The Retreat and Rest Spa at Hansen's Landing with her to Arne's hospital room. Maria was at his side, his hand in hers. She let it go when Kelda entered, but stayed for the meeting Dr. Drury requested. He came in, his tie knotted just so, his face serious. Part of Arne's heart muscle was dead.

"You can't afford a second heart attack. That means some serious changes in your lifestyle. You have to change your diet, exercise daily, reduce work-related stress. All stress." Dr. Drury looked at Arne, then longer at Kelda.

"Sounds like I'll just have to kick back, let the women handle it." Arne was already the most relaxed of the four in the room.

The women handled it. Maria drove Arne home. Kelda went to the hospital accounting office and saw to the paper work. Then she went to the house, her and Arne's house that she had never liked.

Arne seemed to be luxuriating in the comfort of the multi-purpose room sofa. Maria had arranged pillows on it and in the recliner. She had remote controls and gadgets within reach so he could operate the TV, VCR, CD player. A new notebook computer rested on a table along with magazines on boating, golfing, fishing, traveling.

Arne grinned at Kelda. She watched him from the retreat in her mind.

"Hey Kel, you better call Gerda, she's really upset with you. Says it's your duty to put your husband first, you need to stay here with me, bring Ragnar over here if he needs care."

Maria coughed once, picked up the dust-mop she'd been running over the hardwood floor, and left them.

"What did you tell her?" She pictured cabins with cedar siding.

"She knows about Maria and her gran staying here."

"Does she know the rest?" She listened for the Landing creek burbling, cleared of all debris.

He shrugged. "I haven't told her anything. You said you'd handle her."

"I get to tell her you're in love with Maria?" The Landing pictures and sounds dissolved.

"Hey, you heard the doc. Gotta keep the stress level down."

She narrowed her eyes. "Arne, we opened an old trunk of Karli's yesterday. My uncles didn't kill Wallace Taylor. Gerda conjured that up from some of Karli's and Knut's beer talk."

Arne shrugged again. "Whatever."

"Whatever? Whatever, Arne? She controlled your life for years with that lie, and that's all you have to say?"

Arne stretched out, poked a pillow behind his back, clumped another against his chest. "Yeah, I felt like the rope in a tug-of-war between you and her, whoever won got the Landing, I'd just be a frayed piece of rope. Shouldn't have been that way, I know."

"You know?" Kelda said, repeating it in her head.

"The Landing's Hansen land. I know more than you might think about some of what went on. Boat builders and bankruptcy. Knut lost his entire pension. You probably know too, you've been through Karli's stuff. You're right about Gerda, she spends too much. That's going to have to change. I'm leaving that to you and Mac."

"Mac," Kelda said, meaning she'd like to let Mac handle Gerda's spending without her help.

"Arne lifted one hand in a 'whatever' wave. "Maria will handle the flack about living here, move it along slowly, let her get used to it. Maria knows Gerda doesn't like her, but hell, Gerda doesn't much like you either, which makes it easier for Maria to take. Me, I'm tired, Kel. I'm looking forward to resting for a while, and then doing less work. You and Maria can decide what options to call in, how to downsize. We'll lose a little money, but what the hell, it's a tax write-off."

"A tax write-off?" Kelda wasn't keeping up with Arne, who was onto another subject.

"When the doc gives the okay, I'm going out to pound a few nails, maybe show some of the youngsters we've got working a thing or two. You decide on some remodeling at the Landing, I'll come give you a hand. Long as you cook something I like."

He'd give her a hand at the Landing, as long as she cooked. "What do you like that's on your diet?" she asked.

"Everything's on my diet. It's about portion control, remember? You've been telling me that for years. Shit, Kel, lighten up."

Kelda's teeth clenched so hard her jaw ached. It seemed someone had balanced cement blocks on her shoulders. She watched Arne get comfortable, relax, close his eyes.

"Whatever, and a shrug? Whatever, and a shrug, Arne? That's it?"

He opened one eye, shrugged one shoulder, settled deeper into the sofa.

Kelda picked up a golf magazine, considered swatting Arne like one would a fly, slapped the table instead. Arne didn't move.

"Whatever," she said, and went in search of Maria.

The enclosed courtyard off the kitchen was the only part of the house and landscape Kelda liked. A stream trickled to a waterfall and pond at her left; perfectly maintained shrubs and carefully planned arbors and walls for vines surrounded it. A bird bathed in the running water. Maria sat on a bench, hands folded in her lap, eyes sad. A child sent to time-out.

"Maria, I'm going up to the room I used as an office, to make some calls. You and I need to meet with Mac about the business. Any preferences for day and time?"

Maria looked up, her black eyes like rocks in a dish of water. "Oh, Kelda." She stood, let her weight fall against Kelda. "Part of his heart's dead. He's always been so vital, so full of . . . of energy. What are we going to do?"

Another bird joined the first in the stream. Kelda patted Maria's back and thought, *I'm comforting the woman my husband loves, calming her before I explain the situation to our daughters and my mother-in-law.*

Maria sobbed. Kelda patted faster. "We're going to do whatever," Kelda said. "Whatever it takes to get this all sorted and settled."

Whatever and a shrug. Kelda wove a blanket of it, whatever as warp, a shrug as weft, and wrapped up in it while she made her calls.

Set a meeting with Mac regarding Hedstrom Construction.

Told Mac to put the house, boat, and moorage on the market.

Listened to Lauren. Who'd never speak to her again. Because of Maria.

Whatever.

Arranged for divorce mediation. Arne trusted her to keep it fair.

Invited Reva to the Landing for the summer, to live in one of the cottages.

Doodled while Gerda ranted and slammed down the phone.

A shrug.

Talked with Keith Burgess. The state was probing the Smith case.

Talked with Dave Pritchard. Not a good time to visit Tory.

Agreed to meet Dave Pritchard for a drink. In Poulsbo. Tomorrow.

Whatever.

Took a call from Emma. Raymond tilled some soil.

Took a call from Lauren, who wanted to live in a cottage too.

Who wanted to keep Kelda's car just a little longer. While she looked for a job.

Took a call from Raymond. Who'd picked up seed potatoes, and tomato plants.

What about cucumber seedlings? Some squash?

Corn and beans?

Yes, agreed.

Took a call from Lydia.

And wept.

Alone in an empty room, with no books left to absorb the sound.

*3 o'clock is always too late or too early for anything you want to do. - Jean-Paul Sartre, 1905-1980.*

*[See previous reference, Chapter 2]*

# 37
## Arne

Arne felt the motion in his shoulders, the roll of the boat cutting across another's wake. The new boat, smaller than the one Kelda listed for sale. Small enough to be trailered, put in the water wherever he liked. Maria, dark hair, tanned skin, breathed against him, talked to him. Hard to hear over the engine. She looked good on the boat. They hit a deeper swell, lurched.

"Huh?" He jerked up, wondered why the big leather sofa pitched.

"Arne." Maria had both hands locked on his shoulders. Her hair fell around her face. "Arne, it's Kelda. She's crying. Hard. And the door to her study is locked. And she doesn't answer when I knock."

Arne pushed away the pillow he'd been hugging, dragged himself into a sitting position and shook his head. "Nah, not Kelda, she never cries." Hadn't ever, until lately.

"Listen." Maria shook his shoulders again.

He listened. Yeah, crying sounds. "Shit, somebody must have died. Not me, anyway, unless this is a dream." He shook his head again. "Goddamn heart pills have to go, they make me tired."

"Arne, the heart pills are not going. Your body will adjust in time. Dr. Drury said you'd feel tired for a while, that's part of healing, getting your body used to functioning without part of the heart muscle."

"Shit," he said, but even he knew the word carried little weight. Saying it did nothing for him. He smiled at Maria, still leaning over him, her nice breasts pushing against her shirt, almost touching him. He put his hands on them. Felt a flicker in his groin. He stroked her breasts, and the flicker flamed. The breasts moved, left his hands empty.

"Damn you, Arne Hedstrom, I might love you but sometimes I hate you. Your wife is upstairs sobbing and you're down here trying to seduce me. And Gran's right here, in the kitchen."

Hands on her hips, cheeks tinged red. So, he thought, Gran's in the kitchen, she's worried her gran will see. "Hey, Maria, guess what, I've got a hard-on that's going begging. Still some blood pumping through these veins." He made kissing sounds, sucking sounds. "Things'll be okay, you don't need to worry you're getting limp leftovers."

Maria turned, stomped away toward the stairs. He watched her go, black hair down her back, small waist, nice flare to her hips. Left him sitting there. Goddamn. He found the TV control, pushed power, surfed channels. Monday afternoon shit, no game until seven. He closed his eyes, let himself drift.

Wakened to Kelda standing in front of him.

"Goodbye, Arne. Maria and her Gran will keep me posted about your healing. I'll be in touch about the rest."

He watched her drive away in the old black Bronco, thinking she's right, that's not fair, sticking her with that dirty, dented Hedstrom Construction has-been. Couldn't expect Lauren, his blonde beauty, to drive that, though. Figured Maria would have to find something to sell, get Lauren a decent car, let Kelda have her Honda back.

"Arne?" Maria said, hands on her hips again, ready to do battle. "Gran has some soup ready. I bought salt-free crackers and heart-smart spread, and I don't want one word of complaint. Okay?"

Arne snorted. Let Maria help him up from the sofa, help him to the table. Kelda was right. This was one huge, nicely constructed, impersonal house. Maybe they should do what Maria suggested. Live at her place, start readying this one for sale.

*The future comes one day at a time. - Dean Acheson, 1893-1971.*
*U.S. Secretary of State under President Truman, 1949-1953. Played defining role in*
*foreign policy during cold war.*

# 38
# The Landing

Raymond worked the soil in the Landing's vegetable garden, cut seed potatoes and set them to dry and readied stakes while he waited for Kelda's return. He was in the cottage when the old Bronco tottered down the lane. Too late for gardening, too early to offer comfort.

The digging stick and canoe bailer resting on the cottage table reminded him to be patient. These things had come to him, so might she, in time. He wanted to hug her and then hold her close. In truth, he wanted to be with her for the rest of his life.

When the phone rang before seven the next morning, Raymond let the book about herbal soaks fall closed, and picked up the receiver with hope in his heart.

"Raymond, the sun is up, it's a beautiful day, I've got a thermos of coffee and cups, my trowel and slug bait. Let's plant those potatoes before you leave for work."

The soil, even on a sunny May morning, felt cold to his fingers, a perfect contrast to the steaming coffee. He pounded stakes, stretched twine, dug hills for potatoes. They argued a little about spacing; argued too about making the rows so straight.

"Damn," she said, "you men are so linear, you need everything lined up in neat rows. I have the same problem with Ragnar when we plant dahlias."

She picked up a tomato plant that he'd bought from a local nursery, rubbed thumb and fingers over a leaf and took in a deep breath. "Mmm, I can't wait for the first ripe one. I'll eat it right out here. Let the juice drip off my face."

There it was, that fifteen-year-old girl's smile he remembered.

She talked to him in a way she hadn't before, telling him what had happened the day before, what she'd done to get through the phone calls she'd made to her daughters and her mother-in-law. Talked mostly with her head down and her hands busy.

He kept busy too, digging, planting. Listening. Watching.

Kelda stood, rubbed soil off her hands. "My stomach's grumbling; so is yours. I'm going to make us some scones. This soil is good, isn't it?"

"Yes, very good." He stood still, a post.

"Raymond." She looked at him, stepped back, almost staggered. A frown creased her forehead. "What is that look you have in your eyes? Ever since you first touched that canoe bailer?"

Love, he thought. Lust, too, but mostly love. "Hope," he said.

"Oh." She tilted her head and squinted up at him. "Well, Lydia called yesterday, just as things were quieting down. It seemed like she called, anyway. I know you accept that, that messages come into our heads. She told me some things."

"Yes." While he said that one word, Kelda hugged him, and he hugged her back, but she wriggled loose, touched the hair at his temple, and left him. Ran away toward the house.

He leaned on the hoe and watched her, then looked toward the trees and the inlet beyond. *Lydia? How long am I supposed to wait?*

Kelda felt Lydia's presence through the day that began with planting potatoes, and hoped she remained near through meeting Dave Pritchard for a drink and discussion about Troy and Cameo Smith.

Dave wanted to hold her hand. Either one, whichever one wasn't holding her drink. She stirred the drink, vodka-tonic, with the plastic straw, one hand on the straw, other on the glass. Vodka-tonic, a drink she particularly disliked, would improve as the ice melted, and get her on her way back to the Landing without enough alcohol in her system to make driving dangerous.

Dave talked about the scene beyond the window: blue water, sparkling in the early evening sun, expensive yachts and sailboats tied up at the floats or housed in the long rows of covered moorage. He said he'd like a boat.

"We have one for sale. My husband's yacht. I've never cared much for that kind of boating."

"Kelda, why do you keep referring to your husband? You said you're negotiating a divorce."

Kelda studied Dave's face, handsome enough, his brown eyes with their serious look, his graying brown hair. Men with graying hair always looked distinguished and privileged. Things should go their way; they're male and graying. "I'm trying to negotiate a visit with Tory Smith. And with Cameo, someday."

In truth, she appreciated Dave's connections, the information he brought her. Tory would plead guilty to murder in the second degree, and could do as little as ten years. Cameo was still in the psychiatric ward of a hospital, heavily sedated.

"Tory will still be young in ten years," Dave said. "As for us, we need to grab life now."

"Dave, I'm a family therapist, and will be for a good while, even if I no longer earn an income from such work. What you saw in me that interested you has something to do with my professional demeanor. Don't confuse that with attraction."

She followed the words with her best professional Kelda look, and thought about how often she put that on in conversations with men. Never with Raymond Walkingstick, though. Well, not since learning he was the Indian boy Lydia had cared about. When she brushed away the hair at his temple this morning, it had felt like Lydia lifted her hand.

Dave put his hands over hers cradling her drink. "I know it's too soon, you've been through a lot lately. I'll give you time."

He had a look on his face that could have come from the mold Keith Burgess used every time he talked her into another difficult case.

She retrieved her hands and stood up. "I have a nice meat loaf ready to go into the oven back at the Landing. You said you'd like to see the place. Get your car and follow me. You'll get a glimpse of what will be occupying my time from this moment on."

Ragnar stationed himself on the flagstone patio area nearest the main entry, the spot that gave the best view of Hansen Lane when Kelda drove away for her meeting. He didn't intend to leave until she returned. Except for those confounded trips to the bathroom. Old man's bladder.

He took another sip of raspberry wine while Walkingstick dealt cards for their cribbage game they'd set up on the old table generally used to hold seed packages, assorted gardening gloves and gear.

Emma came out, dish towel draped over her shoulder, fingers pushing hair away from her face. "That was Kelda calling, you didn't hear the phone? She's bringing her date, that detective fellow, here for dinner. Be here any minute."

Ragnar hadn't seen Emma so agitated in weeks. Well, days. "Damn it all to hell, Emma, not a date, just a meeting." He studied his cards like they required his attention. No need to let Emma know he didn't much like it either, that detective calling two, three, four times in the last few days. Figured Walkingstick needed a cribbage game for distraction. Figured otherwise he'd sit on the beach whittling 'til he had every finger cut.

"Now Ragnar Hansen, I been knowing you more than seventy years, you think I don't know what's going around in your old head?"

When Walkingstick's head turned to look up the lane, Ragnar knew the wait was about over. Took him another half-a-minute, then he heard cars too, the old Bronco followed by a sleek silver thing.

"Look at that car, looks like a silver bullet," Emma said.

"Man's a police detective," Ragnar said to Emma, but his eyes were on the drive. He watched Kelda pull up in front of the garage she never used and wait for the man to come up out of his car. He and Walkingstick stood, nice and polite, offering hands for shaking when Kelda made the introductions. Kelda had a look in her eyes that said she'd figured them out.

"It's such a beautiful day I'm surprised you're not playing cards out on the great room porch where you can watch boats parading by."

"We're out here watching for deer. Don't want your garden eaten up 'fore it gets going."

"Oh, of course. How conscientious." Then, her voice lower, her arms around him, she said, "I love you, father of my heart. Not to worry, okay?" And he saw her grab Walkingstick's hand, give it a squeeze, saw the man wanted to hold on a whole lot longer.

"I put that meat loaf in the oven when you called," Emma said. "You want me to start on them spuds and carrots for roasting?"

"Please, Emma. More olive oil than butter in the roasting pan. First, will you call Joyce and warn her I'm bringing a guest out to see the cottages? Tell her she's expected for dinner. Come on Dave, I'll show you the lay of the Landing."

Over dinner Ragnar watched Kelda direct the conversation so everyone felt comfortable. Everyone but herself. He knew she had a headache starting, but she kept the talk going, kept it on the fact of looking into developing a small retreat at the Landing, made sure the detective knew she wasn't going to leave the place. He had to work at not smiling about that.

"Joyce and Raymond are the ones who will be putting a proposal together and doing most of the planning," Kelda said. "Joyce is an MBA and Raymond's a corporate attorney. Uncle Ragnar's the CEO, Emma's the Chief of Staff, and I'm writer/producer/director, working mostly off-stage."

First Ragnar had heard of that and remembered what he'd been waiting to tell her. "Found enough parts of a couple-two-three old rowboats to put one good one together. Walkingstick's already started on it, it's in the basement."

"Oh, I love you guys." She got up, dropped kisses somewhere above their heads and went off to the kitchen to fill serving bowls and platters, and bring in the coffee pot.

Ragnar nodded, one good nod. She was underlining something for the detective.

Kelda poured more coffee, distributing it so everyone got a bit. "I'll start another pot."

"You sit down, I'll see to the coffee," Emma said.

"Directing off-stage from where?" Dave asked.

"My mother's sewing room, soon to be library and study if Uncle Ragner agrees. It's the room just off the hall by the stairs. I plan to stretch my brain by writing Hansen history while the others do most of the work."

"Room's been a study and library all along, left for you with Lydia's love. Been waiting for you to be ready, *kär a.*" Ragnar watched Kelda, worrying he'd burst right out of his shirt, the look she gave him. He watched her eyes, their blinking lids, nodded three times when she excused herself. Hansens don't cry. Least not in front of strangers.

*So, Lydia, we can both take a rest. She's going to see to it the Hansen's story gets told.*

Raymond stood with Joyce on the great-room porch while Kelda walked Dave Pritchard to his car. Joyce laughed her lilting laugh, and a bird answered from somewhere, the lilac hedge he thought.

"I don't think this is how Dave envisioned his evening."

"No." Raymond reached into a pocket, pulled out a small piece of driftwood, searched for his knife. Searched for words, too. "What do you think of him?"

Joyce's hands wove the air. "Nice enough, decent looks. Unhappy, and looking for a woman to make him happy. Still a little too caught up in the macho police detective role, but his interest in buying Arne's boat could be a plus. Or a good diversion on Kelda's part. Definitely not her type."

"What type would that be?" Raymond snapped the knife open and shut, open and shut.

"She prefers rowboats. Beyond that, you can ask her yourself, Raymond." She laughed again.

"What's funny?" Kelda asked, coming along in the wake of Joyce's laughter.

Raymond snapped open his knife, looked at the driftwood, looked for an answer. But Joyce took care of it, let him find a breath of air.

"Oh, we're just speculating that the evening didn't turn out exactly as Dave had planned."

Kelda sighed. "He's going to talk with the marina manager about Arne's boat, but I doubt it will suit him. I think he got the message that I'm not anywhere near ready to get involved with a man." She rotated her head and neck, and groaned.

"When you are ready, will you let me know?" Raymond spoke quickly, before thinking could seal his lips, not minding that Joyce heard. She'd figured him out anyway. Seemed like Ragnar had too. He watched Kelda's eyes, searched in the porch-light's shadows for their answer, not expecting to hear words. Not expecting to feel her hand on his, the one holding the driftwood.

"You'll be the first to know, Raymond. I promise. Now, if we're going to pursue this idea of a rest retreat, we need to discuss it in the light of day. First thing tomorrow morning, before Joyce and Raymond head off for their respective paying jobs. I'll have coffee ready by six-thirty, muffins hot from the oven by seven."

Joyce agreed. He agreed. Kelda squeezed his hand again and disappeared into the house.

"Well," Joyce said, "I think we said our goodnights. Come on, I'll walk you to your cottage."

Raymond listened to the gravel crunch under their shoes. Joyce stumbled on the uneven surface. He caught her arm. "You okay?"

"I'm fine." She stumbled again. "Let me have your cane, Raymond. Since you're not using it tonight."

"I'll see you to your door." He thought about that, not remembering to use his cane. Thought of something else. "Where's your flashlight? You always seem so well prepared."

"I didn't have time to think when Emma called. She said Kelda was bringing someone out for a look around the cottages. And then she lowered her voice and said, 'We need your help heading this one off at the pass, Ragnar's that upset.' So, I put the beer I'd opened back in the refrigerator, found some breath freshener, brushed my hair, and put on some fresh lipstick. Just in case I was supposed to use looks and charm."

"Listen," Raymond said. "There, did you hear that? That bird? He's answering your laugh."

But Joyce hadn't heard. Maybe he'd imagined it. He saw her into her cottage, gathered up Seatlh and put his cane back to use, just in case. While water heated for tea he looked through a bird book for a description of the song he'd heard in the darkness. He searched in vain. Either the bird didn't exist, or he couldn't concentrate on the bird song he'd heard.

Instead, he replayed Kelda saying, *You'll be the first to know, Raymond. I promise.*

*I make the most of all that comes, And the least of all that goes. - Sarah Teasdale, 1884-1933. American lyricist, Pulitzer Prize for poem, "Love Songs," 1917.*

# 39
# Kelda

Kelda began her new life by removing the bed and dresser from Lydia's sewing room and creating a reading area with a 1950s chaise Lydia had reupholstered, a walnut lamp table with a brass candlestick lamp and one bookcase that almost reached the ceiling.

She set up a card table to serve as her desk on the opposite wall, with a long, table-height bookcase to hold office supplies. The old treadle sewing machine remained where it had been all the years of Kelda's childhood. Treadling, watching the thread take up lever rise and fall, helped her think through what she wanted to write.

Ragnar checked on her now and then, said he'd rustle up a better work surface than that rickety folding thing and, a few days later, brought in a highly polished trestle table.

"Magna's that was," Ragnar said. "Used as a side server when we were so many sitting down for a meal."

Kelda ran her hand over the polished table top, down the carved legs, across the foot brace. "This was Magna's? Where has it been?"

"In the basement, stored in parts. I dug it out and put it back together."

"Uh huh. Stored in parts, all nicely stained and finished with something that won't let spilled coffee or cookie crumbs mar the wood. Right? Or did you refinish it when you went off to putter a bit?"

"Could be I cleaned it up while you were lost in writing. Could serve as a desk until we get the real thing."

"It would be a shame to put a computer on it."

"Ah, now, it held many a serving bowl in its day as a side-board. It's meant to be used, I'm thinking. We can build shelves and cabinets to fit your needs, just give us a bit of time."

"We? Who's this 'we?'"

"That'd be Walkingstick helping me with the rowboat parts, wanting to learn a thing or two about working with wood. Gives him a break now and again from his nursery work."

"I see," Kelda said, watching her uncle's face for the grin he tried to hide. She'd worried when he drove off in his old pickup for what he called a few things for the rowboat work. The truck now remained outside the garage that had become a workshop with saws whining and sanders droning.

One white rowboat with forest green trim materialized complete with two newly painted oars. Ragnar admitted to a bit of reconfiguring and repair, and newly built seats and floorboard. He'd found side pieces stored one place, keel parts another, all under oiled canvas, all worn from years of use.

Kelda rowed every morning through the remaining spring, all summer and into fall, soon after sunrise. Being on the water early, even on misty mornings, cleared her mind, preparing her for the day's tasks, the changes that set the pattern for the Landing.

Ragnar, her cornerstone, her anchor through the storm of change, sometimes went with her, sipping coffee while she rowed. Joyce went out twice, but preferred the water from the beach where she could look for rocks and shells.

Raymond rowed later in the day, after the stiffness had eased from his leg. He walked in the morning, from his cottage to the old apple orchard where he and a crew worked to create planned areas for native plants, shrubs and trees.

Emma said she preferred solid ground under her feet.

They met formally most days to work on Retreat plans. Joyce gathered information, crunched numbers and developed a proposal for outsiders. Money people first, then potential clients.

"Form a corporation, let it borrow funds," Joyce said. "You've made it clear you don't want to mortgage the Landing or accept Raymond's money for the inlet at this time. The corporation will use the interest on loans as tax deductions. And you keep the bulk of the property as a separate entity."

Raymond arranged for aerial photos and detailed maps of the Landing and compiled technical information about the local watershed and the environmental impact. He had a friend, a former client, whose business was environmental architecture.

"He owes me a favor, he's helping design the working plans for a native-plants garden and nursery. Walking paths, secluded areas, a sales shack that looks rustic with state-of-the-art electronics."

Kelda started a journal with copies of the photos and maps, and snapshots she took as she walked the land. Memory led to memory, with Ragnar's stories enriching her writing.

At a daily Retreat meeting, he tapped the creek mouth and inlet on a photo. "This here's what Lydia called The Indians. Belongs to Walkingstick, seems clear to me. She had one Indian in mind. Joe Williams, called Indian Joe Diggingstick, who fished there and dug clams all the years the Old Ones lived on this here finger in the bay."

"I would like to have a piece along the inlet, at its end," Raymond said. "Here, the other side of the creek from Karli's workshop. But only if I pay for it."

"Can't buy what you own."

"Can't own what I never paid taxes on."

Kelda watched them lock stares. "Look here," she said. "Where the creek empties into the inlet. If Raymond takes ownership of the waterfront south of the creek, the Retreat could be established north of it, where Karli's workshop stands. I don't think we'd have to take out any trees."

"No more than four cabins and a lodge, for four to six guests at a time," Joyce said. "Six guests would mean two couples and two singles." Joyce's hands built cabins in the air. "The lodge won't be that big either. A cozy dining area, a den-like room with comfortable furniture, books, a fireplace; a spa and sauna room, a kitchen. Offices on a second floor."

"Better be a gas-log fireplace," Emma said. "Kelda don't like no wood but alder burning at the Landing. It's my job to keep an eye out for her interests." She'd asked just what a Chief of Staff does, and when she'd been told, said, "Shoot, I been doin' that all along."

Ragnar drove off in his old pickup once or twice a week, worrying Kelda until Emma reminded her he'd driven right up to the day he'd taken to his bed. He'd return with lumber in the back of the truck that he crafted into a work station for computer, printer, storage cabinets and new bookcases. He may have been a logger along with his brothers, but he'd always been a custom cabinet maker at heart.

Kelda moved Magna's old trestle table into a position to visually separate the reading area from the office.

Joyce rearranged her coffee shop work schedule to fit her Landing responsibilities. With Kelda's help, she made the great-room office space into the retreat planning area. Ragnar built an easel stand for her chart-making addiction, her need to think with color markers on paper.

"Look at this," Joyce said. "Raymond's orchard property abuts the south end of the Landing, and his design includes a viewing garden where people can learn plant names, scientific and common, and how Indians and early settlers used them. That fits nicely with the retreat, especially with herbal products for the spas."

She'd met with representatives for companies that sold such products, and had offers for deals and inquiries from licensed herbalists seeking work. Kelda hadn't known such persons existed.

Kelda worried that Liam and Leah Kerry would resent both the retreat at the Landing and Raymond's nursery business across the lane, but they found it the catalyst for a project they'd discussed for years; a fine arts school, with textile arts a main feature.

Patty Hansen helped them redecorate their old farmhouse so it reflected its history, and best utilized space for spinning wheels, looms, and quilting frames. One room, a small bedroom with morning light, became a stitchery room.

While Patty worked at the Kerry's, Erik developed a renewed interest in the Landing. He cleaned the creek and helped Kelda plan walks in the woods that permitted guests to experience the trees and understory without trampling rare plants, like the Fairyslipper.

When Patty finished the Kerry's, she helped Kelda create a museum in the first cottage along the lane. They created a place where people could relax, read, touch or rearrange assorted kitchen antiques on shelves and vintage furnishings. There was wood for the cast iron wood-burning stove, a basket of fabrics by the treadle sewing machine, assorted herbal teas inside a vintage oak icebox.

They enclosed one corner of the entry porch to serve as a mini-kitchen with refrigerator, microwave, hotpot and utensils. The back porch led to the rocky cove where another Ragnar-restored rowboat was available for use. Magna's cedar grove with three small graves edged the cove.

Erik fashioned a path along the creek from the designated cabins and lodge area for guests to follow across the lane to the vintage cottage or into the old growth forest and inlet side of the Landing peninsula. He cleared remnants of the old skid road and positioned rusted remains of early 1900s logging gear as a fence between retreat and private Landing property.

As they worked on preliminaries to establishment of the retreat and drew plans for small buildings and paths, Kelda saw how easily that area would be divided from the privacy of the old Landing house and gardens. Simple signs stating *Private Property* and *Private Drive* could be posted along retreat boundaries.

Joyce reminded them that the retreat area offered enough opportunities to explore natural beauty and peaceful settings that few guests would choose to wander beyond the designated areas. The heart of the Landing, including the old house and dock, and Raymond's rebuilt cottage, would remain unchanged.

Joyce composed a brochure and questionnaire for selected corporations, suggesting a week in nature, a few days even, with healthy foods, rest and relaxation would pay for itself in employee production. The response overwhelmed her.

"A seventy-two percent return in ten days, and ninety-eight percent positive," she said. "One Seattle firm called to ask if they could invest in the development, even buy one cabin for their employees. I thanked them and declined their offer."

When Kelda experienced doubts, which she did at least daily, she opened a journal she'd started the day she'd set up her office in Lydia's sewing room. Taped inside the journal cover was the current property tax bill. A thousand per acre, forty-thousand dollars, twenty- thousand paid, another twenty-thousand due the end of October.

Then she'd escape into a story she'd started thirty-five years earlier, when Lydia died, a fantasy no one would ever see. In it, Lydia Berg married Ragnar Hansen, and gave life to a daughter they named Kelda Ronalda Hansen. The daughter left the Landing for a time. She has now returned to save it from the developer's bulldozers and saws.

# 40

# Raymond

Raymond Walkingstick watched water droplets leave the oars and plip onto the inlet's rippled surface. The inward bound tide pushed him toward the beach. When he got close he'd row back out a way and let the tide carry him again. He enjoyed the rocking, floating freedom of a small boat on moving water, and the memories it brought.

This small rowboat, so loved by Kelda, carried him back through years of mist to his infancy, to his origins as he'd heard them told by the elders. He hadn't been born on the reservation as he thought, but in a dank place, and wrapped in his mother's soiled skirt. She'd hidden in shame, birthed him alone, traveled in fear in the dark of night. His first bath had been in salt water, a part of this same body of water on which he floated, his first cradle a stolen canoe.

Clara Williams, young and terrified, brought him to the village of her people, to her father. There, in the arms of Joe Williams, the infant Raymond survived to live out his destiny as the spirits decreed.

Only recently had he admitted that his conception had been the result of young Clara Williams with a white man connected somehow to the Indian School where she'd been sent. He suspected it had been a forced coupling. Rape, often overlooked in those times, in those circumstances. He'd never known his mother's age at his birth, only that she'd still been in her teens.

He'd spoken these memories and conclusions aloud to Kelda while they rowed from the old Landing dock to the inlet. He'd spoken his life to her, and listened to hers over the last few weeks while the Retreat and Rest Spa at Hansen's Landing took shape on paper and in their minds. They'd argued at times, out on the water, needing a present cause to ease the intensity of revealing their pasts. Argued over land deeds and money until each accepted the other's decision: land would be deeded into his name, and he would invest in a fund earmarked to protect the Landing's future.

He thought about Kelda, across the Sound in Edmonds finalizing the sale of the house she and Arne owned, and the yacht and moorage. He'd asked if she wanted Hedstrom Construction to build the cabins and lodge for the retreat.

"No. Though they do exceptional work. Arne's good, and sets high standards for his crews. But Hansen and Hedstrom have been on an emotional collision course since long before I met Arne. We just acted it out to its end."

He'd waited, silent, knowing she would say more.

"It's not Arne, and it's not me so much as it's mixing two energy forces that should not be mixed. He's imbued with Gerda's energy almost like it's his fate, his position as mother-aligned. That's at least partially due to how his older brother left family matters and messes for Arne. Lauren carries Arne's energy forth. It doesn't have to happen that way. I think Lauren is beginning to sort out how family history can help or hamper, and to make healthy choices for herself."

He'd thought about that ever since, about how alike his mother and his sister became, almost sharing the same energy. And his own energy reflected the emptiness of a father unknown. He'd spent most of his life not knowing himself.

When he'd told Kelda he was there to listen whenever she was ready to talk, he'd expected to do just that. Listen. Sometimes it stunned him how much he talked, the things he said. She asked about his accident, about the damage to his person. He didn't understand the emotional part of his injury, so he explained the physical, the scars and blemishes, and arthritic-like pain.

"There's a cavity, a crater of sorts, in the thigh where muscle tissues were mangled—the abductors, Sartorius, and quad."

"I'm sorry, Raymond. It's hard on both body and emotions. We need to mourn the loss of body tissue and functions like we mourn other losses."

"I'm learning about emotions right along with the use of native plant remedies. As for function, everything still works, though that leg benefits from the cane at times."

"That's good."

She'd smiled, but it was just a smile, a caring Kelda smile, not an intimate smile.

Though he hoped they would move to a more intimate relationship, he accepted what they had. His life was filled with wonder and joy, living at the Landing, being part of the group planning its future, being with Kelda and Ragnar on a daily basis, if even for moments fit into busy lives.

Emma and Joyce had also become part of his daily life. He'd experienced jealousy when he thought Kelda might be interested in Dave Pritchard, the detective so obviously interested in her. Acknowledging that feeling had been important in understanding how he'd long buried feelings. In the end he respected the man for helping Kelda arrange to visit Tory Smith inside prison. She remained sad after that visit, but she talked about her feelings. He learned from her how sadness could heal, not just burrow into the psyche.

There had been light moments with Kelda, too, in their meetings, over dinner, and out on the water. They laughed and joked. He'd thought maybe his face muscles and throat muscles were more damaged than those in his legs, that he couldn't laugh, but Kelda said and did things that gave them cause for use. In the aftermath of one of those lighter moods she'd spoken of fantasies.

"Becoming a writer is a long-nurtured fantasy. Not just a recorder of Hansen history, but a real writer, whatever that is. Do you know what I mean? Do you have any long-held fantasies?"

"Yes." He'd felt those little-used face muscles stretch into a grin, let his eyes rest on her neck and chest. She'd been wearing a tank-top under an open shirt. "I've fantasized for thirty-five years about seeing where those freckles end."

She'd blushed and he thought she would button her shirt, but she didn't; she just watched him, her eyes squinted. After a moment she said, "I think it's your turn to row," and pulled in the oars.

Since then he'd replayed that evening several times a day, worried he'd done harm to their relationship, tried to carry it to a dimension she didn't want yet, quite possibly would never want. Nothing about her behavior in his presence changed, nothing that suggested anger or disgust. Or pleasure or anticipation, either. And so he settled back into enjoying life, letting the spirits carry him where they would.

He'd seen some of her writing, and knew it was good. Reva was responsible for his seeing it. Kelda had allowed her to read several chapters, and Reva begged her to read it aloud after dinner.

"No, absolutely *No*," Kelda said.

"Can Travis read it? There's parts he could publish, like he published part of your Uncle Karli's story about that old murder."

"Sure, he can read it. Anybody that wants to may read it, just not in my presence." She'd looked around the table, stood, pushed in her chair. "If you do read it, any of you, please take time to note spelling or punctuation errors. Make comments, if you like. I'm going for a walk."

He watched her go off into the woods, her daylight sanctuary. He knew she often walked in the wee hours too, out onto the old dock. He'd see her out there, a shadow figure. Soon he wakened about the same time each night, went to his window, considered dressing and joining her.

More than once he got as far as his hand on the doorknob before reminding himself she needed that time and space for her own spiritual renewal. Most nights Seatlh returned to his cottage carrying her scent on his fur. He'd jump onto Raymond's bed, climb onto his chest or shoulders to announce his presence, then curl into his comfort ball, tip of his tail up near his nose. After that, Raymond slept. And dreamed.

*Awake, my heart, to be loved, awake, awake!* - Robert Bridges, 1884-1930.
*Britain's Poet Laureate 1913-1930; doctor by training; literary achievement later in life;*
*author of several Christian hymns.*

# 41
## Kelda and Raymond

Something in Kelda's center felt off-kilter when their group formed their corporation, though each day's progress steadied her. July had come and gone, the dahlias bloomed, and Ragnar was alive. He knew she struggled with the reality of change, and brought her hugs and wine. And in early August a bouquet of lemon yellow dahlias with white tips. She imagined she could smell lemon and soon had the kitchen a sticky mess making a lemon meringue pie.

"Look what you've gone and done to this stove," Emma scolded, scrubbing at hardening yellow spatters, but Kelda knew she was tickled. Too much of the food preparation of late had taken place in Joyce or Reva's cottage kitchens.

Gravenstein apples, ripe and juicy, kept Kelda in the Landing kitchen one entire early September day. After that, she needed kitchen time daily, and resumed cooking dinner meals. Canning season went into full swing with peaches and pears, then pole beans from the garden.

Raymond helped her make dill pickles, to learn how, and then helped with dilly beans.

Ragnar and Emma could bring her up out of little slumps, and there were several, just by being themselves. Joyce could too, with her directness, and by forging ahead with difficult tasks, saying, "It's one of the steps. Some of them are a little hard to take."

Reva's presence helped her heal as the friendship Kelda always knew existed beneath the mother-daughter role-expectations grew so fast. Reva was growing into love with Travis Eklund, and Kelda had the pleasure of seeing her daughter torn between wanting time alone with Travis and time together with the group.

Lauren had taken a job in Seattle that put her in the midst of young people on the move, as she called them, and moved into an apartment with two other young women. She'd enrolled in one post-graduate night school class, something Kelda considered wise.

To Kelda's surprise, Raymond helped most of all; his communication with the spirits opened doors for her. He never actually spoke about spirits, but they were with him. Sometimes he almost glowed. Part of that glow was due to his naturally tawny skin darkening from hours in the sun, but much of it was the awakening of an inner self. She'd seen it happen with clients, but never quite as it did with Raymond.

Their daily trips in the rowboat from dock to inlet and back, watching summer colors fade and fall colors spark, were as cherished as her first cup of coffee with Ragnar, and she acknowledged in her careful counselor-Kelda way that she cared about Raymond. Not just as an extension of Indian Joe and the Old-ones, but for himself.

She knew all at the Landing watched her moods as they progressed on the retreat. A road had to be built, and a bridge across the creek, which required removal of a few maple and alder trees. Karli's workshop had to come down. Kelda left kitchen and writing to work with the crews on those projects. Now and then she cried, and didn't mind who saw. She cried again, pleased tears, when Raymond salvaged the materials from the workshop for use at his nursery site.

When it became clear that six fir trees had to be removed at the building sites, the group conspired to have Kelda busy elsewhere. She found out, and went into a rage that shocked them all. One of the trees was about Kelda's age, the others younger, but all sellable, and they'd planned to present her with a check.

"None will be sold. I want the wood milled for use in the little lodge we'll build, and the large limbs saved for heat in the great-room, or in one of the old cottages. When it's seasoned, we'll burn it and reminisce. I will be there when they come down, as near as the fallers permit. Ragnar will be there, in charge of the falling. What he says goes."

After the chainsaw's roar, a tree's fall seemed a whisper. Kelda dragged limbs, raked needles and cones, and later cooked dinner with pitch still on her hands. Six trees hauled limbless from the landing returned as beams that would support and enhance a Northwest lodge.

On one of her night forays, a warm late October night, Kelda realized she'd grown beyond the sadness at the death of her marriage—she felt a greater loss over the death of those trees. She mused about the fact that the old dock planks had once been trees, and that repairs would require death of more trees. Unless they used recycled synthetic planking. Fake wood at the Landing—difficult to imagine.

She analyzed the way her professional career ended with the Smith case, and how that got tied up in some ways with the unsolved murder of Wallace Taylor. Dave Pritchard gave up on his idea of developing a personal relationship with her, but he became interested in the old murder and searched the archives. He came to the same conclusion the local police and FBI had drawn in 1932: there wasn't enough evidence to charge anyone.

Pritchard told her that his training and gut feeling combined to point to someone from the tribe evening a score. An Indian boy died from alcohol, a half-breed child drowned, evidence pointed at Wallace Taylor's involvement in those affairs.

"There's a story that deserves to be written, Kelda," he'd said the last time they talked. She suspected he was right, and that it would become part of the Hansen history she worked on every day.

She mused about Indian Joe who'd been the Old-ones' friend, the things he taught them about the land, the fact that he was Raymond's grandfather.

Raymond worked with his crew of young men and women, directing them to haul every branch and twig from every downed tree to his nursery property where they chipped it and tilled it back into the earth. They were high school and community college students with tribal connections. Kelda didn't know if they'd abused alcohol or drugs, or been in trouble with the law. She knew only that they saw Raymond as employer, teacher and friend.

Finally, she thought about what Raymond's presence meant in her life. She picked up Seatlh, who had been with her as usual, rubbing against her legs, and carried him to Raymond's cottage.

Raymond had finished his herbal soak and settled with a book on Indian mythology. It reminded him of Jung's work on the meaning of symbols. He'd experienced a strange day, one filled with omens, good omens he thought.

From time to time he glanced up at the fireplace where he'd laid lengths of limbs from one recently downed fir. They weren't seasoned for burning, nor would he burn a fire on such a warm night, but they represented something to him, something about Kelda and what he'd seen in her when she'd ordered the trees milled for building, the limbs cut into burnable lengths. Whatever it was followed him through his days and evenings at the Landing; through times in the rowboat with Kelda, his cribbage games with Ragnar, his baths.

When he first heard a light tapping he ignored it, not recognizing it as a knock, or as his door. Then he heard it again, and rose to answer. His bad leg carried him without its usual complaint. He saw a shadow through the curtained window, a shadow he'd often watched on the dock.

"Hello, Kelda," he said, as though he often greeted her at his door long after dark. Only his brain knew the incongruity between his calm greeting and his internal turmoil.

"Hello." She released Seatlh, smiled. "Raymond, I've been thinking about you. My interest in you as a man, and your interest in my freckles, and whether this is all part of Lydia's plan."

He answered by gathering her into his arms for a kiss. Somewhere, in the ensuing minutes before they made love, he told her he'd loved her for thirty-five years, that though the freckles had always intrigued him, his true fantasy was spending the rest of their lives together.

Later, after they'd made love, and talked, and made love again, he dozed off without a twinge of pain from his hip. He wakened suddenly, disturbing Seatlh who'd curled up with them. "Kelda." He kissed her shoulder, then shook it slightly. "Kelda, won't you want to get back to the house before the others waken?"

She stretched, sat up, held the sheet over her freckled breasts, lighter freckles where sun hadn't darkened them. "It doesn't really matter. They all know we belong together—you and me, and the Landing. They've just been waiting for me to figure it out."

*Love consists in this, that two solitudes protect and touch and greet each other. - Rainer Maria Rilke, 1875-1926.*

*Bohemian Austrian poet & novelist, widely recognized as one of the most lyrically intense German language poets.*

# 42
## Ragnar

Ragnar Hansen poked around in the dresser drawer that held odds and ends of treasures he'd kept over the years, the one drawer he trusted Emma would never violate, until he found the spiral notebook. At long last he would be able to deliver it, this last journal Lydia wrote, the one she instructed Ragnar to deliver only after Kelda knew what it meant to love a man.

He'd placed the notebook in Karli's trunk before he'd soldered it shut, prit-near certain Kelda was destined to live out her life with Arne Hedstrom, okay for a half-Swede, half-German, but not the man she needed.

Ragnar had a bit of a bad moment getting it out of the trunk that day in the basement. Out of the trunk and inside his shirt before Kelda saw it. Got so nervous he dropped a tool on the cement floor, thought it would waken the bats up in the attic. But she'd been so busy arguing with Walkingstick and worrying about an old murder that she hadn't noticed. He opened the notebook, spiral some bent, and read.

*My dear daughter Kelda Ronalda Hansen*

*Saying goodbye to you, leaving you, is what I most hate about this heart disease. I hope the journals I've written over the years help keep me alive in your memory. This special one is for you alone, not for Erik and Greg. What you do with it once you've read it is yours to decide.*

*I don't know when you'll read this, at what age or under what circumstances. Ragnar has specific instructions to deliver it when he believes you are in the proper state of mind. You see, this is a love story.*

*You've read of my anger at Olav for leaving me here while he went off to fight for our country. Perhaps you've wondered, as I often did myself, at my selfishness. My anger, I now know, was born of my fear of revealing to Ragnar and Olav's other brothers, that our love had less strength than I wanted the world to believe. I knew by then that I loved Ragnar, but vowed I'd never let others know.*

*On the night of July 4, 1941, after the picnics and fireworks were over, the boys tucked into their beds, and the others gone into the night, I read a bit more aloud for Ragnar and myself. I'd started a poem by Robert Frost, a favorite poet of all the Hansens, a poem I'd not read before, and completed only the first stanza, which reads:*

Tree at my window, window tree,
My sash is lowered when night comes on;
But let there never be curtain drawn
Between you and me.

*That's as far as I got. Ragnar had just drawn the curtains shut. He looked at me and said, "That's how I'm feeling, Lydia. That I never want a curtain drawn between us. I love you, and I love Olav, but not the same. Don't let him or anger at his love of ships and the sea be a curtain between us."*

*Olav's ship had sailed from Bremerton ten days earlier. He left me with only an impatient kiss; he truly loved the sea. Ragnar and I moved together to his bed, and made love. We, who'd never shared more than an innocent kiss or touch, found the depth of shared love that night. I knew I'd conceived you, that you'd be our daughter, but more than that, the daughter of the Landing. I also knew we conceived a secret, for we chose, right or wrong, to go on as we had been.*

*You know the next events. The bombing of Pearl Harbor, a war, the struggles and joys of life at the Landing, my illness, and Ragnar Hansen's love.*

*Yes, we had a good life, an intimate life, made possible by the Landing and the fact of a shared home. Ragnar loved all of us; me,*

*Erik, Greg, and you. He reared you all with love, agreeing to sacrifice the right to call you daughter because of his love for me.*

*That is the kind of love I hope you find. When you do, you will read this. I hope for and request your understanding and forgiveness, for you were truly conceived in and reared with love.*

She'd signed that part, *Your mother, Lydia.* Then she'd had him sign it too, and he'd written, *Your father, Ragnar.*

There was more, but that's as far as he could read. Damn it all to hell, you'd think by now, eighty and some odd years old, he could read an old journal without crying.

Well, Kelda didn't need to see the notebook this very minute. Later on. Or even tomorrow. He'd give it to her when she worked in the study, where she was most a Hansen, daughter of the Landing. At least she'd see it handed to her out of his hand, not when she chanced across it in some of his things after he'd taken to his bed to die.

He felt Lydia with him, heard her in his head, and knew he had a piece of time to go on yet, now the last truth could be told.

Well, he didn't mind. The Landing was going on, so he would, to

## Acknowledgments

Thanks to my dad, thirteenth and youngest child of Norwegian immigrants, and to his closest brothers and sisters, for giving me glimpses of the proclivities within one large family.

Thanks to my mom, daughter of Swedish immigrants, who spoke often of Native Americans who camped on an inlet on Puget Sound near her home. She was a teacher and an advocate for ending Indian Schools in the area where we lived.

## Velkommen til Poulsbo

Poulsbo is a city on Liberty Bay in Kitsap County, Washington, United States. It is the fourth largest city in Kitsap County. Prior to the arrival of Scandinavian immigrants in the 1880s, the Suquamish people had hunted, fished and harvested marine life in the area for at least 5,000 years. Poulsbo calls itself Viking City and welcomes you with a "Velkommen til Poulsbo" sign.

## About the Author

Jan Walker is the author of five previous novels and four works of nonfiction, including *Unlocking Minds in Lockup,* a treatise on prison education that is also her memoir of going inside prison fences to teach offenders. She spent 18 years teaching in female and male prisons, developing curriculum specific to their needs. She is an advocate for prison reform and for the rights of children of incarcerated parents.

Walker is known for strong character development, and for bringing settings to life in both fiction and nonfiction. She is the publisher at Plicata Press, which has published books for 11 local authors in addition to several of her own works.

Walker grew up on Puget Sound in a Scandinavian community near Poulsbo, Washington. This is her sixth novel and 10th published book.

CPSIA information can be obtained
at www.ICGtesting.com
Printed in the USA
JSHW030824070721
16657JS00001B/45